Alsace

Alsace made-to-measure

Alsace à la carte

Contents

Nature 16

Sporting activities 26

Regional history 32

Arts and crafts 42

A taste of Alsace 52

Recommended eating 58

Wines and spirits 64

Architectural heritage 72

Festivals and celebrations 82

Alternative Alsace 92

Family outings 96

Alsace in detail

The Lower Rhine 102

The Upper Rhine 160

A weekend in Saverne and the northern Vosges regional nature reserve

The northern Vosges regional nature reserve is a protected area covering more than 100,000 hectares/247,000 acres of beautiful scenery. Saverne itself is located at the park's most southerly point. La Petite-Pierre makes a good base with its numerous hotels. Visit the château and its museums (p.110), then catch a spot of fresh air at the Imsthal pool before making your way to the troglodyte homes in Graufthal (p.110), either on foot or by car. Then head back by car to Meisenthal and take a peek in its glass museum (p.111). After experiencing the mystic aura of the *Breitenstein* (a prehistoric menhir), pause at the clogmakers' museum-workshop in Soucht (p.111). Save the afternoon for a fascinating tour of the Château de Lichtenberg (p.106), followed by a visit to the Romanesque and Gothic church of St-Paul-et-St-Pierre in Neuwiller-lès-Saverne. Restored in the mid-19thC., it contains the magnificent St-Adelphus tapestries (p.117). Once back in La Petite-Pierre, enjoy a lovely walk to the Donnenback pond, from where there's an impressive view over the castle from the *Route de Petersbach*. Sunday's agenda is a busy one, taking in Saverne and its surroundings (pp.114-115). Begin with a visit to the Château des Rohan and then stroll through the old town, with a halt at Bockel's, a tempting local chocolate shop. Climb up to the ruins of the Haut-Barr castle (p.115), with its pentagonal keep and ramparts that afford lovely views. Have lunch on the spot or in Taverne Katz (p.114) in the town, before making your way to Marmoutier to visit the extraordinary Romanesque church of a 12thC. abbey (p.138). Return to Saverne, stopping off at St-Jean-Saverne with its tiny Romanesque church of the Benedictine abbey (p.115). Save time for the 'witches' walk', on which you'll discover Mont St-Michel (no connection with the place of the same name in Normandy). The former headquarters of a Celtic cult, it still carries a whiff of paganism (p.115).

A weekend in the
Bruche valley

The beautiful river that leads from the Vosges to Strasbourg travels through a varied and often mountainous landscape. It's a wise plan to stay in the Schirmeck region, and the Metger inn in Natzwiller (p.143) is a good choice. A weekend can disappear all too quickly, so set off on Friday afternoon to the Serva waterfall, in order to treat yourself to some fresh, invigorating air and a good leg-stretch. On Saturday morning, visit the sad remains of the Struthof concentration camp (p.142), the only such camp to be built on French soil. Not surprisingly, the building has a somewhat sinister air, contrasting with its magnificent setting. After your tour, a change of mood is needed. There are some lovely walks around the Coucou pond, the Maxe marshland and the ruins of the Château of Salm. Schirmeck (p.142), which boasts a church, château and wonderful viewing point, is a good spot to end the day, enjoying the beautiful panorama as the sun sets. On Sunday, after an early start, follow the River Bruche to the quasi-twin towns of Mutzig and Molsheim. Mutzig is home to the 'Jacobin' and the château of the Coulaux brothers (p.140). Make some time in your itinerary for Molsheim, an ancient town below the vine-decked foothills of the Vosges; its attractions include the Musée du Prieuré des Chartreux and the fabulous Bugatti collection (p.140). If you have a few moments to spare before lunch, make your way to the charming Dompeter in Avolsheim. Castle devotees should make for Feste Kaiser Wilhelm II in the early afternoon. Then head back to the river to visit the restored Benedictine abbey-church in Niederhaslach (p.141) before embarking on the well-trodden path to Nideck, complete with its castle ruins and waterfall. With a bit of luck, you may even run into the water nymph of Nideck (p.139). By the end of the weekend your legs may be a little weary, but you will have seen some wonderful buildings and landscapes, as well as enjoying fresh air, delicious food and the undoubted pleasure of a good night's sleep.

A weekend in
Colmar

A weekend is just about long enough to explore the delights of Alsace's wine capital. Start your visit at the wonderful Musée d'Unterlinden (p.192), housed in a former Dominican convent. Its hugely varied collection includes several outstanding works of art, the highlight of which is the famous Isenheim altarpiece by Mathias Grünewald, completed in 1515. Allow at least a morning, if not longer, for the museum. The nearby Dominican church dates from the 13th-15thC. It's home to another beautiful altarpiece, known as *The Virgin in a*

Bower of Roses, painted in 1473 by Martin Schongauer (p.193). After a busy first day, revive yourself with a gourmet meal at one of France's finest restaurants, *Au Fer Rouge* (p.194). On Sunday morning the Collégiale St-Martin, located on a café-lined square, is worth a quick peek. Head for the Rue des Marchands and the 16th-C. Maison Pfister, with its exterior murals (p.196). The street continues south to the Ancienne Douane or Koïfhuss (p.194), long used as the Town Hall. You are now entering the renovated Quartier des Tanneurs (p.195). Then make your way into the maze of small streets in the Krutenau district with its half-timbered

homes (p.196). Try not to get lost, and afterwards head for the Pont du Boulevard St-Pierre and the area known as 'Petite Venise' (Little Venice) because of its picturesque riverside views (p.196). If time permits, take a boat ride, embarking from Rue Turenne (p.195). If you're travelling with children, don't forget the Musée Animé du Jouet et du Petit Train on Rue Vauban, with its lovely collection of toys and model trains (p.194). The old town is also home to a museum dedicated to the famous sculptor, Auguste Bartholdi (p.195). As you walk back up to the wonderful Place Rapp (with underground parking), you'll pass the Rue des Têtes and the remarkable hotel and restaurant of the same name, another gourmet destination (p.193). In summer, the old quarter looks very romantic when lit up, but it's at its most magical during the two weeks before Christmas, when it boasts three Christmas markets and at dusk looks like the setting for a fairytale.

A weekend in
Alsatian Jura

Although part of Alsace, this area has a very strong feel of Jura about it – not surprisingly, as its green slopes rub shoulders with nearby Switzerland. The countryside inn in Lutter, dining in an authentic rural atmosphere and resting your head and weary feet in the nearby 17th-C. farm with its comfortable, and yet sophisticated, ambiance. Sunday morning can be spent in the country museum in Oltingue, with its faithful reconstructions of artisans' workshops and 19th-C. interiors and displays of traditional tools and utensils.

Among these you'll find examples of moulds for *kugelhopf* (a kind of bun), possibly similar to the one used to make your breakfast (p.165). On Sunday afternoon, if time allows, the idea of a walk through the Swiss countryside may prove hard to resist. Leaving from Wolschwiller, you'll cross woods and meadows that could be in either France or Switzerland (p.167) – an irrelevant detail, as the views are spectacular in both. Couples on a romantic weekend break can make a point of visiting the smallest museum in France, which is dedicated to lovers. Families can indulge in a few of the water sports on offer in the vast lakes of Courtavon, including swimming, boating and fishing. There are no fewer than seven delightful signposted walks to choose from, covering a total of 135 km (84 miles), and at the entrance to the park you'll find a campsite, bar and restaurant (p.166). You may well return home convinced that you've just spent a weekend in paradise.

The proposed route takes you around Ferrette, an ancient little town with ruined castles and panoramic views, seat of the counts of Pfirt. It leads you through the narrow streets along the 'dwarves' walk', lunching on delicious cheese at Sundgauer Käs Keller before taking part in a bracing round on the 18-hole international Largue golf course, just a few kilometres to the southwest (p.164). You can stay at the

A week around
Mont Ste-Odile

Spend time discovering the delights of this area on foot and by car, and you'll begin to appreciate the sense of calm and spirituality that surround it. Seduced by its beauty and the lush hills and mountains of the Vosges region, you'll start to respond to the land 'where the spirit breathes'. Obernai is a good spot to use as a base, a picturesque and once fortified town, and the ancient residence of the dukes of Alsace. Before girding your

loins for the climb up Mont Ste-Odile, explore the old ramparts, lovely houses, fountains and restaurants of the town, one of the most beautiful in Alsace (p.146). Just a few kilometres to the north, Rosheim is worth a visit, with its Romanesque Maison des Païens, dating from the 12thC., and its medieval town gates. It also contains the restored

St-Pierre-et-St-Paul church from the late 12thC., adorned with Lombardic decoration and sculptures (p.144). Not far away is Boersch, another pretty town boasting a magnificent well (p.145), and the neighbouring hamlet of

St-Léonard has a fascinating marquetry workshop, Spindler (p.145). Several paths lead to Ste-Odile from Ottrott, 3 km/ 2 miles to the west. The most popular is the 'pilgrims' route' that passes the medieval ruins. However, you do have a choice – either the Mur Païen, a prehistoric, or possibly Celtic, structure composed of huge blocks of unhewn stone piled into a wall over 10 km/6 miles long, or via the Niedermunster ruins. The suggested route

leaves from Klingenthal and heads up to the two castles at Ottrott (Rathsamhausen and Lutzelbourg) before returning to Mont Ste-Odile via the Stollhafen rock, which is shaped like a cooking pot (p.146). Once at Mont Ste-Odile, you can enjoy a meal at the pilgrims' inn and take your time exploring and admiring the view (p.147). Still experiencing Ste-Odile's unusual atmosphere, explore the towns of Barr, with its tiny Musée de la Folie Marco (p.148), and Andlau, under the protection of Ste Richarde and her bear (p.148). The health resort of Hohwald is a relaxing spot and the Champ du Feu tower (p.149) is also worth a visit.

A week in Mulhouse and at the Eco-museum of Haute-Alsace

Mulhouse is primarily a heavy industrial and textile conurbation. However, it boasts four or five unusually good industrial museums. Spend the first day in the Musée National de l'Automobile, where the Schlumpf collection is displayed, including the fabulous Bugatti collection. It's a wonderful exhibition space for the history of the automobile and over 500 cars are on display. Children will be fascinated by the videos and simulators (p.226). Day two takes you to the Musée du Chemin de Fer (railway museum), a collection by French Railways (SNCF) outside the centre of Mulhouse. There are huge locomotive engines, cranes, stations, signals, swing bridges, a level-crossing keeper's hut, luxury wagons – everything a rail and rolling stock

enthusiast could want. (p.227). Next is the Musée du Sapeur-Pompier, the fire brigade museum with its antique fire engines and other memorabilia (p.227). A fourth museum awaits your discovery the following day: Electropolis – Musée de l'Énergie Électrique, devoted to the production and applications of electricity (p.227). This can be followed by a visit to the Musée d'Impression sur Étoffes, a museum featuring a vast collection of printed fabric, including 18th-C. Indian and Persian examples and kimonos from Japan (p.227). The zoological and botanical park houses some 1,000 animals and has a particularly good restaurant (p.229). On the following day, spend the morning in the splendid Roman baths (p.229) before enjoying a spot of lunch at the brasserie in Lutterbach (p.231). You can learn how Lutterbier is made in the ancient subterranean cellars. Spend your last two days marvelling at the Eco-museum of Haute Alsace in Ungersheim (20 km/12½ miles), the most beautiful of its kind in Europe. The open-air museum displays half-timbered houses from throughout Alsace, each individual in character. It offers all sorts of fun for adults and children, and on-site craft workers give demonstrations of their various skills. There's also a potassium mine nearby and accommodation and refreshment on site (p.170).

A week in the
Munster valley

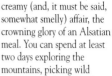

Check into one of the hotels in Munster or Hohrodberg, or perhaps choose one of the many countryside inns, and prepare yourself for adventures in the great outdoors. (Without a reservation, you may have difficulty finding accommodation, so book well ahead.) Munster makes a perfect base for exploring further into the mountain range and other places nearby. It's worth spending a day simply relaxing in the cheese-making town that owes its

name to a Benedictine abbey founded in 634 by Oswald. Around the Place du Marché, storks (*cigognes*) perch on top of most of the roofs and chimneys, eagerly awaited by the locals as signs of good luck. Spend one of your days in Gunsbach, a village just a couple of kilometres to the west, towards Colmar, and

pay tribute to the famous doctor, Albert Schweitzer, winner of the Nobel Peace Prize. He dedicated his life to science, and his books and memorabilia are displayed in a museum (p.205). From Munster itself you can undertake some delightful walks, mountain-bike rides or excursions into the mountains by car. Hard-to-resist attractions include Le Petit Ballon d'Alsace (1,267 m/4,157 ft), with its views of the whole range of the Vosges, the Black Forest and the Jura, a traditional meal in one of the countryside inns and a visit to a cheese-maker. The local cheese is a rich and

creamy (and, it must be said, somewhat smelly) affair, the crowning glory of an Alsatian meal. You can spend at least two days exploring the mountains, picking wild berries and admiring the protected plants and flowers in the high mountain pastures. Save at least a day for the Sentier des Roches (rock path) that takes you to some impressive sites, vast pine forests, cascading waterfalls, dramatic slopes and the glacial cirque at Frankenthal (p.205). Set aside an entire day for the Lac Vert (green lake) in its attractive setting, brimming with trout, perch and pike. Enjoy a picnic in its unspoilt and peaceful surroundings before heading to the Musée

de la Schlitte (museum of sledgers and wood-working), a key to the history of the area's economy (p.207). By now, you will probably have fallen for the charms of this beautiful area and you may regret that you don't have more time to spend.

A fortnight around
Strabourg

Strasbourg, the 'city of the roads', is the capital of Alsace and seat of the Council of Europe, the European Court of Human Rights and the European Parliament. It's also a thriving city worth at least a week of your time, with a central location ideal for exploring the surrounding countryside. Stay in the centre of Strasbourg or its suburbs (p.126-135) and remember that travelling by tram is the best way to get around. Start with a tour of the old town, La Petite France and the Finkwiller district, then visit the Alsatian museum. The Cathédrale de Notre Dame should not be missed, as well as the Musée de l'Oeuvre Notre-Dame. Wait for a good clear day before visiting the Château des Rohan and its museums. Stroll around the Orangerie and visit the buildings near the European Parliament, making sure you leave enough time for the so-called *Ceinture verte* (green belt), a wonderful walk that embraces the city, countryside and river. Drop into a couple of *winstube*

to savour both the food and the atmosphere. In the neighbouring suburb, try the Schutzenberger brasserie in Schiltigheim (p.135) and save time for the lovely medicinal garden in Eschau and the area around the Rhine. A visit to Strasbourg's German neighbour, Kehl, may take your fancy, along with a chance to change the pace of life from urban to rural by exploring the pleasant Kochersberg area. Marlenheim is known for its excellent wines (p.136), Truchtersheim's Maison du Kochersberg (p.137) is an attractive museum, and Handschuheim to the west is the home of the exquisite *flammekueche* (flambéed tart). To the south, visit the Château d'Osthoffen, and take part in the festivals of Erstein (sugar) and Benfeld (tobacco, p.151). Save a day to explore Sélestat, where delights of local food, wine and culture are in store (p.154-155), and visit the Château du Haut-Koenigsbourg (p.158), one of the most spectacular fortresses in Alsace. In Kintzheim, with its old houses, ramparts and castle, the Montagne aux Singes (monkey mountain) is worth a tour (p.158). Towards the north, savour delicious asparagus at Hoerdt (p.124), stroll in the beautiful park of the Château de Pourtalès or the Fuchs-am-Buckel forest (p.124), or discover the Roman village of Brumath (p.124).

A fortnight on the *Route du Vin* in the Upper Rhine

Alsace is synonymous with good wine and food. If you visit in spring, the place is ablaze with flowers; in summer, the local festivals are in full swing. Autumn brings harvest time and a canvas of deep, burnt colour, and late autumn is a perfect time to visit. Two weeks just won't seem long enough. Set out on the *Route du Vin* in the south of Alsace, and you'll soon come across Thann, with its celebrated Rangen wine (p.174). After Guebwiller come the vineyards of Bergholtz, Orschwihr and Soultzmatt (p.191). Small wine-growers are dotted everywhere, their cellars open for *dégustation* (wine-tasting). Skirt Strangenberg and head for Rouffach, city of witches (p.188) and an ancient and once-fortified town. After a break, make for Pfaffenheim (p.190) with its Romanesque church (p.189), Hattstatt, Obermorschwihr, poised on its promontory, and Husseren-les-Châteaux, overlooked by its three panoramic fortresses (p.200). As you descend, you'll reach the fortified town of Eguisheim. Ruined towers built by the family of Pope Leo IX (p.198), rise above the town. One of the outstanding wine-growers, Jean-Luc Freudenreich, has exceptional wines available for tasting, along with the Wolfberger co-operative. Then head for Wettolsheim (p.202), Wintzenheim (near Colmar, p.202) and Turckheim, where an evening meal beckons and the traditional night watchman waits to bid you goodnight. Next day discover Niedermorschwihr with its film-set backdrop (p.202), followed by Katzenthal (p.203), Ammerschwihr (p.210), Kaysersberg, an extraordinary medieval village (p.212) and Sigolsheim (p.210). Spend some time in Colmar, Alsace's wine capital, which is endowed with its own vineyard (p.192). Then visit Bennwihr (p.218), Mittelwihr and Béblenheim before a lengthy pitstop in Riquewihr (p.218), one of France's most beautiful villages. These are followed by Hunawihr (p.220), Zellenberg (p.220), Ribeauville, above which rise three castles (p.211), Bergheim, surrounded by ramparts (p.223), Rorshwihr, Rodern (p.223) and St-Hippolyte (p.223) each seeming more lovely than the last. Hotels for all budgets combine with *winstube* galore, top quality restaurants and a guaranteed warm welcome. All in all, the *Route du Vin* is quite an experience.

A fortnight around
Colmar

Located at the heart of Alsace, Colmar is almost a picture-postcard town, a living museum. Turckheim is a good spot to choose as your base, a picturesque old town with three well-preserved and majestic gates. Your travels will take you no further than a 20-km/12¹/₂-mile radius from the town, but an enjoyable day can be spent exploring its narrow streets, lined with half-timbered houses and climbing the Brand slopes, before a top quality and well-priced dinner in the Auberge du Veilleur. You can follow Alsace's last remaining night watchman as he performs his duties at 10pm (p.200). Just above Turckheim lies Niedermorschwihr, the pearl of the vineyards, with its twisted church tower and famous cellar restaurant, Morakopf (p.202). In Eguisheim, a little further south, stroll around the circular fortified village which nurtured the future Pope Leo IX. Enjoy *choucroute* (pickled cabbage) in the restaurant and spend an unforgettable evening on the premises of wine-maker and magician, Jean-Luc Freudenreich (p.198), relishing his tricks

is well worth a visit, not least for its dramatic evening spectacles. Most villages open their cellars for wine-tastings and for tours of the vineyards along informative and signposted paths (p.199).

of the trade. The *Route des Cinq Châteaux* (five castles trail) leaves from Husseren-les-Châteaux, the highest point in the Alsatian vineyards, and can be completed either on foot or by car. The three castles at Eguisheim afford a magnificent view, adding to their historical interest, and the fabulous Château de Hohlandsbourg, an imposing castle now transformed into a museum,

Spend a memorable day at the pilgrimage site of Les Trois-Épis. The well-marked walks are of only medium difficulty and leave from the coach station. At the summit of Le Galz is a huge monument commemorating the restoration of Alsace to France in 1918; the view is quite extraordinary. Should your visit coincide with Christmas, a fairytale scene awaits, repeated in all the neighbouring villages and their markets. Snowfall is just the icing on the cake.

Alsace à la carte

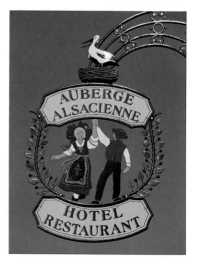

Recommended eating 58

Wines and spirits 64

Festivals and celebrations 82

Alternative Alsace 92

Family outings 96

Architectural heritage 72

Nature

Explore the paths of Alsace, its forests and nature reserve, inhabited by storks and a wide variety of flora and fauna. Or take to the water of its waterways, rivers and canals.

Educational

1. Altenach: Maison de la Nature **p. 163**
2. Bouxwiller: Luppachhof living farm **p. 167**
3. Labaroche: Woodworking and rural heritage complex **p. 217**
4. Niederbruck: Entzenbach living farm museum **p. 173**
5. Sentheim: Maison de la Géologie **p. 173**

Birds

6. Hunawihr: stork and otter sanctuary **p. 221**
7. Munchhausen: ornithological reserve **p. 105**
8. Rouffach: stork sanctuary **p. 189**
9. Urbès: See d'Urbès (lake) **p. 177**

Forests and trees

10. Attenschwiller: arboretum **p. 163**
11. Haguenau: the great forest of Alsace **p. 122**
12. Le Fuchs-am-Buckel: forest walks **p. 124**
13. Mulhouse: forest discovery trails **p. 229**
14. Wissembourg: L'Outre-Forêt region **p.103**

Parks

15. Artzenheim: Eldorado park **p. 233**
16. Katzenthal: romantic Schoppenwihr park **p. 203**
17. Mulhouse: Jardin des Senteurs (scented garden), zoo and botanical park **p. 229**
18. Obernai: Les Naïades aquarium and park **p. 147**
19. Northern Vosges regional natural park **pp. 110-111**
20. Riedisheim: Wallach park **p. 230**

Waterways

21. Colmar: La Lauch and a boat trip from Colmar **p. 195**
22. Kembs: twin canals trail **p. 160**
23. Rhinau and its island **p. 151**

Flora and fauna

24. Haut Chitelet: Botanical gardens at Col de la Schlucht **p. 181**
25. Hohneck: chamois **p.180**
26. Kembs: from Kembs to Shaferhof **p. 160**
27. Kingersheim: tropical aquarium **p. 231**
28. Kintzheim: birds of prey and barbary apes **p.158**
29. Lautenbach-Zell: Moulin insect house **p. 186**
30. Loechlé: Île du Rhin **p. 161**
31. St-Louis: the little Camargue of Alsace **p. 163**
32. Sélestat: La Chapelle du Chêne, an ecological paradise **p. 156**
33. Strasbourg: Haras Nationaux (stud farm) **p. 132**

Trails

34. Bastberg: botanical and geological trail **p. 117**
35. Raedersdorf: botanical discovery trail **p. 167**
36. Ste-Croix-aux-Mines: historic and botanical mining trail **p. 225**
37. Thannenkirch: Taennchel botanical trail **p. 225**

Lakes

38. Metzeral: mountain lakes **p. 208**
39. Sewn: fishing lakes **p.172**

Alsatian landscapes

40. Le Ballon d'Alsace **pp. 172 and 182**

Museums

41. Colmar: Musée d'Histoire Naturelle et d'Ethnographie **p. 197**
42. Kingersheim: Musée Océanographique **p. 231**

The Alsatian countryside, a delightful jigsaw

Vosges

Alsace's two *départements* are protected by the two large nature reserves of northern Vosges and Ballons des Vosges. The varied landscape of mountains, glacial cirques, lakes, rivers and hills are home to a wide variety of flora and fauna.

The wide expanses

Known as the 'blue line of the Vosges' during World War I, the Vosges mountain ridge is located in the Haut-Rhin. A tourist route follows its course for 80 km/50 miles via

The Grand Ballon

the Grand Ballon (1,424 m/ 4,672 ft), taking visitors from the Col du Bonhomme to Thann. The wonderful landscape includes the distinctive summits, rounded by the forces of erosion, as well as mountain pastures, peat bogs and lakes hidden in the forests. To the west, the horizon stretches into Lorraine and to the east it extends to the Plaine d'Alsace and Germany.

The terrain of the northern Vosges

The northern Vosges landscape has its own contrasts, including rocky escarpments, forests and plains. Around Cleebourg and its vineyard, the flat-tiled, warm-coloured roofs of village houses bring colour to the scene. Further east, the wooded Sauer valley unfolds along the rivers. The dense forest area of the northern Vosges, designated by UNESCO as a biosphere reserve in 1989, heads towards Saverne, made up of spruce (80 per cent), as well as oak and beech trees.

A marshy landscape

Humid marshland and peat bogs occur both deep in the valleys and high on the slopes, giving rise to unusual aquatic ecosystems and a varied flora and fauna. Insects buzz around in large numbers when the water dries up in summer. The area demands a very special form of protection to resist the advance of the forest, and in the northern Vosges regional nature reserve Highland cattle

Highland cattle imported from Scotland

from Scotland have been introduced. Their impressive curved horns and wonderful thick coats make them quite a tourist attraction and they can negotiate terrain that no tractor can.

The wine-growing region of Haute Alsace

The wine-growing region is mostly concentrated between the Vosges, dotted with fortified castles, and the

marshy terrain, lie mostly to the south of Strasbourg with just a few to the north, comprising over 200 sq km/ 77 sq miles of flat, aquatic landscape. The humid terrain is deeply carved by the tributaries of the river Ill, interrupted from time to time by verdant forests. Long considered the poor relation of the vineyards

LE SUNDGAU, ROUTES DE LA CARPE FRITE

ponds and lakes, the source of carp, a local speciality. Houses here are more robust and austere, with a very individual version of half-timbering and fewer geraniums at the windows, due to the more severe climate.

Plaine d'Alsace. The slopes, planted with vines in perfectly straight rows, surround the pretty villages where ramparts and watchtowers rise above the multicoloured façades of the houses, with their geranium-clad windows. In autumn the vineyards are full of people harvesting the grapes who are happy to discuss and explain their craft.

The *rieds*

The Rhine dominates this part of Alsace, and the plains are liable to flooding in the winter. The *rieds*, areas of

of Piedmont, the region is nevertheless rich in crops such as corn and cabbage.

Sundgau, Alsace's southernmost area

The area south of Mulhouse is known as the 'Alsatian Jura'. The Sundgau landscape echoes neighbouring Jura in its limestone cliffs and narrow gorges, along with its spruce and beech forests and many

ABUNDANT ORCHARDS

Alsatian orchards growing apples, pears, cherries and *mirabelles* (a European variety of plum) are vital to the manufacture of local *eaux-de-vie*, and growers are encouraged to promote new varieties. Wild cherries from the orchards that hug the small roads or flourish in the fields have a lovely, slightly acid flavour, unique to the species. They are also grown in the protected orchards in the north, or those that thrive naturally in the Pays Welche. If you're unfamiliar with mirabelle liqueur, try a glass after a meal or in ice cream, tarts and jams. It's really quite delicious.

Alsatian wildlife,
from the ferocious lynx to the migrating stork

The wildlife of Alsace is particularly rich and thriving, thanks to local environmental concern and the guaranteed protection of two Vosges nature reserves. Animals and birds exploit the diverse habitats of the region: high pastures, forests, vineyards, rivers, villages, as well as the *rieds* of the floodable plains.

A good milk producer, the Vosges cow's annual average yield is over 4,400 kg/9,700 lbs of milk, from which Munster cheese is made.

The lynx

The lynx, which had become an endangered species in Europe, was reintroduced in 1980 to the forests of Haut-Rhin, arousing interest in hunters and those who live in the mountains. The feline carnivore has large green eyes and delicate ears crowned with a small brush, as well as very acute eyesight. Look out for the tracks of the 20-odd lynx that live in the forests, particularly in the winter, but don't confuse lynx with the wild cat, which has a long, bushy tail.

Cows from the Vosges

Originally from Switzerland, the Vosges cow is easily recognisable in the summer as it grazes in the pastures of the Ballons du Sud. It has a very distinctive colouring, sometimes speckled, and its back and belly feature two large white stripes. The head is short, the nose relatively large and the animal's curved horns are tipped with black.

The Monarch of the Glen

In the Vosges, a stag is a relatively common sight among the roe deer and bucks. This is his domain,

and selection of the clan's leader takes place on autumn evenings during the rutting period. Adult stags engage in violent combat until the *troat* (a long, raucous cry) rings out to signify victory. The champion will rule over his terrain for another year, surrounded by a harem of does.

A forest full of bucks

Within the flood plains of the Rhine, the Ill Wald forest extends over more than 1,500 ha/3,706 acres of humid terrain. A dynamic and fascinating ecosystem with over 110 tree-dwelling species has established itself in the region. A site of special ornithological interest, it is home to some 52 remarkable bird species, from the marsh owl to the curlew. It also contains the most important wild population of bucks in France – over 300 of the magnificent animals with their speckled coats and flat antlers.

The curlew

The curlew shelters in the marshes of the Alsatian *ried*, and its characteristic 'coo-ee', a deep and melancholic sound, can be heard during long winter evenings.

Although the birds are vociferous during the courtship period and after the young have hatched, the curlew lowers its long curved beak and keeps a low profile during the incubation period, while nesting in the short grass of the marshes. Grey-brown in colour with a white rump, it is easily identified by its hesitant, long-legged gait; highly alert, it flies off at the slightest sound. Unusually for the bird world, the colouring of the male and female birds is identical.

The hoopoe

The hoopoe is a spectacular and easily recognisable bird with a pink-brown body, broad black and white wings and a bouncing flight. It has a fan-shaped, black-tipped crest that is opened at intervals both on the ground and in flight, when it looks like a magnificent butterfly. The hoopoe lives among the vines and migrates in late autumn to Africa and southern Sahara, having stocked up on insects and grapes at harvest time. Listen out for its call, a soft, far-reaching *hoop-hoop-hoop*.

The lucky stork

The stork is a symbol of Alsace, where it is seen as a sign of prosperity and good fortune. A large, black and white wading bird with red beak and feet, it builds a substantial nest in a high, inaccessible place. The female lays up to four eggs and sits on them for just over a month; the young fly the nest about two months after hatching. The bird is threatened during its long migration south by hunters and traps, but it is being re-established in Alsace. Several pairs have chosen to make their permanent home in villages around the wetland areas.

The flora of Alsace,
scents of natural well-being

A lsatian flora is as diverse as the habitat in which it grows – a region including acid forest terrain, humid peat bogs, siliceous vineyards and chalky soil. Hundreds of species of indigenous trees and flowers thrive, to be spotted during botanical walks and in the public gardens. Alsace is a delightful area for nature lovers.

Orchid

A remarkable pine tree

The Hanau pine is a Scotch pine peculiar to the Bitche region. A tall species (around 40 m/130 ft) with a pointed crown, rectilinear trunk and no lower branches, it's a red-orange colour at the top. A protected tree in the forests of the northern Vosges, the Hanau pine has been the subject of much research. It's thought to be a cross between the Wangenbourg mountain pine and the high plain pine from the Haguenau forest.

Scotch pine

Myrtles and bilberries

The myrtle, a species of bilberry, is found growing wild in the forest of the Vosges or cultivated as a larger berry on the forest-clad slopes of the region. Its dark blue fruit are appreciated by humans and wild animals alike. The cultivated variety is harvested only after seven years' growth, and is usually made into jam, wine and liqueur. Bilberries can also be marinated in vinegar or served with an aperitif.

A carpet of cotton grass

In spring, the humid peat bogs are covered in a carpet of tassels formed by white flowers called cotton grass (*eriophorum vaginatum*). At the end of the season, all that remains at the top of the tall and tender stalks is a white pompon whose soft and silvery-white seeds fill the air, borne on the wind. Traditionally the flowers were used to stuff cushions or as lamp wicks.

The purple foxglove (*digitalis purpurea*)

The silica-rich and acid soil of the region makes perfect conditions for the foxglove, known as the 'gant (glove) de Notre Dame'. These glamorous purple flowers grow to a height of between 60 cm and 2 m (2 ft and 6½ ft) in sunny locations within the forest clearings or on the slopes. The digitalin extracted from the leaves is violently poisonous, but very effective when used for medical purposes, such as regulating the heartbeat.

Sweet woodruff (*asperula odorata*)

Nicknamed the 'little lily of the valley', *asperula odorata* has small white flowers and splayed stems. It flourishes in the beech forest undergrowth and is harvested in late April and early May. Its leaves are macerated in *eau-de-vie* to give a very subtle, slightly peppery flavour to the alcohol, used in cooking. Alsatians use sweet woodruff in a variety of ways, including a rather delicious brew traditionally drunk on May Day (*Maitrank*) and a jelly which accompanies foie gras or sorbets.

A wild tulip

The wild tulip (*tulipa sylvestris*) has narrow, lance-like leaves, a single flower and a fragile stalk that grows to 20-30 cm/ 8-11 inches. It can be found in siliceous terrain and its solitary flower, which opens during April to May, sometimes has delicate tinges of red and green. It is a protected species in France and Switzerland.

Orchids galore

You'll spot many species of orchids on the chalky, fallow ground. Among the easiest to identify are the bee orchid (*ophrys apifera*) and fly orchid (*ophrys insectifera*), patterned to appear like the bee and fly (hence their names). The bee orchid looks like the rear of a small bumblebee, with elliptical leaves and pointed flowers with pink sepals, whereas the velvety fly orchid has narrow shiny leaves, brown flowers with green sepals and a bluish patch at its base. Both orchids prefer lime conditions.

Orchid

THE BENEFITS OF *ASPERULA ODORATA*
Asperula is hung in garlands or boxes from the beams of Alsatian homes. A versatile and useful plant, it has a range of beneficial applications. It is used as a tonic and also to detox the body; both requiring a diluted infusion, taken at regular intervals. Asperula has a number of culinary uses and may also be dried and made into a decoction to apply to dry skin patches.

From sandstone to potash,
geology of the region

The Vosges mountains range from the sandy northern peaks, the *Vosges gréseuses*, to the high granite southern mountains, the *Vosges cristallines*. Geology and appearance change with every valley, from the oil-bearing north and the mines of central Alsace, to the Ballons du Sud and the potash mines.

Rounded summits

The term '*Ballon*', used to describe the Alsatian summits, is thought to reflect their rounded shape, although it could have derived from

The highs and lows

The high crystalline mountains – predominantly granite in content – complement the lower

The Grand Ballon

the word '*belen*', referring to the Celtic god Bel. There is some evidence that the range was used as a solar observatory in Celtic times. The geology of the range makes it appear much higher than it actually is, with the Grand Ballon, high in granite content, standing at 1,424 m/4,672 ft and offering a wonderful panorama over the Black Forest and the Alps. Hohneck Ballon reaches 1,361 m/ 4,465 ft and Petit Ballon is, unsurprisingly, the lowest at 1,267 m/4,157 ft. The massif is clad with dense forests and its high pastures are dotted with Alpine flowers.

sandstone range to the north as two contrasting parts of the whole, distinctive landscape. Sandstone was used to construct most of Alsace's monuments, including the cathedral in Strasbourg and

the fortified castles of Nideck and Lichtenberg, with their unusual, petrified appearance. The troglodyte houses in Graufthal in the Zinsel valley are dug out of a 70-m/ 230-ft cliff.

Troglodyte dwellings at Graufthal

The silver-bearing Vosges mountains

Around Ste-Marie-aux-Mines and Ste-Croix-aux-Mines, the Val d'Argent (silver valley) has over 2,000 mines, responsible for the area's renown in the 16thC. The mountains are particularly rich in mineral resources and silver, lead, copper and other metals have been extracted since the Middle Ages. The mines are narrow, cut into the rock with hammers and chisels to roughly the height of a man; progress was often limited to only 6 cm/2¹/₂ inches per day. The industry

went into gradual decline, and by 1939 all the mines were closed. Today, efforts are being made to resurrect the area's mining heritage, and some mines have been reopened to the public. All necessary safety precautions are taken for the tours.

A RATHER UNUSUAL MARKET
Last weekend in June

The mineral market of Ste-Marie-aux-Mines is famous throughout Europe. It brings together serious collectors of rocks and fossils along with an enthusiastic public. There are over 700 exhibits on display, sometimes rare examples, found locally or from as far away as Russia, Poland, Madagascar, America, Belgium, the UK and Morocco. Ammonites, fossils, jasper and semi-precious stones are on sale at reasonable prices. The origins of the fair, and the interest in mineralogy to which it responds, lie in the Val d'Argent, where traditional markets were held to sell the produce from local mines.

Striking oil

Pechelbronn (in the Bas Rhin) was known in the 17thC. for the curative applications of its oil. The first oil exploitation in Europe began here, with the opening of a refinery in 1857. It remained active during the first half of the 20thC. and closed in 1960. The mines and boreholes remain, together with hand-operated pumps and other memorabilia of the Alsatian 'brown gold'.

Potash country

The world's largest deposit of potash was discovered in Wittelsheim in 1903. A local landowner, Amélie Zurcher, together with Joseph Vogt, established a successful enterprise which was to survive both World Wars. The potash basin of Alsace extends today around Mulhouse, and its principal contemporary use is as a fertilizer. The international reputation of Alsatian potash is partly due to Hansi's striking blue enamelled plaques featuring a stork and Strasbourg Cathedral. However, most of the wells have now been closed (see box p.171).

Sporting activities

Alsace is a wonderful place in which to improve your fitness while enjoying walking, hiking, horse riding, cycling and a range of water sports.

Walking trails

1. Lauterbourg: Hauts du Canton path **p. 104**
2. Marlenheim: three chapels' trail **p. 136**
3. Mont Ste-Odile: Mur Païen ('pagan wall') trail from Ottrott **p. 148**
4. Munster: *Sentier des Roches*, GR 531 **p. 205**
5. Pfaffenheim: trail around sacred sites **p. 190**
6. Rouffach: mountain walks **p. 189**
7. Strasbourg: *Ceinture verte* (green belt) walk **p. 135**
8. Thann: marked trails, (vineyards, foothills) **p. 175**
9. Turckheim: Brand vineyards' wine trail **p. 205**
10. Urbès: trail around mountain lake **p. 177**
11. Villé: tour by car and on foot **p. 152**
12. Wasserbourg: walk towards the Petit Ballon **p. 207**
13. Wettolsheim: wine trails through the vineyards **p. 202**
14. Wolschwiller: walk crossing over from France to Switzerland **p. 167**

Horse-riding

15. Brinckheim: Koer equestrian centre **p. 163**
16. Junghöltz: Munsch farm **p. 187**
17. Labaroche: Hacienda ranch **p. 216**

Cycling and biking

18. Marmoutier: mountain bike trails **p. 138**
19. Wissembourg: cycle paths into Switzerland and back **p. 102**

Golf

20. Mooslargue **p. 162**
21. Ammerschwihr **p. 210**
22. Soufflenheim **p. 120**

Water sports

23. Courtavon: water-sports complex **p. 166**
24. Erstein: watersports **p. 150**
25. Huningue: Whitewater course **p. 162**
26. Kembs: boat hire **p. 161**
27. Kruth-Wildenstein (dam): watersports **p. 177**
28. Mulhouse: water-sports complex **p. 230**
29. Reiningue: Doller sailing centre **p. 231**

Fishing

30. Lac d'Alfeld **p. 172**
31. Lac Blanc **p. 214**

From the air

32. Munster: hot-air balloon rides **p. 178**
33. Schnepfenried: hang-gliding **p. 180**
34. Vieux-Ferrete: microlites **p. 165**

Winter sports

35. Le Champ-du-Feu: cross-country skiing **p. 149**

Health and fitness

36. Le Fuchs-am-Buckel: La Cour du Honau **p. 125**

Other

37. Bartenheim: eco-karting **p. 160**

Alsace on foot,
tracks and trails for all

There is no shortage of marked paths in Alsace. The Club Vosgien operates its own walking clubs, chalets and signposting activities. Several GRs – *Sentiers de Grande Randonnée* (long-distance footpaths) – cross the Vosges, providing a great way of seeing the area (and keeping fit).

The Fédération du Club Vosgien

The famous Vosges walking club was formed in 1872 to promote tourism for walkers and other nature-related activities. It has 34,000 members and its headquarters are in Strasbourg, supporting a large number of local associations. Drawing on volunteers, it develops, signposts and maintains some 16,500 km/10,250 miles of walking trails. The club also publishes guidebooks and maps, showing waymarked paths of varied lengths and difficulty and has an informative website: www.club-vosgien.com.

In contrast to the gentler Lorraine side, the slope of the Alsatian Vosges is abrupt, sometimes giving a steep descent to the plain.

Trails and signposts

The Club Vosgien is the only official French body responsible for signposting footpaths. Trails are distinguished by colours,

'Please take your litter with you'

GR paths

A variety of long-distance footpaths cross the Vosges range: the GR 5 (Holland-Mediterranean) follows the ridge, from Donon to Fesches-le-Châtel (260 km/162 miles), the GR 53 from Wissembourg to Schirmeck (167 km/104 miles) and the variants – GR 532, GR 533 and GR 534.

including the yellow GR 532, green GR 533 and red lozenge GR 534 (combined with the red and white markings of the FFRP – *Fédération Française de la Randonnée Pédestre*). The European paths are marked with white symbols inside a green square, whereas local paths are waymarked with crosses and triangles. looped circuits sport different circles of colour.

Be prepared

A family walk without stops normally proceeds at a pace of around 3-4 km ph/2-2¹/₂ mph. Wear a good pair of walking shoes and take a rucksack for picnics and refreshments, especially water. Please take care not to litter the paths. Alsatians respect their environment and will expect you to do the same. The chalets and *gîtes d'étape* of the Club Vosgien, the

Panda *gîtes* and the bed and breakfasts in the parks are all good places to rest your head and weary legs.

Criss-crossing the country

The paths in Alsace include the European paths E2 (North Sea-Mediterranean, 2,500 km/1,554 miles) and E5 (Atlantic-Adriatic, 1,500 km/932 miles). There are other paths such as 'the three countries' (450 km/ 280 miles) and the 'Interregio' (220 km/137 miles), between France, Switzerland and Germany. The *Sentier de la*

Sarre is 250 km/155 miles in length and the *Tres Tabernae* travels between the Palatinate (Germany) and the Vosges range (160 km/100 miles). The *Sentier Stanislas-Kléber* travels over a 300-km/ 187-mile stretch between Lorraine and Alsace.

Thematic trails

There is no shortage of themed walks in Alsace, including the Central Alsace walks and trails (PR), the gastronomic paths in the northern Vosges and the nature walks in Alsace's Petite Camargue. Other paths cross the Vosges and the borders. They allow you to investigate the natural parks, fortified castles and mining heritage of the area. Wine trails are among the easiest in terms of terrain and can be completed in a couple of hours, with the aid of information boards about the wines and how they are made. There are no less than 12 wine trails to choose from, and they end in a *dégustation* (tasting) in the local village.

Alsace's Petite Camargue

Sports and recreation,
for all seasons

Alsace is a great place to enjoy your favourite sport, whether it's golf, fishing, skiing, cycling or horse-riding. The lovely tranquil environment is complemented by plenty of accommodation throughout the year, as well as hearty meals to reward visitors.

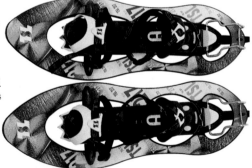

Skiing

Downhill skiers have over 50 lifts to choose from in the Vosges in Haute Alsace, and there are snow-making machines and special lighting for night skiing (5-10pm) in Markstein and Lac Blanc. Cross-country skiing fans can enjoy a total of 1,000 km/621 miles of marked trails, notably at Markstein, Trois-Fours, Lac Blanc, Bagenelles and in the Champ du Feu massif. There are also good facilities for snowboarding, ski jumping and tobogganing. For further information visit the website: www.skifrance.fr

A winter wonderland

Snowshoeing is a very popular sport in the Vosges and is organised by the nature reserves who run expeditions lasting half a day (or longer) to track animals. In Markstein, Schnepfenried and Lac Blanc, baby lifts and toboggan runs have been installed, and tows are free for children under four. Dogsledding expeditions are also available.

Up, up and away

The average height of the Ballons of the Vosges and sheer cliffs on the Plaine d'Alsace make them the perfect environment for hang-gliding. There are schools of instruction in airborne sports, and you can launch yourself from Le Bonhomme (595 m/ 1.952 ft), Lapoutroie (450 m/

Lac Blanc

1,476 ft), Hochstein (329 m/ 1,080 ft), Fellering (360 m/ 1,181 ft) and Treh-Markstein (790 m/2,592 ft). Sightseeing flights in planes, microlites and hot-air balloons are also available in the Vosges massif (pp.178, 180, 165).

ON HORSEBACK FROM NORTH TO SOUTH

Alsace offers many opportunities to enjoy trekking on horse-back. The *Comité Départemental du Tourisme Équestre du Haut-Rhin* in Colmar (see coloured pages) publishes a brochure with details of centres, activities, accommodation and itineraries of varying lengths, together with information on saddleries, harnesses and vets. A visit to the Haras Nationaux in Strasbourg (p.132) is a good way to start gathering information.

Water, water everywhere

A wide choice of water-based activities is available in Alsace, including the recreation centres at Colmar and Kembs (pp.161, 195) and mini-cruises on the Rhine. Houseboats with six to eight berths can be hired to travel the Alsatian canals, and further river trips are available on the waterways of Strasbourg and Colmar (pp. 126, 192). Quiet, flat-bottomed boats travel along the Ill and the Lauch (pp.130, 195) and canoeing and kayaking can be practised on the majority of the rivers, with over 600 km/ 373 miles of navigable waters in the summer months (pp. 150, 233).

Fishing fanatics

The mountain lakes have colourful names – Blanc (white), Noir (black) and Vert (green). They provide a haven for

fishing fans who want to practise their techniques in a beautiful and peaceful environment. You'll need to buy a permit

(*carte de pêche*), which is free for under 16s, and to familiarise yourself with national and local regulations. Permits and information are available at tourist offices and cafés near popular fishing spots. Hopefully you'll be rewarded with carp, pike and other fish (see coloured pages at back of book).

Alsace on two wheels

For those who prefer to view the countryside from a saddle, there are cycle paths that follow the route crossing the Vosges from north to south, or between Alsace and Lorraine. You can cycle (without luggage if you wish) across the border or along the left bank of the Rhine via the Hardt, or alternatively explore the vineyards. Tours can be arranged which include accommodation, gourmet stops and train travel. Maps and guides cover the hundreds of cycling paths that exist in Alsace – the real preserve of the cyclist (see coloured pages at back of book).

Regional history

Alsace preserves traces of its prehistoric past, its social history and its industrial heritage as well as its many past conflicts.

Archaeological interest

1. Bliesbruck, Moselle: French/German archaeological park **p. 122**
2. Biesheim: Musée Gallo-Roman **p. 233**
3. The Donon: Celtic site **p. 143**
4. Mulhouse: Roman baths **p. 229**

Judaism in Alsace

5. Bouxwiller **p. 116**
6. Struthof: remains of concentration camp **p. 142**

Military history

7. Bennwihr: martyred village **p. 218**
8. Labaroche: Linge memorial and museum (WWI) **p. 217**
9. Marckholsheim: Maginot Line and memorial museum **p. 157**
10. Masevaux: *Route Joffre* **p. 172**
11. Reichshoffen **p. 108**
12. Sigolsheim: national memorial to *Première Armée* (WWII) **p. 210**
13. Turckheim: Musée de la Poche de Colmar **p. 200**
14. Vieil-Armand: national monument and necropolis **p. 171**

Castles and forts

15. Andlau and Spesbourg **pp. 148 and 149**
16. *Rocher de Dabo* **p. 139**
17. Husseren-les-Châteaux and Eguisheim **pp. 200 and 198**
18. Fleckenstein and Hohenbourg **p. 106**
19. Grendelbruch **p. 142**
20. Haut-Koenigsbourg, Kintzheim and L'Ortenbourg **pp. 158 and 159**
21. Huningue: Musée d'Histoire **p. 162**
22. La Petite-Pierre **p. 110**
23. Lichtenberg **p. 106**
24. Neuf-Brisach **p. 232**
25. Osthouse **p. 150**
26. Ottrott **p. 145**
27. Pourtalès (castle) **p. 125**
28. Rastatt (Germany): Schloss Favorite **p. 104**
29. Ribeauvillé: Châteaux de Ribeaupierre **p. 221**
30. Saverne: Château des Rohan; Château du Haut-Barr **pp. 114 and 115**
31. Thann: Château d'Engelbourg **p. 174**
32. Windstein **p. 106**

Industrial heritage

33. Krems: hydraulic power station **p. 161**
34. Marckholsheim: hydro-electric power station **p. 157**
35. Merkwiller-Pechelbronn: Musée du Pétrole **p. 109**
36. Ste-Marie-aux-Mines: silver mines in St-Barthélemy and St-Louis-Eisenthur; Musée de la Scierie Vincent (sawmill museum) **p. 224**

LORRAINE

Épinal ●

FRANCHE-COMTÉ

Ancient stones,
the legacy of the past

The history of Alsace began in the area surrounding the Rhine, the frontier marker. In 58 BC, during the Roman conquest, Julius Caesar forced the Germanic tribes to retreat to the east of the Rhine, establishing the demarcation of the Roman Empire.

Jupiter Taranis, at Haguenau historical museum

The Mur Païen

Before the Romans

Prehistoric remains from 600,000 BC have been found in Achenheim and Hangenbieten and archaeologists have also discovered an important collection of Bronze and Iron-Age objects in the Haguenau forest region, along with burial grounds. Evidence of the first Celts can be seen in Lembach and the Pandours ditch near the Col du Saverne, and the strange *Mur Païen* ('pagan wall') that winds around the top of Mont Ste-Odile is probably a prehistoric defensive structure. The *Breitenstein*, or *Pierre des 12 Apôtres* ('stone of the 12 Apostles'), is an ancient standing stone in the northern Vosges, covered with strange carvings.

Gallo-Roman times

Celtic tribes arrived in Alsace between 1500 and 2000 BC, different groups settling in diverse parts of the region: Haute-Alsace, Alsace Bossue, Outre-Foret and Basse Alsace. The Roman invasion in 58 BC was followed by a period of prosperity, in which vineyards and villa estates were established. The decline of the Roman Empire saw the arrival of the Alemans (or Alemani), an agricultural people who were in turn driven out by the Franks in the 5thC., heralding the Merovingian period. In 750 AD Alsace was divided into Nordgau and Sundgau, which roughly translate into the Haut-Rhin and Bas-Rhin regions of today.

ROCKS, CULTS AND CASTLES

The Circuit des Roches trail in Dieffenthal has existed for centuries. Behind the church is an unusual geological site, a rocky granite area eroded into ball-shaped formations. This strange place is full of Celtic associations and it's here that the *schiewaschlawe* festival takes place, during which flaming wooden discs are thrown. The Spring equinox is also celebrated during the night of the first Sunday in Lent. The Rocher du Sacrifice is another evocative historical site. Its panoramic view of the Château de l'Ortenbourg and the Château du Haut-Koeningsbourg, dominating the vineyards of the plains below, is quite breathtaking.

Mercury, Westercamp museum at Wissembourg

Jewish sites in Alsace,
a deep-rooted heritage

oday many Jews still live in Alsace, despite the terrible losses suffered by the population during World War II. The region's large Jewish community is one of the most significant in France.

Jewish presence in Alsace

During the Roman period, Jews established themselves in the towns in the Rhine valley. Their communities gradually diminished until the 18thC.,

German Jews to the area. Their religious autonomy was reduced under the First Empire and the communities began to decline once again, leading to an increase in emigration.

The Jewish legacy

There are more than 200 official Jewish sites in Alsace, including synagogues, cemeteries, *mikvés* (ceremonial water basins) and collections of Jewish artefacts in museums. Hebrew inscriptions such as those on the outer walls of Neuwiller-lès-Saverne, are not uncommon, and the synagogues in Colmar, Thann, Haguenau, Struth and Ingwiller are all important

Ingwiller synagogue

when the 20,000 Jews living in Alsace comprised more than half of France's total Jewish population. After the French Revolution, Jews were granted civil rights and new decrees gave them the right to pursue their trades, attracting many

aspects of Alsace's heritage. The Jewish cemetery in Ettendorf is the oldest in Alsace, and covers a large area on the hillside with its 1566 steles. Strasbourg's Rue des Juifs is home to the remains of a 13thC. ceremonial bath.

CULINARY SPECIALITIES

Some Jewish dishes are specific to Alsace, such as *chalet* (apple clafoutis), which is eaten at Rosh Hashanah, the Jewish New Year. Herrings with cream and *tsémetkuech* (cinnamon cakes) accompany tea or coffee at Yom Kippur. Unleavened bread is rolled into small balls or *matzekneipfles* that are served with beef soup. Plaited loaves of bread known as *berchess* are eaten on the Sabbath and, finally, other specialities include *strudel* (apple pastry with raisins and cinnamon), a Jewish carp dish and *pichkelfleisch* (beef cooked in brine).

Strudel

Fortified castles
and defences, all along the Rhine

The name 'Alsace' was recognised as far back as the 7thC. and became more widely known under Adalric, father of St Odile. Under the Carolingian rulers of the 8th-10thC., the land was divided into Nordgau and Sundgau, each ruled by a count. Medieval fortified castles were built at strategic points in the Vosges and ramparts often protected towns on the plain.

Thirty Years War (1618-1648), Alsace became for the most part French and during the French Revolution was divided into two *départements*, the Bas-Rhin and Haut-Rhin. Today the region is entirely French.

Kientzheim

Fleckenstein

Alsace divided

From the 9thC. onwards Alsace fell under the influence of the Alemans, tribes of German origin. In 1354, the Decapolis of Alsace was formed from 10 cities to resist the excesses of the feudal system and to provide a defence against the power of the nobility. Gradually, these cities (Strasbourg, Mulhouse, Colmar and Haguenau among others) freed themselves from their overlords. After the

A feudal system

Many fortresses were built during troubled times and under the impetus of Eguisheim (11th-12thC.) and Hohen-staufen (12th-13thC.). The two *départements* contain over 150 ruins, restored in varying degrees, which can be reached along marked paths, although it may require some effort. The magnificent fortress town of Neuf-Brisach was one of the most beautiful, constructed by Vauban in the 17thC. to defend the Rhine.

The defence system

To the north, the castles of Fleckenstein, Falkenstein, Schoeneck and Windstein were the first to emerge from the wooded massif. Lichtenberg, Fleckenstein and Hohenbourg formed manmade eyries, perched on the mountainside, and the nearby Frankenbourg, Grand Geroldseck, Wasenbourg and Wagenstein castles are also impressive. Some castles were destroyed during the Thirty Years War while others survived until the French Revolution. Today, the headquarters of the northern Vosges regional nature reserve are housed in the restored Petite-Pierre castle.

Neuf-Brisach

Kintzheim

In central Alsace

Further south, among the other impressive ruins, the Château d'Ottrot, Château de l'Ortenbourg (encased in its outer wall or *chemise* – 'shirt'), Landsberg, Haut-Andlau and Spesbourg castles sit on wooded ridges or on the edges of the vineyards. Kintzheim castle has been restored and its courtyard is home to the *Volerie des Aigles*, where 80 birds of prey perform in spectacular training flights. It is dominated by the imposing Haut-Koenigsbourg, which casts its shadow over the other castles on the slopes of the Vosges. The train from Strasbourg takes you down towards Mulhouse and offers excellent views of the castle.

The armoury at Haut-Koenigsbourg castle

2,484 ft). It was given to Kaiser William II in 1899 and an architect from Berlin, Bodo Ebhardt, restored the ruins between 1900 and 1908, drawing on archaeological finds and archives. The neo-medieval complex was returned to France with the Treaty of Versailles and became a national monument, its furniture a legacy of its German past. Exhibitions and festivals are often held within the castle's austere walls.

Romantic ruins

The hills of the Vosges in the Haut-Rhin are dotted with picturesque ruins, situated in the forests and at the edge of the vineyards. Among the most famous are the towers of Ribeauvillé, Kaysersberg and Hohneck and the castles of Eguisheim, Pflixbourg, Schrankenfeld and Windstein. Near the Rhine, the ruins of Landskron defend the great river. In the Sundgau, within Jura, the castles of Ferrette and Morimont dominate the limestone cliffs.

The castles at Ribeaupierre

Haut-Koenigsbourg

Haut-Koenigsbourg

This prestigious fortress overlooks the Plaine d'Alsace from its rocky promontory above Sélestat (757 m/

JEAN RENOIR

Jean Renoir's film, *La Grande Illusion*, was shot during the winter of 1937 in Haut-Koenigsbourg. It portrays the relationships between captives Jean Gabin and Pierre Fresnay and a German officer, Éric Von Stroheim, in a wartime prison. An idealistic and pacifist work, the film has often been classed among the 12 best in the world. The small tower door through which the actors descended still carries a sign used in the film.

Memories of war,
great and tragic campaigns

I t's impossible to visit Alsace, the frontier zone between France and Germany, without passing a variety of military sites. Between 1870 and 1945, the region experienced three wars and underwent three changes of nationality. The tale of this beleaguered area is retold in Alsace's historic sites.

Alsace and Lorraine

The military struggles over the regions dominated the 19th and 20thC. The Franco-Prussian war (1870-71) brought German rule over Alsace and Lorraine. After World War I, the territories were returned to France, only to be re-occupied by the Germans in 1940. In 1944, the 1st French Army under De Lattre de Tassigny and the 2nd Armoured Division under Leclerc both re-entered the region as liberators, at Mulhouse and in Strasbourg respectively. Strasbourg once became the capital of Alsace in 1949, and the headquarters of the Council of Europe.

General Mac-Mahon

Memories of battle

The northern Vosges saw considerable conflict in the Franco-Prussian war. The bloody battle of Froeschwiller took place on 5 August 1870 not far from Woerth, and General Mac-Mahon was defeated near Wissenbourg,

opening the door for the Prussian invasion.

The Maginot Line

After World War I, Alsace became part of France once again. The mission of creating a defensive line from the North Sea to the Alps, consisting of casemates and underground fortifications, was given to the War

Minister, Paul Painlevé, and his successor André Maginot (1877-1932), after whom the defences were named. Within 10 years the 'French wall' was constructed, featuring 58 works along the northeast border and 50 in the Alps. However, it was not able to stand the sustained attack of German parachutists, aircraft and tanks in 1940.

STRUTHOF CAMP

During World War II, occupying German forces constructed the Natzwiller-Struthof death camp, the only one of its kind in France. It lies in a wooded and austere setting, often under snow,

and in 1944 held 7,000 prisoners in a camp designed to take 1,500. Many Jews, Russians, gypsies and members of the Resistance died there and a huge memorial pays tribute to the victims. Some of the prisoners' cells and two huts have been made into a museum.

Alsatian identity,
an eclectic affair

SPEAKING FRENCH

You will hear different dialects spoken around the province, including *Elässisch*, a High German dialect, known as Alemannic or Alsatian. A Romance dialect, *Welche*, is spoken in the Orbey, Lapoutrie, Labaroche, Le Bonhomme and Fréland *communes* which are collectively known as Le Pays Welche. In Labaroche you may even hear a local version of Old French, and in Strasbourg the street signs are bilingual, bearing both *Strasse* and *Rue*. Bring plenty of phrase books!

Language, patriotism, religion, family and friends are all important to the people of Alsace. They have preserved and protected their regional character across the centuries, despite their turbulent past and changing rulers. The Alsatian identity remains firmly in evidence today.

From the other side of the Vosges

Alsace is well known in France for its serious and disciplined nature. Family and community life, based around local festivals and solidarity, together with the strength of the Catholic, Protestant and Jewish faiths, are all important and binding features of Alsatian society.

The distinctive Alsatian dialect, an Alemannic language with French syntax, is still spoken. Wherever you are in the world, if someone says 'Yo, Yo!', you'll know you're in the presence of an Alsatian.

The influence of Alemannic roots

Alsace has 750 choirs, 92 brass bands and 200 windbands, often subject to influences from across the Rhine. Painted furniture, wrought-iron signs, a passion for good food and drink – all these are shared with their German neighbours, perhaps accounting for the large numbers of Germans that you meet in Alsace. However, Bavarian and Alsatian styles are clearly distinct; signs feature different designs, for example, and recipes are definitely not the same. The Alsatian identity is conveyed very clearly through its many publications, newspapers and books.

Famous Alsatians,
warriors, artists and philosophers

A lsace has been the birthplace of many famous men and women across the centuries, among them military figures, writers, artists, philosophers and industrialists. Several Alsatians have left their indelible marks in history.

François-Christophe Kellermann (1735-1820), the victor of Valmy, became a marshal. Rapp (1771-1821) fought in Egypt and Russia, and Lefèbvre (1755-1820) helped Bonaparte during the *coup d'état* of 18th Brumaire (10 November 1799).

Jean-Frédéric Oberlin

Four generals, one empire

Four First Empire generals – Kléber, Kellermann, Rapp and Lefèbvre – came from Alsace. Jean-Baptiste Kléber (1753-1800) was born in Strasbourg and his statue stands in Place Kléber. His victories include Mayence, Fleurus, Maastricht and the Egypt campaign.

The philosopher and pastor

Jean-Frédéric Oberlin (1740-1826) was a theologian and pastor in the small village of Waldersbach. Along with his wife, he set out to improve the lives of his parishioners.

He founded playschools for the children, invented educational tools, helped to develop agriculture and traditional crafts, promoted a small local textile industry and set up a mortgage society. He was a great admirer of Jean-Jacques Rousseau and the greatest philosophers and minds of the revolutionary era would come to consult with him. Oberlin is still venerated across France today.

Auguste Bartholdi

Auguste Bartholdi (1834-1904), sculptor, was born in Colmar. His most famous work is the Statue of Liberty in New York, cast in bronze and over 33 m/108 ft in height. Bartholdi also produced the remarkable *Lion de Belfort*, carved into the sandstone rock of the citadel. Reproductions of both statues can be found in Paris.

Statue of Maréchal Rapp at Colmar

Bartholdi was the official artist of the Second Empire and the Third Republic, and several French towns feature his patriotic statues.

Friend Fritz). This popular novel (the basis of an opera by Mascagni), gives a faithful portrayal of Alsatian life. The two friends went on to write other novels, including *L'Invasion* and *Le Conscrit de 1813* (The Conscript of 1813), further establishing the image of Alsace in France. After the 1870 Franco-Prussian war, Alsace was handed over to the Prussians by the Treaty of Frankfurt, which served to inspire several artistic and literary movements.

Uncle Hansi

On the eve of World War I, the Alsatian caricaturist and watercolour artist Jacques Waltz, better known as Hansi (1873-1951), published his *History of Alsace*

Ribeauvillé, by Hansi

as told to the Children of France and *My Village*. With great humour, he depicted grotesque-looking German soldiers and the likeable peasants and villagers in regional costume in a satirical version of the modern comic strip. Hansi was also an accomplished artist whose talented oil paintings and watercolours depict the regional landscapes around Colmar. He finally became the curator of the Musée d'Unterlinden. His posters are valued as social documentation of the era.

L'Ami Fritz, an Alsatian novel

Émile Erckmann (1822-1899) and Alexandre Chatrian (1826-1890) were joint authors in 1864 of *L'Ami Fritz* (Our

The house of L'Ami Fritz *in Wissembourg*

PFLIMLIN AND EUROPE

The politician Pierre Pflimlin (1907-2000) played a significant role in 20th-C. Alsace. He was a member of Parliament, a minister, President of the MRP (a national republican party) and mayor of Strasbourg. His politics were rooted in the European concept and Christian socialism. As President of the European Parliament, he sought to open up the Alsace region to new enterprises and trading opportunities with the countries of the Rhine.

Albert Schweitzer

Albert Schweitzer (1875-1965) was a theologian, philosopher, musician, musicologist and missionary doctor. Born in Kaysersberg, he became a pastor in Strasbourg before studying medicine and travelling to West Africa, where he founded a hospital in 1924. He wrote, studied and gave organ recitals to help develop

his hospital. After 1945 his writings warned of the dangers of the atomic bomb. and he was awarded the Nobel Peace Prize in 1952. Schweitzer died in Lambaréné (in Gabon), and his name is revered throughout the world.

Arts and crafts

Alsace has a rich tradition of arts and crafts, ranging from its famous domestic stove to pottery and crystal. It is also home to a growing number of fascinating local heritage museums.

Museums

1 Fréland: Forge and blacksmith's museum **p. 217**

2 Ungersheim: Eco-museum of Haute-Alsace **p. 170**

Festivals

3 Benfeld: tobacco festival **p. 151**

4 Erstein: sugar festival **p. 150**

Potteries

5 Betschdorf **p. 121**

6 Soufflenheim: pottery city **p. 120**

Markets

7 The Trois-Épis pilgrim site: New Year market **p. 203**

8 Thann: decorated egg market **p. 175**

Heritage

9 Graufthal: Clogmakers' museum and workshop **p. 111**

10 Guebwiller: Musée du Florival (ceramics) **p. 186**

11 Husseren-Wesserling: Musée de Textiles et des Costumes (textile and costume museum) **p. 176**

12 Klingenthal: historic weapons factory (mainly knives) **p. 146**

13 Muhlbach-sur-Munster: Musée de la Schlitte (museum of sledgers and woodworking) **p. 207**

14 Pfaffenhoffen: Musée de l'Image Populaire (local arts and crafts) **p. 119**

15 Ste-Marie-aux-Mines: Maison de Pays (industrial heritage) **p. 224**

16 Sarre-Union: Science and crafts museum **p. 112**

17 Soucht (Moselle): Clogmakers' museum **p. 111**

18 Zillisheim: the 'forgotten trades' trail **p. 169**

Miscellaneous

19 Colmar: Arts & Collections d'Alsace (gift emporium) **p. 195**

20 Kaltenhouse: earthenware stove workshop **p. 123**

21 Labaroche: woodworking and rural heritage complex **p. 217**

22 Marmoutier: organs **p. 139**

23 Meisenthal (Moselle): Glass and crystal shop) **p. 111**

24 Muttersholtz: Gander fabric shop **p. 156**

25 St-Léonard: Spindler marquetry workshop **p. 145**

26 Turckheim: the Bois Fleuri studio (decorated wood workshop) **p. 201**

27 Villé: distilleries **p. 153**

FRANCHE-COMTÉ

● Vésoul

Wissembourg

A4

⑰ ㉓

⑯

Lower Rhine ⑤

Moder

⑭ Haguenau

⑨ A4

⑳ A35 ⑥

A5

Zorn

Saverne

ALSACE

㉒

N4

Bruche

Strasbourg

Molsheim

Donon
(1,009 m/
3,310 ft)

N422

Champ
du Feu
(1,110 m/
3,642 ft)

⑫ ㉕

N83 ④

GERMANY

N420

③

Le Climont
(966 m/
3,169 ft)

A35

㉗

A5

Sélestat

㉔

⑮ N59

Ribeauvillé

①

㉑ ㉖

⑲ Colmar

⑦

Freiburg

⑬

N415

Hohneck
(1,361 m/
4,465 ft)

Fecht

Petit Ballon
(1,267 m/
4,157 ft)

⑩ Guebwiller

Grand Ballon
(1,424 m/
4,672 ft)

Rhine

⑪

②

A35

Thann

⑧

Ballon
d'Alsace
(1,250 m/
4,101 ft)

N83

Mulhouse

⑱

Upper

A36

A5

Belfort

Altkirch

D419

A3

Rhine

Basle

SWITZERLAND

0 5 10 15 20 25 km

0   10   20 miles

Traditional furniture,
the heart of family life

Furniture makers in Alsace work principally in wood, a plentiful local material. Skilled woodworkers, using a refined style and a technique akin to marquetry, have for centuries produced chairs, beds and cupboards, some quite elaborate and decorative.

The Alsatian chair

The wooden Alsatian chair with its angled legs is very typical of the region. It began life in the houses of the aristocracy but gradually became associated with rural life. The tilted back is shaped like a torso, with wide shoulders, narrow waist and rounded seat. The chair is usually either painted or decorated with carvings, featuring entwined hearts or animal motifs.

Family fortunes in wood

The Alsatian wardrobe, the traditional symbol of a family's wealth, is tall and wide and rests on round feet. It is almost square, with columns and large cornices. Depending on the financial status of the family, it is sometimes inlaid with marquetry and is usually made from pine wood veneered in oak or walnut. Its flower motif, with six brown and white star-shaped petals, is similar to the one you'll find on wardrobes from Lorraine. They are sometimes painted (often with a marble pattern), just like those in Scandinavia, and feature flowers or naïve rural scenes.

The alcove bed

An authentic Alsatian bed is designed to be housed in an alcove away from the rest of the main room, or *stub*. It is generally relatively small, but wider than its counterpart in Brittany, sometimes taking up half the room. In northern Alsace the bed alcove would be left open, but in the colder Sundgau region it has doors to keep the sleepers warm.

Visual imagery

Alsace has a strong tradition of religious imagery in its domestic decoration. It may include ex-votos and *hinterglasmalereien* (naïve painted paper images under glass) that hang in various rooms to ensure divine assistance. *Goettelbriefe* (baptism

blessings) make popular ornaments, and are often framed along with good wishes from godparents (known as *taufwunsch*) to protect the children of the house. The greetings may be painted by the godmother or godfather, or commissioned from local artists.

Symbolic designs

Geometric designs, lozenges, stars and swastika-style solar symbols all appeared on European and Basque country furniture until the 19thC. The intertwined serpent has religious associations and the crown and

Detail of a marquetry chest

they should contain 35 skirts given to the bride by her parents. The multicoloured wooden chest

Coat of arms on the Colmar town hall

two-headed eagle is a symbol of the Holy Roman Empire. The more idiosyncratic heart motif appears on numerous pieces of furniture and pottery in Alsace, as well as cake tins (*springerle*).

Chests and caskets

Chests were traditionally given in Alsace as marriage gifts. Custom dictated that

remained popular in rural areas from the Renaissance to the end of the 19thC. More solid and sturdy pieces were decorated with sculpted columns and arches, and sometimes featured inlaid marquetry work. Smaller caskets were kept on a table and often used for documents and important family correspondence.

Marquetry

Pieces featuring wooden inlaid work were very costly, and consequently usually found in the more prosperous regions in the 16thC. The marquetry was applied to furniture and panelling, as well as to clocks and chests. At the end of the 19thC. the woodworker Charles Spindler revived the art of marquetry in his St Leonard workshop, designing pieces which

involved great skill and attention to detail, often using slices of wood veneer less than a millimetre thick. The natural nuances and grain of the wood made the completed furniture true masterpieces.

USING WOOD FROM ALSACE

Alsatian carpenters and cabinetmakers created distinctive and elegant pieces of furniture, which were often panelled and involved partitions and coffered tops. Polished walnut added to the prestige of wealthy owners, while pine was used as a cheaper alternative, often painted for decorative effect. Cherry, maple and fruit tree woods were used to make chests, corner cupboards and ornate cradles.

Fabric and textiles
for all tastes and budgets

The textile industry – spinning, weaving, dyeing and printing – has always played an important role in Alsace. Workshops still use traditional techniques, using wood blocks to print designs and embroidering the most intricate details by hand.

Fine fabrics
Napoleon III's doctrine of beauty in utility was fully achieved by the textile workers of Alsace. This important regional industry still thrives in the Ste-Marie-aux-Mines valley today, producing top quality mohair, dyed in brilliant colours with wonderful results.

Printing on fabric and paper
At the beginning of the 19thC. Jacques Schaub created designs for the textile industry using intertwined floral motifs. Around 1814 the first lithography workshop allowed designs to be transferred on to paper and reproduced on a large scale. Techniques of engraving and fabric printing were further improved by Godefroy Engelmann, a fabric merchant's son from Mulhouse who became a lithographer and chromo-lithographer. Modern studios in Ribeauvillé still successfully reproduce popular designs from the 18th and 19thC.

Printed calico or *indiennes*
Daniel Koechlin imported the first samples of *indiennes*, printed cotton fabrics, to France in the 19thC. He then unravelled the secret of the famous *rouge turc* (Turkish red) dye, bringing riches to Mulhouse. The Musée de l'Impression sur Étoffes (museum of printed fabrics) charts the history of the industry. It is housed in a former industrial building that belonged to the Société Industrielle de Mulhouse, founded in 1825 by 22 industrialists, including Koechlin, Schlumberger, Zuber and Dollfus – the last, as an artist, was particularly sensitive to colours. The textile museum and design school provide a valuable source of information and research on *indiennes* and their origins.

An 18th-C. fabric design

Cashmere from India
Patterns on cashmere were inspired by rugs and fabrics from India, some dating from the 17thC. They were the height of fashion during France's Second Empire and elegant society ladies would drape themselves in printed wool shawls, patterned with a

Jean-Henri Dollfus

paisley design in black and orange, deep red or green. Such items have become prized items in antique shops today.

The Tissuthèque in Mulhouse

The textile library, established by the industrialists of Alsace in 1833, is open to designers from all over the world and contains over 3 million documents and 1,700 fabric samples, with further material available on CD-Rom and the Internet. Gaze at a flourish of geraniums on a black background, or exotic birds newly discovered by early colonial explorers, and you can imagine the romance and excitement that such patterns first evoked.

Lace and patchwork

Lace was a feature in Alsatian homes as early as the 18thC. It was used on bonnets and

THE SOCIAL DREAM OF WESSERLING

Surrounded by 200-year-old trees, the buildings of Husseren-Wesserling are clustered around the main square near the château. The houses, chalets and workshops make up a self-contained town hugging the banks of the Thur. The renovated Musée du Textile et des Costumes (museum of textiles and costumes) is housed in a former industrial building in a vast park, where the Boussac fabric factory used to operate. Learn about the history of the great industrial families and of costumes, together with the processes involved in producing fabric from raw material.

The park housing the Musée du Textile et des Costumes

collars, and still appears today on Alsatian costumes worn at local festivals. The tradition of patchwork was inspired by the Amish, an American movement joined by colonists from the Val d'Argent who left for the New World in the 17thC. Every year in the valley, the *Carrefour du Patchwork* (patchwork crossroads) brings together Alsatians with a passion for constructing wonderful quilts from different pieces of fabric.

Vosges linen

Known as *koelsch* (pronounced 'kelch'), this linen fabric usually has a checked design in blue and white or red and white. In former times this durable fabric was largely made at home and was used to make bed covers, napkins, curtains or waistcoats for traditional costumes. It is still made by hand today, but can be very expensive. When mixed with cotton it is more affordable.

Koelsch

Pottery and earthenware,
from fine art to everyday use

Different rustic styles of pottery are created in Alsace by the local craftspeople. They range from the most simple jug to the most magnificent oven dish used to cook *baeckeoffe* – a hotpot of pork, beef and lamb, marinated in wine, which is a firm favourite of every Alsatian family. In the 18thC. the beautiful faience of Paul Hannong brought much wealth to Strasbourg.

Popular pottery

Soufflenheim, to the east of Haguenau forest, is the capital of Alsatian ceramics. Pottery was made in the area as far back as the Bronze Age, as witnessed by shards of broken pottery found in the burial mounds. However, it was not until the 19thC. that the craft really began to flourish and became the city's main commercial activity. Pieces are turned and moulded on a wheel, and then decorated with traditional motifs such as daisies, cockerels, birds and fish.

mixture. Once dry, the item is covered in a glaze that becomes hard and transparent when it's fired in a kiln.

workshops. This small town is a lovely place, famous for its blue and grey jugs, pots and vases, and over a dozen local studios are still in operation. A fascinating museum chronicling the history of the craft is housed in an old

Adding some colour

By using a mixture of clay, water and metal oxides, a potter can introduce colour to his pieces – normally in shades of green, blue, yellow and brown. The design is applied with a brush attached to a small bowl full of the

Grey and blue

Sandstone ware is the traditional pottery used to preserve and cook food in Alsace. For almost two centuries, grey sandstone pieces decorated with blue patterns have lined the shelves of Betschdorf's

Grey and blue pottery from Betschdorf

farmhouse; it features an interesting collection of pottery from the Middle Ages right up to present day examples. A reconstruction of a workshop is displayed in the barn alongside.

Traditional pottery from Soufflenheim

A salty glaze

Thrown by hand, modern Betschdorf ceramics still retain their characteristic colouring – a grey sandstone base with a cobalt blue decoration, applied with a paintbrush before firing. The final glazed effect is achieved by adding rock salt during the last stages of the firing process. The salt breaks down chemically in the heat, creating a transparent, protective layer over the pottery.

Monochrome blue

In the 18thC., porcelain from Delft and Rouen greatly influenced the work of Alsatian manufacturers Charles-François and Paul Hannong. Designs inspired by

creations of 17thC. gold- and silversmiths, resulted in octagonal plates and delicately rimmed bowls, decorated in blue. Strasbourg pieces made between 1709-1740, have decoration with distinctive black outlines embracing diluted cobalt blue designs.

Hannong flowers

In the late 18thC., the wonderfully naturalistic floral designs of Paul Hannong's ceramic works were the glory of Strasbourg. Inspired by 17thC. botanical plates, they often featured insects and butterflies, with the most amazing attention to detail. *Trompe l'oeil* plates and pâté dishes were among the highlights produced by the Hoechst manufacturers, strongly influenced by German designs.

The *kachelhoffe* of Alsace

Earthenware stoves have provided a very efficient form of heating in Eastern France for many centuries. The *kachelhoffe* is traditionally the most important piece of

A design by Paul Hannong

furniture in the house. Heat is transmitted throughout the house by the radiation from the earthenware itself and the circulation of hot air within the structure. More than two-thirds of the energy released by the burning wood or coal is converted into heat – a remarkably efficient process.

Glass and stained glass,
clearly beautiful

S ince the 16thC., Alsatian glassmakers have sought to imitate the decorative enamelled glass from Venice and Central Europe, producing glasses, tankards and flasks, engraved or painted with heraldic, religious, floral or hunting motifs.

The 'captain's decanter'

Wide-bottomed wine carafes are known as *bouteilles du capitaine*, perhaps because of their stable base, suitable for a rocky table. Large wine glasses with tall green stems are called *hock* glasses, or *roemer* if they are shorter, more squat in shape and equipped with trumpet stems, often ridged.

Small flasks, big name

The prestigious house of Lalique was founded at the beginning of the 20thC. It still produces crystal, glasses, carafes and decorative items at its factory in Wingen-sur-Moder in the northern Vosges. René Lalique (1860-1945), a key figure in the Art Nouveau movement, is famous for his beautiful perfume bottles and vases, decorated with motifs from the natural world, such as swans, serpents and dragon-flies, together with floral designs and female figures.

Stained glass windows

Stained glass has been an important architectural feature since the early Middle

Stained glass window at Marmoutier Abbey

Ages. With the advent of new techniques and colours, painting on glass became a popular activity in the 16thC. Local masters of glass painting were concentrated around Alteckendorf, and the subtle, lead-based colours adorn glass in homes as well as churches. The art of glass painting demands great skill and patience and is widespread in Eastern France.

WOOD, WATER AND SAND

The earliest glassmakers in the northern Vosges drew upon good local supplies of wood (to stoke the fires), water and sand. To protect their furnaces they built huts, known as *Stützenhütte*, along the banks of the river, where fern ashes mixed with sand improved the melting process. They added a pinch of arsenic, sodium nitrate and lime to remove any traces of iron in the sand. Traces of the glassmakers are still visible today – clearings were abandoned when-ever they moved on in search of fresh wood supplies.

Glassmaker in Meisenthal

The art of metalwork,
from iron to pewter

Blacksmiths and ironworkers form the basis both of a guild and a craft that have long operated in Alsace. They construct and decorate iron signs, locks, door knockers, chests and handles as well as pewter vessels.

PIPING HOT WAFFLES

Craft and culinary skills combine in the Alsatian waffle iron. Two plates, round or rectangular and usually dimpled or decorated, are operated by two long arms, and when closed and placed over the heat, their markings are left on the hot dough of the waffle (*gauffre*). The waffles feature coats of arms, naïve motifs or family names, and are works of art in themselves. Old-fashioned irons have now become rare collectors' items.

A waffle iron from Bouxwiller museum

gates to local vineyards and outside the studios of artisans, and sometimes even include a signature. They hang from long iron poles and feature all kinds of emblematic motifs, such as animals, plants, crowns and vine shoots. The craft is still alive and thriving in the region.

Metal flourishes

Alsatian locksmiths belong to the guild of blacksmiths. Metal-clad safes and elaborate ornamental locks on chests and Renaissance wardrobes reveal the skill and attention to detail involved in this form of metalwork.

The handles are works of art in themselves. When polished, the metal ornamentation complements the natural wood tones of the pieces of furniture on which they feature.

Pretty in pewter

Craftsmen working in tin and pewter created wonderful pieces, particularly in the 16th and 17thC., similar to those made in Germany and Switzerland. Experts in both metalwork and engraving, the decorative details feature heraldic motifs, human figures or hunting scenes. The vessels could hold several litres.

Works of art and publicity

The most impressive iron signs date from the 17th and 18thC., influenced by designs from across the Rhine. They give details of the relevant guild or title of the aristocratic owner, and can be seen at the

A taste of Alsace

From fried carp to *flammekueche*, not forgetting *choucroute*
(*sauerkraut*) and Munster cheese, Alsatian specialities are varied
and quite delicious.

Fruits and vegetables

1. Feldbach: St-Loup estate (fruit orchards) **p. 169**
2. Hoerdt: asparagus **p. 124**
3. Mietesheim: horseradish and apple juice **p. 119**
4. Niedermorshwihr: Christine Ferber's preserves **p. 203**
5. Obermorschwihr: Marbach Abbey (medicinal plants and infusions, homemade fruit juices) **p. 191**
6. Sigolsheim: pick your own myrtles (a type of bilberry) **p. 210**

Wines

7. Colmar: regional wine fair of Alsace **p. 196**
8. Eguisheim: Alsatian wines from Jean-Luc Freudenreich **p. 198**
9. Gueberschwihr: wine festival, *Fête de l'Amitié* – winemakers' open day **p. 189**
10. Kientzheim: cellar of Paul Blanck & Son **p. 211**

Cheeses

11. Breitenbach: Saesserlé farm, mountain cheeses (*tommes*) **p. 209**
12. Lapoutroie: Graine au Lait cheesemakers **p. 216**
13. Le Markstein: Uff Rain farm-inn **p. 179**
14. Muhlbach-sur-Munster: Lameysberg farm-inn **p. 207**
15. Munster: *Route du Fromage* (cheese trail) and Munster valley *tourte* **p. 204**

Chocolates

16. Saverne: Jacques Bockel, chocolatier extraordinaire **p. 115**
17. Strasbourg: Christian, chocolatier and pastry chef **p. 131**

Alcohol

18. Lapoutroie: Miclo distillery **p. 216**
19. Villé: distilleries **p. 153**

Markets and festivals

20. Lapoutrie: St-Nicolas market **p. 215**
21. Saales: market of country produce **p. 143**
22. Thannenkirch: cherry festival **p. 225**

Fish

23. Carspach: fried carp **p. 168**
24. Orbey-Pairis: trout farm near the Lac Noir **p. 214**
25. St-Amarin: trout **p. 175**

Farm produce

26. Hachimette: Cellier de Montagnes (farm shop) **p. 217**

Flammekueche

27. Handschuheim: Auberge à l'Espérance (typical Alsatian inn) **p. 137**

Snails

28. Mittelhausen: snail farm **p. 137**
29. Osenbach: snail festival and races **p. 190**

Gingerbread

30. Gertwiller: Lips (speciality shop) **p. 148**

Choucroute,
the keynote of Alsatian cuisine

Strasbourg is the capital of *choucroute*, a cabbage-based speciality. The word is related phonetically to the German *sauerkraut*, and the dish has been a staple of Alsatian cuisine for centuries.

A potted history of *choucroute*

Cabbages have been cultivated for over 4,000 years. They originated along the Mediterranean and Asiatic coastlines, and the practice

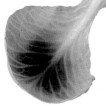

of fermenting cabbages has been carried out in China since the 3rdC. AD. *Choucroute* appeared in Central Europe in the 13thC. and arrived in Alsace in the 15thC., when it was known as *gumpostrûkt*.

Prepared as a sour dish, cabbage featured on 17th-C. monastic menus and at rural festivals, before making its way west to

Paris during the French Revolution, and finally appearing on the tables of 19th-C. brasseries throughout France.

Brassica oleracea

Alsace is responsible for 72 per cent of France's cabbage-growing and *choucroute* production, with the next largest region, Champagne-Ardennes, producing 16 per cent. The varieties of *choucroute* cabbage derive from the species *Brassica oleracea*, a large white cabbage. Its seeds are initially sown in a nursery and then replanted in thoroughly prepared soil two months later. The cabbage is harvested between July and November, either by hand using a long-bladed knife or by machine.

Putting the '*chou*' into *choucroute*

The green cabbage (*chou vert*) is sorted, stripped of its outer leaves and stalk, sliced and sprinkled with sea salt. The strips are placed in vast cement vats and further generous doses of salt are added, after which boards are placed on top of the *choucroute* and the vats are firmly sealed. The salt helps extract the water from the cabbage and it is then allowed to ferment for

2 to 6 weeks, emitting a rather pungent odour as it matures. The brine is then drained off and the cabbage placed in sealed containers for 2 months or more. Once ready it must be packaged within 2 hours.

The nutritional benefits of *choucroute*

The cabbage in *choucroute* is transformed through a process of natural lactic fermentation caused by glucose. It gradually increases in acidity, allowing it to be kept for several months without deteriorating. Nutritionally it's full of fibre and a good source of vitamins A, B, C and K. It was eaten by Dutch sailors in the 18thC. to help prevent scurvy – a disease caused by lack of fresh fruit and vegetables – during their long sea journeys. Today *choucroute* can form part of a healthy diet and is not too high in calories as long as it's not eaten with overly rich accompaniments.

GRANDMOTHER'S C...

Serves 6-8.
Ingredients: 1.5 kg/3 l...
2 onions, 1 bottle of R...
salt and pepper, 10 bl...
berries, 2 cloves, 1 *bo*...
400 g/14 oz smoked s...
250 g/9 oz smoked bacon, 2 po...
500 g/17½ oz slightly salted pork loin, 1 dozen Strasbourg sausages, 1 kg/2 lbs potatoes.
Wash cabbage and remove stalk. Peel onions, blanch the pork knuckles and loin, slice the lard. Line a large casserole dish with the pork rind. Place the *choucroute* in the dish and add the onions, cloves, juniper berries, whole peppercorns, *bouquet garni*, lard and the pork and lamb. Pour in the wine and add a pinch of salt and pepper. Cover with the lid and cook at low temperature for around 3 hours. Add the peeled, par-boiled potatoes and the smoked bacon and simmer for a further 30 minutes. Serve with the meat and poached sausages.

Choucroute in company

Typically, *choucroute* is served as an accompaniment to charcuterie – sausages from Strasbourg, Montbéliard or Morteau, cervelas, salamis and blood puddings. It's cooked in wine, beer or champagne and can be served with bacon, chops, smoked or boiled pork, or with fish, pheasant or guinea fowl. If it has been carefully marinated and well cooked, it makes a perfect accompaniment and can be seasoned with a variety of flavours, such as cumin, fennel, horseradish, parsley, juniper- or elderberries, savory and dill. Authentic *choucroute* bears little relation to the bitter tinned varieties produced industrially.

Munster cheese, authentically Alsatian

Munster is without doubt one of the oldest cheeses in France. Made with unpasteurised milk and gently matured, it is a creamy, strong-flavoured variety, which was first made in the mountain pastures in the 15thC. Traditionally made by hand, involving a long, labour-intensive process, it forms an important part of the local cuisine. The best time to try Munster is during the spring and autumn months.

The town of Munster

A cheese of pedigree

It appears that Munster cheese owes its origins to the Benedictine monks who came over from Ireland and established a monastic foundation in the Munster valley at the end of the 7thC. The name itself derives from *monastère* (monastery). Dairy farmers (*marcaires*) still make the cheese in the Vosges for local consumption. Most of its production takes place in the Vosges *département* and it's then matured in Alsace. Industrially produced Munster is a poor substitute, possessing little flavour and a much less pungent aroma. Connoisseurs prefer their cheese served naturally, but some enjoy it at the end of a meal with a little dish of cumin or caraway seeds.

Making Munster

In Alsace, the milk used to make the Munster cheese is drawn just once a day (twice in Lorraine and around Lapoutroie and Orbey). It takes 5 litres/1.1 gallons of milk to make around 500 g/ 17½ oz of cheese. The liquid is first placed in a large copper vessel, then the cheese-making process commences. The milk is heated to 38°C/100°F, and rennet is added to provoke coagulation. The resulting milk curds are cut into cubes and put into moulds allowing the whey to drain off.

PRETZELS

The salty, knot-shaped biscuits, *bretzel* or pretzel, 'through which the sun can be seen three times', make delicious accompaniments for cheese.
In former times, New Year pretzels could be as much as 60 cm/ 23 inches long and 35 cm/14 inches wide – large enough to be worn as necklaces or bracelets. Pretzels are made from dough dunked in salty boiling water and then baked in a fierce oven. They may be stuffed with cheese or ham, or sprinkled with seeds, and today are often eaten as a sort of Alsatian sandwich (*moricette*) to accompany a glass of beer or wine. Pretzels also go well with Munster cheese and, sprinkled with grains of rock salt, they simply melt in your mouth. You can munch on a fresh pretzel as a snack at any time of day.

Maturing Munster

During the maturing process that lasts around 3 to 6 months, each cheese is rubbed

by hand with a salt and water mixture. It becomes a yellow-orange colour and its crust is smooth and creamy. Each *marcaire*

(cheesemaker) has his individual method, but it's invariably a long and labour-intensive process. The *Taste-Fromage* fraternity, devoted to cheese tasting, was founded in 1987 in Munster and meets several times a year. The *Route du Fromage* (cheese trail) starts at the town of Munster itself before passing through Soultzbach, Wasserbourg, Le Petit Ballon and

Landersen. It finally joins the *Route des Crêtes* (ridge route), taking in La Schlucht, Soultzeren, Col du Wettsein, Le Glaborn and Hohrod.

Gnocchi with cheese

Kaesknepfle, gnocchi with cheese, have been enjoyed since ancient times. The Romans knew them as 'globi', and they sustained the soldiers of the Third Punic War (149-146 BC). They are not difficult to prepare. Simply take 300 g/10$^{1}/_{2}$ oz of flour, mix with the same quantity of *fromage blanc*, three eggs and a pinch of salt. Let the dough rest before forming it into small balls no larger than an egg. Poach in boiling water for around 10 minutes, then drain and serve with hot melted butter. What could be easier or more delicious?

Bibeleskäs

Bibeleskäs is the name given in Alsace to the 'maiden's cheese', a dish of fresh *fromage blanc*, sometimes with a little *crème fraîche*, served in ramekin dishes with onion, parsley and chopped chives or fine slices of the white section of leeks. Add salt and pepper to taste and serve with hot grilled potatoes and a large chunk of crusty country bread – quite delicious!

Recommended eating

Delicious food in Alsace can be enjoyed in a variety of establishments, such as *winstube*, inns or *marcaireries* (farm-inns run by dairy farmers and cheesemakers).

Hostelries

1. Rosheim:
   Le Rosenmeer
   p. 144
2. Roufflach:
   Château d'Isenbourg
   p. 188

Farm-inns

3. Hohenbourg
   (château):
   Le Gimbelhof
   p. 107
4. Le Bonhomme:
   Le Brézouard
   p. 215
5. Le Markstein:
   Salzbach
   p. 179
6. Le Platzenwasel:
   Uff Rain
   p. 179
7. Metzeral:
   Christlesgut
   p. 208
8. Wasserbourg: Le
   Kahlenwasen
   p. 207

Restaurants

9. Ammerschwihr:
   Aux Armes de France
   p. 210
10. Colmar: Au Fer Rouge
    and Aux Trois
    Poissons
    p. 194
11. Hagenthal-le-Bas:
    Chez Jenny
    p. 166
12. Hoerdt:
    À La Charrue
    p. 124
13. Kaysersberg:
    Hassenforder and
    Schlossberg cellar
    p. 212
14. Mulhouse:
    Tour de l'Europe
    p. 230
15. Riedisheim:
    La Poste Kieny
    p. 230
16. Rouffach:
    À la Ville de Lyon
    p. 188
17. Schweighouse-sur-
    Moder:
    La Cassolette
    p. 123
18. Sélestat: Jean-
    Frédéric Edel
    p. 154
19. Strasbourg: Le
    Buerehiesel (in the
    Parc de l'Orangerie),
    Le Crocodile,
    La Brasserie
    Schutzenberger
    pp. 127, 131, 135

Inns

20. Handschuheim:
    À l'Espérance
    p. 137
21. Illhaeusern: Auberge
    de l'Ill
    p. 233
22. Le Bonhomme:
    Auberge du Vallon
    p. 215
23. Lutter:
    country inn
    p. 167
24. Merkwiller-
    Pechelbronn:
    Le Puits VI
    p. 109
25. Natzwiller: Metzger
    p. 143
26. Turckheim:
    Le Veilleur
    p. 201
27. Westhalten:
    Le Vieux-Pressoir
    p. 191

Taverns

28. Saverne: Katz
    p. 114

Hotel-restaurants

29. Colmar:
    Maison des Têtes
    p. 193
30. Hohrod: Hôtel-
    Restaurant d'altitude
    Panorama and farm-
    inn (*marcairerie*)
    p. 209
31. Kaysersberg:
    Chambard
    p. 212
32. Lapoutroie:
    Le Faudé
    p. 216
33. Munster:
    À la Verte Vallée
    p. 204
34. Ribeauvillé:
    Clos St-Vincent
    p. 211

Specialities

35. Carspach:
    La Couronne
    (fried carp)
    p. 168
36. Eguisheim: Le Caveau
    d'Eguisheim (*chou-
    croute, baekeoffe*)
    p. 198
37. Lameysberg:
    cheeses and pies
    p. 207
38. Le Silène: Roman
    cuisine at
    archaeological park
    in Bliesbruck-
    Reinheim, on French/
    German border
    p. 113
39. Vieux-Ferrete:
    Sundgauer Käs
    (cheese)
    p. 165

Winstube

40. Bergheim: Winstub
    du Sommelier
    p. 233
41. Strasbourg
    p. 135

Great savoury dishes,
full of substance and style

Traditional Alsatian dishes are filling and based largely around *charcuterie*, such as Strasbourg sausages and ham. Trout, pike-perch, carp and snails are often served, but *foie gras* (fattened goose liver) holds pride of place, a delicacy that has been enjoyed since Roman times.

huge and appreciative acclaim. The marshal was rewarded with a plot of land in Picardy, and the chef received the sum of 20 pistoles.

Pâté à la Contades
Jean-Pierre Clause settled in Strasbourg in Rue de la

The origins of Alsatian *foie gras*
In 1778, a young local chef, Jean-Pierre Clause, created the first goose liver *pâté en croûte* (wrapped in a crust) for the Maréchal de Contades – the governor of the Alsatian province who also played host to many lavish dinner parties. The dish was named *pâté à la Contades* and became all the rage after it was served at the court of Louis XVI in Versailles where it gained

Mésange, where he became the first manufacturer of *foie gras*, introducing truffles into the recipe. His pâté soon gained an international reputation. There is a vast difference between goose and duck liver, and between the *foie gras* from southwest France and Alsace. The Alsatian version, using goose liver, simply melts in the mouth and is complemented perfectly by a glass of Gewurztraminer wine. As there are

relatively few geese in Alsace, manufacturers travel to the markets in the southwest and in the east to obtain them. Today, over 40 variations on Jean-Pierre's recipe are on sale in the delicatessens of Alsace.

Flammeküeche
Known in French as *tarte flambée*, this is one of the most popular Alsatian dishes. It's made with a mixture of onions, chopped pork and cream, placed

Foie gras with spices, Artzner & Feyel

on a very thin, finely rolled, pizza-like pastry base and cooked in a very hot oven for 10 minutes. The ingredients are almost always the same, with fresh produce and very fine pastry providing the key to the dish's success. Served with a crisp salad, it makes a delicious meal at a reasonable price.

fleischknaepfles are meatballs, consisting of pork, beef and veal, and there is also a variety made from liver called *lewerknaepfles*, which have a particularly delicate taste. All of these appear on menus in restaurants and are served with herbs and spices, such as coriander, which vary between

GLORIOUS GAM

Deer, hare, wild boar – the forests of the Vosges are home to a wide variety of game, as well as a large selection of wildfowl, including pheasant, partridge, wild duck and quail. In autumn, roasted game and wildfowl are both enjoyed, accompanied by a delicious bilberry sauce. You'll find them on the menu of the local inns and restaurants, but the dishes are at their best when served in the homes of the hunters themselves. Jugged hare served with Alsatian noodles (*spaetzles*) covered in bilberry sauce is an experience which is hard to beat.

Baeckeoffe

Boiled potatoes are common ingredients in Alsatian cooking. They feature in *baeckeoffe*, a magnificent hotpot, with pork, lamb and beef, all marinated in dry white wine from Alsace. The dish can take a whole morning to prepare as the meat is cooked for 3 hours before the raw, sliced potatoes are layered into the dish (sometimes this takes place on the following day). The *baeckeoffe* was traditionally cooked in the village baker's oven, and although it appears less frequently in restaurants today, it is customary to give thanks when it's served.

Knaepfles

Knaepfles are small balls made from potato. The richer

individual establishments. At the beginning of the 19thC. Maximilian I, King of Bavaria, sent for an Alsatian cook, Mme Kayser, to cook at his court in Munich, solely in order to enjoy an authentic dish of *lewerknaepfles*.

Schiefala

This Alsatian speciality (pronounced 'chifela') is a classic dish served in the *winstube* of Strasbourg. It is made with shoulder of pork, salted and smoked, and cooked in a stock. It is then sliced and served with potato salad and small onions, complemented by a delicious, hot horseradish sauce, served on the side.

Schiefala is a traditional recipe from the Haut-Rhin and goes equally well with a green salad or a well-made *choucroute*.

Cakes and desserts,
for the sweet-toothed

Desserts, cakes, doughnuts and gingerbread are traditionally served at the end of Alsatian meals, but they can also be savoured with a cup of coffee or a glass of wine. They also play a key role in local festivals.

Kugelhopf

Kugelhopf is a familiar speciality in Alsace. Its name derives from the German word *Kugel*, meaning ball, referring to its dome shape, and *Hopf* or hop, referring to the

brewer's yeast used in its recipe. The distinctive fluted and twisted mould used to make the hollow cake can be found in souvenir shops all over the region. The *kugelhopf* is baked with raisins and almonds and is sprinkled with sugar. You'll see the cake at festivals, at the breakfast table and when the time for apéritifs comes around.

Fromage blanc tarts and creams

Sugar is often added to a *fromage blanc* tart and lemon zest may also be included to give it that extra sparkle, along with vanilla sugar, raisins or ground almonds. On festive days confectioner's cream is added as a special treat. *Siaskas*, a very nourishing and filling dessert, is popular in the Munster valley and often served in the farm-inns of the Vosges region. Fresh *fromage blanc* is divided into small portions, topped with cream, sprinkled with sugar and kirsch. *Wyncrem* (cream with white wine) is served with macaroons.

Siaskas

Fruit tarts

There are as many varieties of fruit tart in Alsace as there are fruits to put in them. These include blueberries, plums, rhubarb, pears, apples,

cherries and yellow mirabelle plums. Tarts can be sweet or savoury, eaten warm or cold, and may be made from orchard or forest fruits, when they are sometimes sprinkled with ground cinnamon. In the countryside an evening meal often consists of vegetable soup followed by a slice of fruit tart, with no main course in between. A recent addition to the list of favourites is the Austrian *linzertarte*; made with raspberry preserve and dusted with cinnamon.

Festive doughnuts

Fasenachtskierchles – a form of doughnut – were traditionally handed out to children and important local figures at carnival time, when they served as a reminder of the spirits of the dead. Today children go round houses to collect these doughnuts during celebratory fireworks or when the ancient Celtic game of *schieweschlawe* (flaming disc throwing) takes place. In rural areas, it's customary to give the hens the first doughnut fried, to ensure large and frequent eggs. Made with brewer's yeast, the dough is flavoured with kirsch (a cherry-based liqueur).

Lebküche

Since the 15thC., *lebküche* or spice cake (a type of gingerbread) has adorned the Christmas tables of the Marienthal monks. The honey-based cake can be flavoured with aniseed, ginger, cinnamon, cloves, coriander, chocolate or nutmeg. *Lebküche* is at its most plentiful and popular in the Christmas markets and around the feast of St Nicholas in early December. Antique moulds for the cake are very elaborate, but today *lebküche* comes in simple rectangles, decorated with the image of St Nicholas stuck on with honey. Gertwiller has been considered the *lebküche* capital of Alsace since the 18thC.

SPRINGERLE

The recipe for this traditional cake includes aniseed, but its most remarkable feature is its naïve decorative motifs. The designs, pressed into the pastry, are highly symbolic, including images of hearts, plants, beasts and horse-riders, as well as Biblical quotations. Secular themes include marriage, love, traditional costume, trades, hunting, heraldry and humorous designs.

Christmas cakes

Cakes appear as seasonal treats in Alsace, particularly around Christmas. *Bierewecke* (fruit cake) is made with raisins, nuts, almonds, dates and spices. Christmas cake, *Chrischtstolle*, is shaped symbolically in the form of swaddling clothes, to commemorate the slaughter of the Innocents. *Bredeles*, another Christmas treat, are buttery biscuits flavoured with vanilla, lemon, aniseed or almonds. You can celebrate New Year with a delicious local brioche, *Neujohrwecke*.

Wines and spirits

Alsace is an important wine-growing area, its vineyards, stretching from Thann to Wissebourg, are located in a beautiful and fertile landscape. Join the famous *Route du Vin* to discover its different grape varieties.

LORRAINE

Museums

1 Kientzheim: museum of Alsatian wine and wine-growing **p. 211**

2 Ribeauvillé: museum of vines and viticulture **p. 211**

Wines

3 Colmar: regional wine fair of Alsace **p. 196**

4 Eguisheim: Jean-Luc Freudenreich's Alsatian wines **p. 198**

5 Ottrott: red wine **p. 145**

Distilleries

6 Lapoutroie: guided tour of the Miclo distillery **p. 216**

7 Villé: distilleries **p. 153**

Festivals

8 Turckheim: Brand regional wine fair **p. 201**

Breweries

9 Lutterbach: micro-brewery **p. 231**

10 Riquewihr: Gilbert Holl's micro-brewery **p. 219**

Wine-tasting

11 Gueberschwihr: winemakers' open day at *Fête de l'Amitié* wine festival. **p. 189**

12 Husseren-les-Châteaux: cellar tour **p. 200**

13 Kientzheim: cellar of Paul Blanck et Fils **p. 211**

14 Lapoutroie: Musée des *Eaux-de-Vie* **p. 216**

15 Niedermorschwihr: Caveau du Morakopf **p. 202**

Wine trails and walks

16 Eguisheim: Grands crus wine trail **p. 199**

17 Ribeauvillé and Riquewihr: *Route du Vin* **pp. 218-223**

18 Turckheim: wine trail through Brand vineyards **p. 201**

19 Wettolsheim: vineyard trails **p. 202**

N4

Épinal

N57

FRANCHE-COMTÉ

●Vésoul

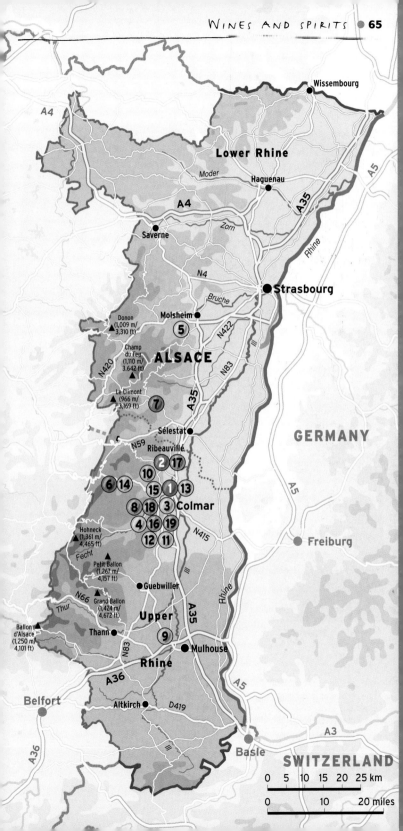

The wines of Alsace,
perfect complement to local produce

Alsace boasts three AOCs, *Appellations d'Origine Contrôlée* – Alsace, Alsace Grand Cru and *Crémant d'Alsace* (a sparkling wine). Seven red, white and rosé grape varieties enjoy a hot and dry climate, making dry, clean tasting and fruity wines. The 170 km/106 miles of the *Route du Vin* meander through two *départements*, including many wine-growing villages dotted with tempting pitstops known as *winstube*.

The wine growers of Alsace

The wines of Alsace are identified by grape variety, not by geographical region, estate or village. For example Pinot Noir, Alsace's only red variety, can come from a number of wine-growing areas and may taste differently as a result. Often the name of the region does not appear on the label. Small wine-growers form co-operatives, whereas medium-sized growers are responsible for their own production. Large wholesale wine merchants buy-in grapes.

Light wines

Sylvaner is a real thirst-quencher, a dry and light wine with a fruity note that goes well with seafood, fish and charcuterie. It should be drunk young. Pinot Blanc is a rounded wine with a fresh, supple character and a spicy nose; it is easy to drink. Riesling is dry, sophisticated and subtle – pale yellow in colour, it is the star of the white grape varieties grown in Alsace. It's a lively, elegant wine which goes just as well with fish as with *choucroute*. Muscat d'Alsace is dry and has an aromatic grapey nose, making it a perfect apéritif and party wine. It can be served with cheese and dessert, but production of Muscat d'Alsace can be irregular.

in restaurants. *Klevener* results from a blend of Pinot Blanc grape varieties and Tokay Pinot Gris, and is grown on more than 160 ha/395 acres of sunny soil in the Vosges region of northern Alsace. Dry and fruity, it releases an intriguing flavour that develops slowly on the palate.

Full-bodied wines

Pinot Gris from Alsace, known as Tokay Pinot Gris, has a round and powerful flavour with a complex bouquet that complements dishes such as *foie gras* and roast meat. It is very different in character from Hungarian Tokaï. Gewurztraminer is a well-balanced, heady and richly aromatic wine with an intense bouquet and softer spicy palate; it is often served as an apéritif or with dessert and goes well with *foie gras*. Its cousin, Traminer, is a good stand-alone drink. Pinot Noir goes well with game, poultry and cheese. It makes a fruity rosé or more complex red wine with a marked cherry aroma and taste.

Other grape varieties

Other wines are served in the *winstube* of Alsace, consisting of blends of several varieties of white grapes. *Zwicker*, also known as *Edelzwicker*, is both popular and high-quality, and can be drunk throughout the meal. It's served by the carafe

Late harvests and 'noble rot'

Late harvests (*vendanges tardives*) can last over a month, from early October to mid November. They benefit from the region's 'Indian Summer' during which soft autumn mists give way to still-warm sun. The grapes are harvested carefully – some of them are 'botrytised' and classified as *grains nobles* (noble rot). The extra ripening time produces a subtler, sweeter and more complex wine, requiring a few years to develop fully in the bottle, and wines made using this delicate method are often more expensive. Vineyards on the River Rangen, in Thann, for example, have steep, sun-drenched slopes and produce wines that command both respect and a high price.

HOW TO DRINK WINE

Alsatian wine should be served chilled but not too cold, at temperatures between 8-10°C/46-50°F, from delicate glasses with long, green stems. The wines are generally drunk when young (one to five years after harvest), although some are left to age longer, such as the *grands crus*, late harvests and vintage wines. *Crémant d'Alsace* is a sparkling wine served at 5-7°C/41-44°F in a fluted or tulip-shaped glass. Fresh and fruity, it is delicious either as an apéritif to a meal or with dessert.

Alsatian beers,
a drink for all seasons

Alsace is one of the few regions in France where wine- and hop-growing take place alongside each other. In fact, breweries abound in Alsace, and each master brewer brings his own techniques to the complex process. No fewer than 16 stages are involved in brewing beer, from malting to final bottling, and these all shape its individual taste.

6,000 years in the making

Beer was known to the Ancient World and is believed to have originated in the region between Palestine and Mesopotamia. It was a sacred drink of the Ancient

The Heineken brewery

Egyptians, who called it 'liquid bread', and it subsequently spread across Europe. Brewing in Alsace dates from Celtic times, when Gallic tribes developed their celebrated barley beer. The recipe was improved and refined in the 9thC. by monks, who added hops to the brewing process. In Alsace, monastic breweries appeared in Wissembourg, Pfaffenhoffen and, most notably, in Strasbourg.

An historic industry

Arnoldus Cervisarius founded the first Alsatian brewery in 1260, and in 1268 the first guild of brewers was established by St Louis. In Strasbourg, the corporation took the name of *Tribu des Tonneliers* ('tribe of coopers'), but only with the French Revolution did brewing develop into a significant industry. In 1803, Strasbourg had 250 breweries, but today only six remain in Alsace (Fischer, Heineken, Karlsbrau, Kronenbourg, Meteor and Schutzenberger), but they produce 56 per cent of French beer.

Four Alsatian ingredients

Beer is made with pure water, barley, hops and yeast, all of which exist in high quality in the Vosges region. Barley, for example, is grown at the heart of the Ried and hops in the small valleys of Kochersberg and Ackerland. Each plays a key role: barley transforms into malt, providing colour and flavour; hops introduce a touch of bitterness and yeast transforms the sugar into alcohol. Water is also an important factor: 8 litres/ 1.76 gallons of water are needed to make 1 litre/0.22 gallons of beer.

Hops

CHICKEN IN BEER
Serves 6
Ingredients:
1 chicken (1.5 kg/ 3 lbs), small bottle of light beer (*bière blonde*), 4 shallots, 100 g/3½ oz of butter, large pot of cream, 200 g/7 oz mushrooms, parsley, salt, pepper, small glass of juniper liqueur.

Joint the chicken and fry the pieces in 50 g/1¾ oz of butter and a small quantity of oil. Add the finely chopped shallots and cleaned, sliced mushrooms. Fry till golden and mix with liqueur and beer. Season and simmer over a gentle heat for around an hour. Remove chicken, place on a plate and keep warm. Reduce the juices and add remaining butter and cream. Pour sauce over the chicken, garnish with parsley and serve with Alsatian noodles (*spaetzles*).

From hop to glass, a complex affair

The beer-making process requires many stages, beginning with grinding the malted barley to flour, and adding water. The mixture is then heated and stirred, whereupon the starch in the grain begins to break down into sugar. Non-malted grain is mixed in to form a mash, which is filtered to produce the stock or wort. Hops are added, and the mixture is heated and then filtered. Fermentation is now allowed to take place, after which the resulting liquid is stabilised through pasteurisation. Yeast is then added to convert the sugar to alcohol. After maturation, the yeast is removed and the beer is filtered and bottled. You can see these stages for yourself in a guided tour at one of the breweries, before sampling the finished product.

Micro-breweries

The old historic breweries in Alsace are an important part of the region's heritage but are not usually open to the public. Among the beers from the Alsatian micro-breweries are Lutter'bier from Lutterbach and Hollbeer from Riquewihr, unfiltered and amber in colour. Sharrach beer from the Lauth brewery in Scharracherg-heim suits all palates, and is available as both a dark and a light beer, and in many different varieties. Lanterne and Trois Brasseurs (three brewers), from Strasbourg, are highly fermented, and the Uberach beers are made with water from the springs of the Moder valley. If you enjoy beer, the Alsatian brewers will leave you spoilt for choice.

How to drink beer

Beer can be light, amber-coloured or dark brown. Connoisseurs inspect its transparency, the texture of its froth, the density and size of its bubbles. A quick sniff reveals much about a beer's character; it can be spicy on the nose, fruity or 'hoppy', smelling of chocolate, caramel or honey. A good beer is best served at a temperature of 6-8°C/43-46°F.

Eaux-de-vie in Alsace,
the essence of local fruit

I n Alsace, cherries, mirabelle plums and raspberries are used to make sweet liqueurs, served in small glasses in restaurants and homes across the region. The museum dedicated to this *digestif* tells you everything you need to know on the subject, and even the fragrance of the liqueur is a delight.

Sensual scents

In the orchards of Lorraine the trees are laden with mirabelle plums and in the Rhône valley delicious William pears flourish on the branches. To appreciate why pear liqueur is so expensive, you need to realise that 28 kg/62 lbs of pears are needed to make just three bottles of alcohol. Fruits destined for liqueurs are distilled in Haute-Saône, but it's the *kûrzstehlala* of the Villé valley, a short-stemmed cherry, that makes the best *kirsch* (cherry liqueur) in Alsace.

Mountain fruits

In the heights of Alsace you'll find the white alisier, a variety of *sorbus*, and a limited amount of liqueur is distilled in the mountains around Ammerschwihr. Juniper berries are also found in the mountains, with their strong scent redolent of Nordic *eau-de-vie*. Wild and cultivated raspberries and strawberries are also used to make liqueurs, and blueberries are harvested in the mountains and blackberries

from the hedgerows. The long roots of the yellow gentian are distilled to make *Enzian*, and connoisseurs are also fond of a liqueur made with dog-rose hips.

A few useful tips

Eaux-de-vie should be kept away from bright light, and drunk fairly soon after it has been opened to avoid oxidation. Small glasses are ideal, as they allow you to enjoy the aroma of the orchards and mountains in which the berries ripen before harvest.

THE ROUTE DU KIRSCH

The 'Kirsch trail' follows the Val de Villé from Sélestat, with a succession of distilleries, starting in Thanvillé. In this mountainous region, with its rich soil, the Morello and wild cherries have a very acidic and watery flesh. *Kirschwasser* is the oldest form of *eau-de-vie* and a substantial quantity of cherries is needed – 18 kg/40 lbs to make just a single litre (0.22 gallons) of *eau-de-vie*. There are few remaining stills and distillers in local farms, and their future is uncertain, so you should act quickly if you want to sample their brews.

This perfume gradually develops when the *eaux-de-vie* are kept in a refrigerator and served chilled.

The waters of Alsace,
source of natural goodness

The geology of Alsace is very varied and gives rise to several excellent springs – fewer in number than in neighbouring Lorraine, but just as beneficial and therapeutic. The spring water of Alsace has been appreciated for centuries and is available today in bottled form.

Carola water

Colour-coded Carola bottles appear on the tables of restaurants and homes all over Alsace. They feature a blue label for still water, green for the slightly sparkling version and red for fully sparkling version, and the still water is ideal for preparing food for infants as it's low in nitrates. It has a slightly acid taste with a momentary bitter aftertaste.

sparkling. The spring waters of Ribeauvillé were famous as far back as the 15thC., but they were only rediscovered at the end of the 19thC. by a doctor, J.E. Chrétien Staub, who named them after his wife, Caroline. The thermal baths that were established around the spring only operated for a few years, but the bottling plant is still flourishing.

Celtic mineral water

Celtic mineral water from Niederbronn-les-Bains has been licensed for consumption since 1966. Today it's sold in major supermarkets in plastic and glass bottles. There's a

Franciscan water

In the 13thC. a Franciscan monk named Tschamser brought the particular taste of the water to the attention of the inhabitants of Soultzmatt. In 1838 a spa resort was established, under the guidance of a Monsieur Nessel, who commercialised the water 30 years later. The Lisbeth spring, from which the water is drawn, emerges at 275 m/902 ft. Nessel water has a limited production and is recommended for digestive complaints. The spring was declared a site of public interest by Napoleon III.

The monks of Murbach

Wattwiller has its source in the heart of the regional nature reserve in the Vosges. The Romans recognised the purity of the water, and in the 8thC., monks from Murbach Abbey made it famous. It's used to treat skin diseases, rheumatism and kidney ailments, and people come from all over France and Germany to enjoy its therapeutic benefits. Wattwiller has been available commercially since 1993.

The abbey-church in Murbach

Architectural heritage

Alsatian architecture is both varied and fascinating, including examples of Gothic, Romanesque and Baroque styles. There are mountain homes, half-timbered houses, farmhouses, buildings with multi-coloured façades – some contemporary, others centuries-old.

LORRAINE

Municipal buildings

1. Barr: Musée de la Folie Marco
   p. 148

2. Benfeld: Hôtel de Ville (town hall)
   p. 151

3. Bouxwiller
   p. 116

4. Mulhouse and its 19th-C. heritage trail
   p. 229

Religious heritage

5. Andlau: Ste-Richarde church
   p. 148

6. Dambach: St-Sébastien chapel
   p. 152

7. Domfessel: fortified church
   p. 113

8. Ebermunster: magnificent Baroque church
   p. 155

9. Marmoutier: abbey-church
   p. 138

10. Mont Ste-Odile
    p. 147

11. Murbach: St-Léger abbey-church
    p. 187

12. Neuwiller-lès-Saverne: St-Pierre-et-St-Paul church
    p. 117

13. Niedermorschwihr and spiral belltower
    p. 203

14. Ottmarsheim: abbey-church
    p. 232

15. Soultzbach-les-Bains: houses, churches and château
    p. 206

16. Thierenbach: Notre Dame basilica
    p. 187

17. Wintzfelden: lapidary museum (religious gemstones)
    p. 191

Rural heritage

18. Fréland: museum of regional arts and traditions (Pays Welche)
    p. 217

19. Gommersdorf
    p. 168

20. Orbey: Musée du Val d'Orbey (arts and regional traditions)
    p. 215

21. Pfaffenheim: trail of sacred sites (chapels, dolmen etc.)
    p. 176

22. Storkensohn: oil mill and museum of rural mountain workers
    p. 176

23. Ungersheim: Eco-museum of Haute-Alsace
    p. 170

Towns and villages

24. Colmar: museums, districts, River Lauch boat trip, La Petite Venise ('little Venice')
    pp. 192-197

25. Eguisheim
    p. 198

26. Haguenau and St-Georges church
    p. 122

27. Kaysersberg: houses and museums
    p. 212

28. Molsheim
    p. 140

29. Oberhai
    p. 146

30. Ribeauvillé
    p. 211

31. Riquewihr and its museums
    pp. 218-220

32. Rosheim: houses, St-Pierre-et-St-Paul church
    p. 144

33. Rouffach
    pp. 188-189

34. Saverne
    pp. 114-115

35. Sélestat
    pp. 154-155

36. Strasbourg: cathedral, museums, 'capital of Europe'
    pp. 126-135

37. Thann: Musée des Amis de Thann, collegiate church
    p. 174

38. Turckheim
    p. 200

39. Wissembourg and the Romanesque churches of northern Alsace
    pp. 102-103

Alsatian houses,
sandstone and gables

H ouses in Alsace have many things in common, as well as some subtle differences too. Some houses are adorned with oriel windows, others bear patterns and embellishments on their half-timbering that vary with the region. The roofs are generally covered in flat, brown tiles.

House with oriel window in Turckheim

Window in sandstone frame in Sélestat

The sandstone of Alsace

Stone houses stand alongside wooden ones, and in Alsace they are generally detached from one another, sometimes even facing in different directions. In the Hanau region, stone hewn from the sandstone quarries is used to frame the windows and sills. The entrance to the house is usually on the wall giving on to the courtyard and leads to the kitchen. To one side, overlooking the street, is the living room or *stub*. In the more prosperous regions, including the wine-growing areas, oriel windows adorn the façade of the homes, together with balconies that can be sealed firmly in the winter months. Oriel windows were precious sources of light for buildings in narrow streets

and offered good vantage points from which to see, be seen and keep an eye on the streets below.

Half-timbering in the vineyards

Half-timbering is a distinctive feature of the multicoloured façades of Alsatian houses. Blue, yellow, red and green appear regularly, sometimes to excess, as embellishment on the outer walls; the older, whitewashed colours are softer,

Hôtel du Tisserand in Gommersdorf

the more modern acrylic colours are bolder. Balconies laden with petunias and pink and red geraniums add another splash of colour for a picture-postcard effect. A small kitchen garden is often located outside the village and its fortifications.

Mountain farms

The large farm buildings and outhouses of the Vosges region are built in a single block, occupying the harsh mountain slopes. They are simple constructions, especially in the Val de Villé and Le Pays Welche, with a low, long stable and a dairy. The granaries perch on the slopes and are accessed via a rear entrance. Some of the *marcairies* (dairy farms) have now become farm-inns offering hospitality to tourists.

Town hall in Colmar

Farms in Sundgau

In Sundgau, traditional Alsatian farmhouses are large enough to accommodate both people and animals with the living area, barn and stables all grouped under one roof. They have an internal courtyard, steeply sloping roofs, a small garden and surrounding walls. The roofs extend over the sides of the building to protect them from the weather, and sometimes its half-timbers are adorned with symbolic motifs, such as the tree of life, solar wheels and the diagonal cross of St Andrew.

Village fountains and wells

Every square in an Alsatian village contains a fountain or well, often featuring red sandstone columns supporting a statue of the local patron saint, an historic figure or a heraldic emblem. In Andlau, the female bear met by St Richarde, wife of Emperor Charles le Gros, takes pride of place. The wells in Riquewihr and Kaysersberg remain regular meeting points for local people, and ponds, which were formerly drinking troughs, are commonplace in the northern Vosges.

Town halls

The town hall was very important in the market towns of the Middle Ages, symbolising municipal power and authority. The elaborate buildings often feature oriel windows, pinnacles, twin staircases and graceful, carved stone balconies. Good examples of this ornate

Well in Sélestat

municipal style can be seen in Ensisheim, Obernai, Rouffach, Kaysersberg, Molsheim, Guebwiller and many other villages. In Strasbourg and Colmar, the town hall remains a prestigious public building and a key symbol of local life.

HARVESTING THE WOODS OF ALSACE

Over 80 per cent of wood produced in Alsace is destined for the construction industry, which has supported the livelihoods of loggers, sawyers and craftsmen for centuries. Timbers were transported down the steep slopes on sledges (*schlittes*), drawn in the winter by horses. The rustic fjord ponies, well adapted for this heavy work, provided the only means of transporting huge tree trunks from the forest.

Religious art,
from Romanesque to Baroque

The church of Saint-Léger at Guebwiller

France, Germany and Italy have all left their mark on Alsace's religious heritage over the centuries, and variations on the Gothic architectural style have given rise to the region's most impressive religious buildings.

St-Thiébault collegiate church in Thann

Romanesque style

The Romanesque churches of Alsace are simple, classic structures, often in the shape of the Latin cross with short lateral arms. The walls have few apertures and the façades are sparsely decorated. The lantern tower is placed above the transept crossing and is often embellished with Lombardy banding, as found in the churches of Murbach, Marmoutier, Gueberschwihr and Neuwiller-lès-Saverne. The columns are simple and unadorned, but the portals sometimes feature remarkable sculptures. The doorway of the St-Pierre-et-St-Paul church in Andlau has a frieze depicting animals, monsters and realistic and allegorical scenes. The churches in Lautenbach and Rosheim also have interesting features.

Gothic churches

Gothic art harmonises closely with the Alsatian and Alemanic spirit,

Strasbourg Cathedral

and it has achieved an exceptional aesthetic quality in Alsace. The magnificent cathedral in Strasbourg, for example, is one of the finest architectural expressions of the style. The cathdedral's 'archivolt', a series of vaulted arches, replaced the rustic ceilings of earlier churches. The restored St-Laurence doorway, dating from the late 15thC., features some elaborate sculptures depicting the martyrdom of St Laurence, and is a fine example of the High Gothic style that flourished in the Middle Ages, lasting until the 17thC. The collegiate church of St-Thiébault in Thann is also worth a detour.

FAMILIES OF ORGAN-MAKERS

The Silbermann family, traditional organ-makers, was well known in the 18thC. Examples of their work can still be seen today in Marmoutier, Ebersmunster, Altorf, Strasbourg, Wasselonne, Soultz-les-Bains, Molsheim and Gries. In the 19thC. the Stier-Mockers and Callinet families introduced new elements into the manufacture of organs. The Kern, Mühleisen and Koening companies continue this historic tradition.

Church organ by Silbermann (1778)

Notre Dame Cathedral in Strasbourg

This is one of the finest Gothic cathedrals, built with pink sandstone from the Vosges. It was ravaged by fire several times in the 12thC. and its restoration

Notre Dame de l'Assomption church in Rouffach

took over two and a half centuries. At the end of the 13thC., the architect Erwin of Steinbach took charge and added a new façade, remarkable for its huge number of statues. In the 15thC. a beautiful spire raised the structure to a height of 142 m/466 ft, flanked by four turrets with winding stairways. The six-storeyed pyramid was designed by Jean Hültz of Cologne.

Mendicant orders and High Gothic

The austere influence of the Franciscans and Dominicans can be felt in Colmar, Rouffach and Wissembourg. Gothic churches expanded into vast vaulted choirs, as seen in the ruins of the Franciscan church in Sélestat, and the lines of the columns became purer and more sober. Towers and turrets vanished and the churches of the mendicant orders had solid, powerful profiles.

Baroque angels

In the 18thC., Baroque became the dominant architectural style and can be seen at its finest in the early 18thC. abbey-church in Ebersmunster, with its brightly painted decoration and stucco work and a huge crown-shaped baldaquin. The Notre-Dame

Strasbourg Cathedral

basilica in Thierenbach, built in 1723 in the Austrian Baroque style, is also worth a detour.

Traditional organs

In Alsace, the church organ has a long-standing tradition. Sometimes classed as historic monuments, the most ancient organs are those in Strasbourg cathedral (1489) and in Bouxwiller (1688). The Bas-Rhin has no fewer than 740 organs, making it one of France's most richly endowed *départements*.

Ebermunster Abbey

Great houses,
in the country and the town

Symbols of past prosperity, the great houses of Alsace can be seen in towns and in the prosperous villages that border the vineyards. Compared to the numerous fortified castles, palaces are relatively rare, and some châteaux in the countryside remain in private hands.

Maison Pfister in Colmar

Magnificent homes
As you stroll through the Petite France quarter in Strasbourg and Krutenau in Colmar, glance upwards at the splendour of the houses. The stone buildings boast oriel windows and sculpted canopies, with gables perched on top in the style of Flemish architecture. Note the windows decorated with leaded lattice or crown glass (small pieces of round glass used in medieval window panes).

Majestic structures
Alsatian châteaux (pp.36, 106) were for the most part fortresses. Palaces and mansions were rare between the Renaissance and the 18thC. The Rohan Palace in Strasbourg, built by Robert de Cotte and featuring a classic façade and impressive furnishings, is a fine example

of an Alsatian palace. In the country, fortified castles were sometimes converted to domestic splendour, such as the Maison du Parc in La Petite-Pierre, within the northern Vosges regional nature reserve.

Country castles
Wasserburgs, defensive castles surrounded by water, have preserved their original

Husseren-Wesserling

architecture to a large extent, and most remain in private hands. However, the castles at Osthoffen, Osthouse (with an unusual portal featuring stone elephants), Thanvillé, Scharrachbergheim, Bischeim with its English garden (in the Bas-Rhin), as well as Reichenberg, Wesserling, Bucheneck and Wagenbourg (in the Haut-Rhin) are all open to visitors.

A novel folly
Louis-Félix Marco, a bailiff, constructed the Folie Marco at Barr in the 18thC. A small

and luxurious manor, now converted into a museum, it re-acquired the Schwartz brothers' collections of furniture in 1963. Pieces of furniture, porcelain, pewter and mementoes of local history have been displayed

The Rohan palace in Strasbourg

Folie Marco in Barr

Château des Rohan in Saverne

in their original rooms. The main façade of this classic building has four storeys overlooking the street and a magnificent stairway leading to the collection.

The architecture of Strasbourg

The 16thC. homes in Strasbourg are made of rough-cast brick or wood, and feature gables, turrets with stairways, oriel windows and ornate portals. Notable half-timbered houses include the Maison Kammerzell (built in 1589 and decorated with frescoes and splendid woodcarvings), the former Corbeau inn and the Maison Au Pigeon. The Musée Alsacien, housed in a former aristocratic house, is itself

an interesting example of local stone and brick architecture, as is the former Hôtel des Bocklins.

The German Renaissance

In Alsace, architectural development came to an abrupt halt with the outbreak of the Thirty Years War. Construction slowly resumed in the 17thC., inspired by Renaissance buildings; and their continued influence on Alsatian classicism is displayed in the chancellery in Bouxwiller.

Maison Kammerzell in Strasbourg

COLMAR, BEHIND CLOSED DOORS

Private mansions and town houses abound in the centre of Colmar. Their lovely and often very sophisticated 18th-C. interiors are sometimes masked by austere façades. Elsewhere, impressive porches open on to Rue Berthe-Molly and Rue Chauffour. The Lycée Bartholdi (a secondary school) is the work of Ixnard and dates from 1785 while the college library's painted ceiling, by J. Melling, depicts the Muses of Parnassus. The Hôtel Arlesheim is adorned with allegorical subjects, and the doors of the house where Voltaire lived (in 1753) are decorated with mouldings.

A new architectural style, German Baroque, was introduced by the Bishop of Strasbourg, who drew upon German Baroque artists in the construction of his castle in Saverne.

Luxurious residences

Financiers and industrialists were responsible for the lavish 19thC. villas in Alsace. The middle-class homes of Mulhouse reflect this important development, such as the Ermitage villa, built in 1868 for a wealthy manufacturer of calico fabric, the Maison de la Cour des Chaînes (an 18thC. factory) with its painted ceilings, and the Villa de la Bourbonnière. Another example of the genre is the Villa Mantz, built in 1840 and inspired by the architecture of Palladian villas.

Alsace's rural heritage,
off the beaten track

Today, Alsace's rural heritage is all too easily overlooked. The countryside features several unique historical sites and structures which are rare witnesses to an eventful, secular past.

At the crossroads

Small crosses, no more than 2 m/6½ ft in height and made of local sandstone, can be found at the junctions of many trails and tracks. Walkers often stop at these monuments to admire the landscape or to determine the next section of their route. Most of these crosses (*croix de chemin*) date from between the 16th and 19thC. and they are often placed at impressive viewing points.

Watchtower in Kaysersberg

Watchtowers

Entrance gates and watchtowers often appear in the surrounding walls of villages. Although originally built for strategic purposes, they are now home to storks' nests rather than watchmen. These towers reach heights of 25-30 m/82-98 ft in the vine-growing areas and examples can be seen in Ribeauvillé, Kaysersberg and Thann. In Riquewihr the watchtower,

known as the *dolder*, was first erected in 1291 and was reinforced during the 15th and 16thC. A belfry often sat on

Boundary stone in Hanau forest

the top of the medieval towers, which provide remarkable views over the plain and mountain range beyond.

Boundary stones

Half-hidden in the Hanau forest are boundary stones featuring the heraldic symbols of Alsace and Lorraine on opposite sides. Near the Moselle, the designs are very different, incorporating coats of arms and dates. These markers have survived many threats of destruction, posed less by weather than by the demands of modern farming.

Imperial benches

Dotted along the Route des Vosges, from the north towards

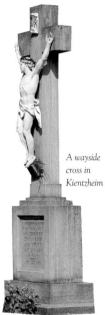

A wayside cross in Kientzheim

the Kochersberg region, are a number of unusual sandstone benches. In the time of stagecoach travel, long intervals could be spent waiting in the countryside, and the benches, topped by a sandstone roof, provided useful shelter for people and luggage. They were first introduced in 1811 to mark the baptism of Napoleon's son, the King of Rome. More were built in the Second Empire and those that survived have now been restored.

Nicknames and surnames,
a regional legacy

The origins of local nicknames and surnames go back over the centuries, and each village has its own. The traditions of local and ethnic rivalry, expressed through jokes and name-calling, are deep-rooted in Alsace.

Historic nicknames

Inhabitants of Brumath used to dunk their potatoes in vinegar before eating them

The Alsatians and their neighbours

Even before World War I, many French people considered the Alsatians to be of Alemannic (German) descent, nicknaming them *têtes carrées* ('square heads'). For their part, the Germans called Alsatians *Waggèsbier* ('lager louts').

Rivalries from within

'In the Bas-Rhin (Lower Rhine) there is nobody; in the Haut-Rhin (Upper Rhine) there is birdsong.' This is how the inhabitants of the Haut-Rhin defend their region. The Bas-Rhin locals avenge themselves by mocking the accent and slang of their Haut-Rhin neighbours, who are said to speak as if they have a permanently sore throat. Sometimes,

however, local rivalries can be overtaken by events. People from Altdorf, located on a hill, used to deride dwellers in Eckendorf as 'the bog people'. The latter, living in a valley, would call their opponents 'foggy bottoms'. Today the valley is united and descendants of the former antagonists live together in one village known as Alteckendorf.

(which tastes quite nice, actually), and as a result they were known as *essibatscher* ('vinegar splashers'). Inhabitants of

Oermingen were described as *ziwelkoepp* ('onion heads'), whereas people from Sélestat are 'duck chasers' or 'onion crushers' (*ziweletreppler*). Those living in Strasbourg were derided as *meiselocker* ('tit-trappers'), referring to the ancient custom of hunting the city's birds, a tradition practised by local children.

Festivals and celebrations

Street performers, arts and craft fairs, markets and festivals... Alsace loves to celebrate, especially at Christmas.

Markets and fairs

1 Brumath: onion festival (end September) **p. 124**

2 Gundolsheim: flea market (summer) **p. 191**

3 Rouffach: organic fair: bread, wine and cheese (early June) **p. 189**

4 St-Louis: book fair (mid-May) **p. 163**

5 Wasselonne: annual fair (end August) **p. 138**

Christmas

6 Colmar: illuminations (Friday and Saturday at end of year); Christmas markets (first weekend in Advent) **p. 193**

7 Kaysersberg: Christmas markets (from early December) **p. 213**

8 Mulhouse: Christmas market (last week in November to 31 December) **p. 229**

9 Strasbourg: *Christkindelmärik* ('Christ Child' Christmas market) **p. 134**

10 Thann **p. 174**

11 Les Trois-Épis: New Year's market (between Christmas and New Year) **p. 203**

12 Village-Neuf: living Nativity scene (24 & 25 December) **p. 161**

Alsatian traditions

13 Benfeld: tobacco festival (August) **p. 151**

14 Blodelsheim: harvest heritage festival (last weekend in July, even years only) **p. 171**

Arts and Crafts

15 Courtavon: festival of the three lilies **p. 167**

16 Gueberschwihr: open cellars for *Fête de l'Amitié* wine festival – (penultimate weekend in August) **p. 189**

17 Illhaeusern: festival of boatmen (second weekend in July) **p. 233**

18 Lapoutroie: St-Nicholas market (around 6 December) **p. 215**

19 Marlenheim: wedding of *L'Ami Fritz* (weekend of 15 August) **p. 136**

20 Metzeral: *Transhumance* festival (end May) **p. 208**

21 Mulhouse: Journées d'Octobre festival (early October) **p. 229**

22 Orbey-Tannach: water festival (first weekend in July) **p. 215**

23 Ribeauvillé: pipers' festival (first weekend in September) **p. 222**

24 Seebach: *Streisselhoch-zeit* (traditional country wedding) (mid-July) **p. 103**

25 Sélestat: Corso Fleuri (2nd Sunday in Aug) **p. 155**

26 Stosswihr: Frankenthal wedding festival (second week in August) **p. 209**

27 Thann: 'burning of three firs' festival (30 June) **p. 175**

28 Turckheim: traditional night watchman (1 May-30 October) **p. 201**

29 Zellenberg: S'Wieladà (around 15 August) **p. 221**

Local produce

30 Colmar: regional wine fair of Alsace (around 15 August) **p. 195**

31 Erstein: sugar festival (last Sunday in August) **p. 150**

32 Osenbach: snail festival (April-May) **p. 190**

33 Rodern: Pinot Noir festival (third weekend in July) **p. 223**

34 Saales: market of country produce (Fridays, July-September) **p. 143**

35 Thannenkirch: cherry festival (second weekend in July) **p. 225**

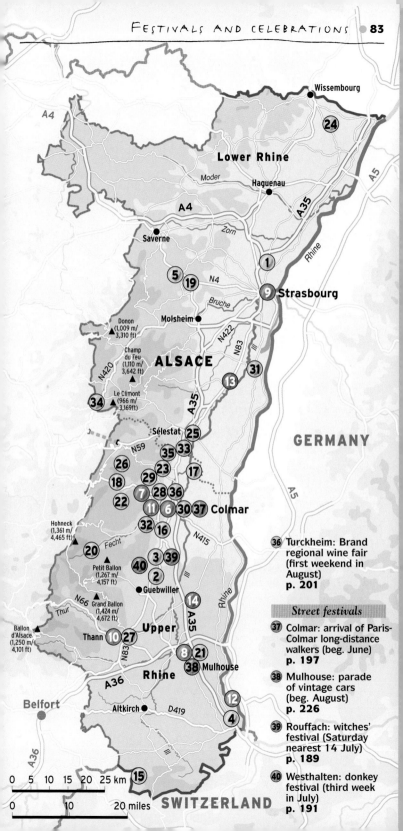

36 Turckheim: Brand regional wine fair (first weekend in August) p. 201

Street festivals

37 Colmar: arrival of Paris-Colmar long-distance walkers (beg. June) p. 197

38 Mulhouse: parade of vintage cars (beg. August) p. 226

39 Rouffach: witches' festival (Saturday nearest 14 July) p. 189

40 Westhalten: donkey festival (third week in July) p. 191

Customs and traditions,
celebrations all year round

Tradition and heritage are deeply significant for the people of Alsace. They have been at the root of its festivals and fairs over the centuries, with individual towns and villages celebrating their history through dance, music and costumed processions.

The *kilbe*

Traditionally, the *kilbe* offered the young men of Alsace the opportunity to go from one village to the next, drink as much as they wanted and meet as many eligible young

women as they could. In Hirsingue, in the 19thC., the event was held in September and lasted for 5 days. Today, a *kilbe* is celebrated on the local patron saint's day, the day of the village festival or on any special occasion. Essentially a dance affair, often involving traditional costumes, it allows the locals to enjoy themselves to the full.

Sundays in Alsace

Preparations for the day of rest start on Saturday afternoon in Alsace, when shops shut

earlier than usual. In the villages everything is closed on a Sunday, so make sure you've done all your shopping in advance. The pavements are cleaned, and in the parish church the organist rehearses new pieces for Sunday morning mass. Brass bands parade, music and dancing enliven the streets and, on a more sombre

note, dawn serenades are sometimes conducted at the memorials to those who lost their lives in the region's battles.

The *messdis*

Messtag (pl. *messdis*) is a popular event, similar to a *kilbe*. They are often held during the festival of the local patron saint in the villages, providing a welcome opportunity for families to come together and enjoy a *flammekueche* (flambéed tart) or a plate of *kesselflasch* (pork delicacies). White wine is the order of the day, and popular dances and frenetic waltzes take place, to the strains of an accordion. The most important *messdis* in Alsace are held in Wintzenheim on the Sunday after Shrove Tuesday, in Truchtersheim on the Sunday after 15 August and in Marlenheim at the 'marriage of *L'Ami Fritz*', (also 15 August). *Messtag* in Furdenheim is held on the third Sunday in September.

The first Christmas trees

Strasbourg's first Christmas tree is thought to have appeared in 1605, decorated with paper flowers, apples and sweets. Christmas tree candles first arrived in 1757, along with glass decorations. There's a reference to a Christmas tree in Turckheim in 1597, but Sélestat has an even earlier description of the town's decorated tree, dating from 1521. In 1600, the town hall of Sélestat boasted a tree adorned with apples.

The huge Christmas tree in Kléber Square, Strasbourg

The bounty of Nature

Since the Middle Ages, the federation of market gardeners has marked the occasion of their patron saint's day (St Roch) on 16 August. Young men accompany a procession to the church, carrying baskets of vegetables on their shoulders. Even more unusual is the guild of *zewelatrepplers* ('onion tramplers'), founded in Sélestat. Their name derives from the traditional practice of treading new seeds into the ground with planks of wood attached to their shoes. Members of the guild wear a varnished wooden onion and are (allegedly!) adept at eating raw onions without flinching.

Flea markets and attic clearances

As the days grow warmer, Alsatians relish meeting friends and neighbours at the flea markets held in the small streets of the village or town. You are unlikely to unearth an undiscovered Rembrandt or Picasso, but there are lots of things to entertain you, as well as the chance to try a grilled sausage at one of the many stalls, washed down with a mug of beer. Nowadays, all too many items are made of plastic, but if you have a good rummage, you may find the odd interesting old clock or engraving.

THE ROUNDS OF THE NIGHT WATCHMAN

The night watchman was once a common sight in European towns and villages. He can still be seen in Alsace today, going about his business in Sélestat and Turckheim. It was the night watchman's job to light and then extinguish the town lamps and keep a watchful eye on the place during the hours of darkness. Today, his role is to amuse tourists with historic tales as he does his rounds, lamp, horn and halberd in hand, crying out at every street corner his warning of the dangers of fire.

Festivals and fairs,
the seasonal cycle

There's a festival in Alsace to mark every season, if not every week. The Alsatians love celebrating, whether to honour a patron saint, mark a family occasion or commemorate an historic event. For many tourists, such local festivities are the high point of their visit to the region.

Christmas markets

The now widely fashionable Christmas markets, whose origins lie in the ancient markets of the Rhine, are strongly supported in Alsace. They were traditionally held during the weekends leading up to Christmas, stocked with local produce and gifts made in domestic kitchens or knitted or embroidered by Alsatian women. Christmas markets today are rather more commercial and professional affairs, but they remain picturesque and atmospheric occasions. Locally produced smoked *charcuterie*, pastries, breads and honey are among the culinary highlights.

Carnival time

Alsace celebrates its royal carnival with *schangelas*, rolled doughnuts in the shape of chicken's legs, and *knieplatzer*, flat doughnuts traditionally moulded on the knees of the women bakers. The winter festival is also celebrated in the villages of central Alsace and Sundgau with the hurling of wooden, flaming discs – a legacy from Celtic times. The effigy of a witch or 'winter' figure may be burnt at the stake, depending upon the area. In Habsheim, near Mulhouse, the witch figure is charged with all the evils of the village, which are expelled when it is destroyed.

The spring festival

Spring festivals, such as the one in Dambach-la-Ville, often take the form of a walk in Alsace. In some regions the small white asperula flower, with its star-shaped petals (p.21), is the central theme of the spring walks, especially in the

LE 8 MAI RANDONNÉE DE L'ASPÉRULE À NIEDERSTEINBACH

villages of the northern Vosges. Known as the *Randonnée de l'Aspérule* (asperula walk), these occasions celebrate the natural powers of the plant, which is used for flavouring food and alcohol, as well as for therapeutic purposes.

Wedding ceremonies

In Marlenheim, weddings keep alive the tradition of *L'Ami Fritz*, hero of the 19thC. novel by Erckmann and Chatrian (p.41). Locals wearing traditional costumes

Streisselhochzeit (*traditional wedding*) *at Seebach*

play the roles of mayor, curate, guests and verger. Other costumed participants line the streets, accompanied by a traditional band. The peasant wedding is also re-enacted during the *Streisselhochzeit* in Seebach, a celebration of haymaking time. These festivals date back to 1937.

Festival of St John

On 24 June, the summer equinox is celebrated with the festival of St John the Baptist. Each village builds a pyramid-shaped bonfire or *fackel*, centred around a conifer, reaching a height of up to 20 m/66 ft. Once dusk falls, the

fires are lighted and dancing begins. This lively and noisy celebration, thought to derive from Celtic Beltane fires, lasts until the final embers die.

Pfifferdaj

Pfifferdaj (day of the fifes) is one of the most traditional festivals in Alsace. It dates from medieval times, when the counts of Ribeaupierre, installed in the château overlooking Ribeauvillé, were patrons of musicians and performers. At the beginning of September, entertainers came to pay homage to their overlords, and a folk festival, complete with music, dancing,

Poster for Pfifferdaj

a huge procession, was held in honour of their patron saint, Notre-Dame de Dusenbach. The fife (*pfiffer*) was a popular instrument at the time, and the Pfifferhaus in Ribeauvillé is said to be the old head-quarters of itinerant musicians. Today the *pfifferdaj* is held on the first Sunday in September in various locations, including Ribeauvillé and Bischwiller.

St Nicholas

St Nicholas' huge white beard and jolly red cheeks are familiar to every Alsatian child. A Turkish bishop of the 4thC., and patron saint of Greece and Russia, legend has it that he visited an inn, the owner of which had cut the throats of three small children in order to serve them to his guests. Having converted the owner to Christianity, St Nicholas took the children out of the salting-tub, restored them to life and despatched them to school. Nowadays, he is said to bring ginger-bread, oranges and other delicacies to the well-behaved children of Alsace – their mischievous contemporaries meet the Bogeyman instead!

Tales and legends,
once upon a time in Alsace…

Fairies, dwarves, ghosts and witches lurk in the mountains, springs and valleys of Alsace. The ruins of the castles harbour secrets and tales too scary to be told on dark, wintry nights…

Bouxwiller church

The patron saint of Alsace

St Odile is the patron saint of Alsace, and during the 7thC. her life was recounted in many legends. The daughter of Adalric of Hohenbourg, Odile was rejected by her father when she was born blind. However, she miraculously regained her sight after being baptised, and her father was also converted by this event and his daughter's faith. He finally acknowledged Odile and gave her his summer residence and mountain fortress, Hohenbourg castle. In 680, Odile founded the first abbey for the women of Alsace, housing more than 130 nuns of noble lineage. St Odile is buried in the convent's chapel, and the sacred site enjoys a magnificent panoramic view of the Vosges and the Plaine d'Alsace (p.147).

The dwarves of Ferrette

Once upon a time, *erdwiebele* (dwarves) inhabited the Gorge aux Loups to the south of Ferrette. They were great metalworkers and everything they used was made of silver, even their garden and kitchen equipment. The dwarves were eternally youthful, although they did not have children themselves, and they were very helpful to the people of the valley. However, their long cloaks always covered their feet, intriguing some young women of Ferrette. One day, they went to the dwarves' gorge and sprinkled very fine sand on the ground. At dawn, the dwarves headed for the wood, leaving behind the footprints of goats in the sand. The young women made fun of the footprints, and the dwarves were so mortified by their laughter that they have never been seen from that day to this.

Fritz the cooper

Fritz Himmel, a cooper, loved to drink and gamble at Mother Kummel's inn in Saverne. One day, having lost all his money, he bumped into the devil, who offered him 1,000 pieces of gold for his soul. Fritz agreed, returned to the inn and gambled away most of his new-found fortune. He then met two giants who were spreading terror throughout the region. They fought among themselves for the remainder of Fritz's money, finally killing each other. The Lord of Gonzenheim was so grateful that he rewarded Fritz with another 1,000 pieces of gold, enabling him to repay his debt to the devil.

St Richarde's bear (794)

Richarde was the wife of the Emperor Charles le Gros ('the fat'), a jealous man who locked his beautiful wife up in Kirchheim. The lord of Andlau arrived to defend his kinswoman's honour, and Richarde left, having decided to build an abbey. A pilgrim prophesied that she would found her abbey on the spot where she saw a female black bear digging in the earth. Strangely enough, when in Andlau, Richarde came across a bear that was trying to bury

THE SACRED TRIANGLE

A powerful magnetic axis is said to link the triangle formed by the Donon mountains, Mont Ste-Odile and the Champ du Feu, to the west of Obernai. If you hold a pendulum, a positive energy circuit makes it swing between the Rothau campsite to the gap between the mountains. An ancient Druid warning reminds those susceptible to the magnetic field of the full moon's effects on the Earth. However, this does not deter walkers from enjoying the beautiful landscape on the route along the Mur Païen to the foot of the Donon.

The Champ du Feu

its dead offspring, and she comforted the animal, stroking its head. The beautiful empress brought the young cub back to life in her arms, and a few months later a wonderful convent was built in Andlau. The bear is commemorated in a sandstone sculpture on the site.

The tale of Strasbourg's two Christmas trees

On Christmas Eve, the markets of Strasbourg were brimming with toys and cakes. The story goes that a kindly grandmother was saving her pennies to buy sweets for her grandson. The child, wanting to buy a gift for his grandmother in return, went into the woods and cut down two fir trees. He tried to sell them, but, sadly, without success. Master Heidel, a local head nurseryman, took pity on the boy and gave him a gold coin in return for the trees, together with some turkey and a delicious cake. The following day the nurseryman's sons planted the trees behind the Ste-Aurélie church. During the night, the trees grew so high that they can still be seen to this day.

Alsatian costume,
an outfit for every occasion

I n Alsace, festivals are the perfect occasion for the locals to don traditional regional costume. Red waistcoats for the men and large black headdresses for the women are common in Alsace, with the design of the costumes varying from valley to valley.

Distinctive dress

Since the Franco-Prussian war of 1870, Alsatian women have acquired a rather idealised image. Their traditional costume includes a large, black, bow-shaped headdress with a three-coloured rosette, and a long red skirt adorned with black velvet ribbons. An apron is worn over the top. This costume was commonly worn in Lower Alsace, allowing emigrants from the region to recognise each other when living abroad. The red, white and blue rosette, together with the apron, traditionally embroidered with cornflowers, poppies, daisies and corn ears, also provided distinctive symbols for fellow Alsatians.

One of Hansi's illustrations

Patriotic costumes

Following the 1918 Armistice and the liberation of Alsace in 1945, thousands of costumes were manufactured to illustrate Alsatian patriotism. Some were rather imaginative, bearing little relation to the traditional skirts, such as the black *schlupfkapps* of the Lower Alsace. Regional costume had now become an artificial symbol, expressing patriotism through a red waistcoat and black velvet trousers. In illustrations by Hansi, such costumes portrayed an inaccurate image of Alsace.

Authentic peasant costume

Over the centuries, traditional peasant clothes have evolved hand in hand with commercial and rural life of the valleys. Dairy farmers (*marcaires*), for example, had their own costume in the Munster valley, while the dress worn in the Vosges had a marked influence on that of

it sports brocaded velvet with inset patterns, in black, violet or dark blue. At home, the Alsatians swap their *bruschti* for a *peter*, a knitted black woollen jacket, which is warmer and easier to wear. Elegant young people wear them today in coloured silk.

Black hats and white bonnets

The black felt hat took on a variety of designs from the

the Bruche valley. Some parts of the costume, such as the waistcoat, 'skirt' or hat, could be worn happily by both sexes, while the distinctive headdress became the symbol of a married woman.

The headdress

The falling price of ribbon, silk and lace in the 19thC. made elaborate headdresses generally more accessible. Decorated with knots and strings, they were tied under the chin and covered the wearer's cheeks and ears. Some of the designs worn at festivals are quite remarkable, in particular those seen in Kochersberg in Lower Alsace, adorned with brown silk damask and floral patterns. Others, such as in Wissembourg, are made of embroidered tulle, or have large black knots on a gold bonnet. The different motifs identify the religious or social status of the women wearing them.

Elegant and comfortable waistcoats

The red waistcoat (*bruschti*) is worn over the shirt to help protect the wearer from the cold. In Lower Alsace, it has lapels and buttons, while further south,

INTERPRETING COSTUME

Landscape and climate are key factors in the design of traditional costume, but religion, social class or membership of a guild were also important. In the past, one glance could reveal the wearer's status and origins. Young women wore red knots, young men caps or bonnets, while red skirts were worn by Catholics and green by Protestants. The etiquette of costume can still describe a person like a calling card. Conscripted soldiers, for example, wear plumed and multicoloured attire during festival in the Obernai region or in Upper Alsace, and orange flowers adorn the head-dresses of young married women.

17thC. In its more decorative form, it was worn mostly by the middle classes, while the peaked hat of the Sélestat region had military connotations. The most popular headwear of the Alsace region included the white cotton bonnets with long embroidered points for the men of Lower Alsace, the Russian fur hat of Seebach, the upturned pot-shaped hat of the Hoerdt region and the dairyfarmer's embroidered leather hat sported in the Munster valley.

Alternative Alsace

Alsace has its own mysterious, fascinating and thematic trails that draw upon history and tradition. Discover more about the region on some inspiring and unusual journeys.

Trails

1 *Route du Vin* (wine trail), 180 km/112 miles, Marlenheim to Thann **p. 136**

2 *Route de la Carpe Frite* (fried carp trail), from Altkirch to Oltingue **p. 168**

3 *Route de la Truite* (trout trail), from Remiremont to the gateway to the Hautes Vosges; gives access to Vallée de la Thur, Thann and Cernay **p. 176**

4 *Route des Cinq Châteaux* (5 castles trail) **p. 199**

5 *Route Joffre* 18 km/11 miles from Maseveaux to Thann **p. 172**

6 *Route des Crêtes*: farm-inns, *marcairies* and wonderful mountain landscapes, covering 80 km/50 miles **pp. 178-181**

7 *Route du Fromage* (cheese trail), Munster to Petit Ballon **p. 204**

8 Grands Crus trail: Hunawihr, Zellenberg, Beblenheim, Bennwihr, Mittelwihr and Riquewihr **pp. 218-220**

9 *Route Verte* (green route): historic and cultural sites in Contrexéville, Vittel, Épinal, Le Tholy, Gérardmer, Munster, Turckheim, Colmar, Horbourg-Wihr, Neuf-Brisach, Breisach-am-Rhein, Freiburg-im-Brisgau, Kirchzarten, Hinterzarten and Titisee-Neustadt **pp. 184, 192-197**

10 *Route Historique Romane d'Alsace* (Romanesque route): a trail of Alsace's Romanesque remains, from Wissembourg to Feldbach. 19 stages covering over 120 11th- and 12th-C. monuments **pp. 204-209, 232**

Witchcraft

11 Le Bastberg: witchcraft in Alsace **pp. 102-103**

Legends

12 Nideck: château and waterfall (mythical haunt of a water nymph and some local giants) **p. 117**

Miscellaneous

13 Colmar-Metzeral: Micheline train **p. 139**

14 Limersheim: excursions and discoveries on a tobacco trail **p. 197**

15 Niederbronn: healing springs **p. 151**

16 Soultz: instruction in water divining **p. 187**

N4

LORRAINE

N57

Épinal

Remiremont

FRANCHE-COMTÉ

Tourist routes,
see a different side of Alsace

There are a number of tourist itineraries in Alsace, not surprising for a region of this size. The signposted, thematic routes focus on food and wine, history and nature, and stretch from north to south and between Lorraine and the Rhine. The trails are a great way to discover Alsace's culinary specialities or heritage sites.

The *Route Verte* (green route)

The cross-frontier *Route Verte* was created in 1960 by the mayor of Colmar. Seen as a symbol of friendship between Lorraine, Alsace and the Bade region, it encompasses many historic and cultural sites. There are 15 successive *communes* (administrative subdivisions) along the route that stretches from the west to the east and includes culinary pitstops such as Contrexéville, Vittel, Épinal, Le Tholy, Gérardmer, Munster, Turckheim, Colmar, Horbourg-Wihr, Neuf-Brisach, Breisach-am-Rhein, Freiburg-im-Briesgau, Kirchzarten, Hinterzarten and Titisee-Neustadt.

The *Route Romane* (Romanesque route)

From the north to the south of Alsace, between Wissembourg and Feldbach, there are 19 stops along this thematic route. Over 120 monuments bear witness to the richness of

The Gérardmer valley

Alsatian art that developed between the 11th and 13thC. , integrating the artistic and architectural influences of the neighbouring regions of Burgundy, Lombardy, Lorraine, Franche-Comté and the Rhine valley. This itinerary takes you through the history of Alsace from the dramatic impact of the Carolingian kingdom to the prosperity of the Hohenstaufens.

The *Route des Crêtes* (ridge route)

The *Route des Crêtes* is one of Alsace's best-known routes. It runs along the ridge of the Vosges from the Col du Bonhomme to Thann, visiting the many mountain farm-inns, which combine farming and hospitality.

St-Léger church in Guebwiller

Access to the high pastures is possible from each of the valleys of the Vosges and wonderful panoramas follow one after the other. The *Route des Crêtes* stretches for 80 km/ 50 miles and takes in the Col du Bonhomme, Col de la Schlucht, Markstein and the Grand Ballon before heading down towards Vieil Armand and Cernay.

The *Route Joffre*

This lovely itinerary bears the name of the Commander-in-Chief of the French forces, Field Marshal Joffre. Created during World War I to assist communications between the Doller and Thur valleys, its military role was resumed during the winter of 1944-45, prior to the advance of French troops for whom it

Military monument on the Route Joffre

was the sole means of access to Thann. Today the *Route Joffre* is a tourist itinerary connecting Masevaux and Thann over a stretch of

18 km/11 miles. From Thann, you can also make your way up to the *Route des Crêtes* and pick up the *Route du Vin*.

The *Route du Vin* (wine route)

The *Route du Vin* is France's most famous gastronomic itinerary. In Alsace, it zigzags along the 180 km/112 miles

between Marlenheim and Thann, exploring the local wine-growing villages known as the 'pearls of the vineyards'. Tasting cellars allow the visitors to try different wines and there are several *sentiers viticoles*, waymarked tracks that wind through the heart of the vineyards.

The *Routes de la Carpe Frite* (fried carp routes)

The *Routes de la Carpe Frite* were created in 1975 in Sundgau to promote the regional culinary speciality, imported from the eastern regions. The fish, caught in the pools of Sundgau, are traditionally served in piping hot fried slices, accompanied

ALSACE MEETS LORRAINE

Two tourist itineraries take in both Alsace and Lorraine. The *Route de la Truite* (trout route) makes its way from Remiremont to the Hautes Vosges and then on to the Thur valley, Thann and Cernay. It's a good way to join the *Route du Vin* and follow the Munster cheese itinerary, or to climb up towards the *Route des Crêtes* or, as a third alternative, the *Route Joffre*. The *Route du Bois* (wood route) is divided into three loops and nine circuits, extending over a total of 500 km/ 312 miles. There are information points which explain the history and development of the landscape which, in Alsace, are situated in the Ballon d'Alsace, Munster, Haut-Koenigsbourg and La Petite-Pierre.

by mayonnaise and fresh green salad. This trail is a wonderful way to discover the sites hidden in the quiet valleys of the Ill and the Thalbach, to the south of Mulhouse between Altkirch and Oltingue.

Family outings

Traditional festivities with delicious snacks and treats, plus parks specially adapted for children's use, are all in store for young visitors to Alsace.

Festivals

1. Blodelsheim: harvest heritage festival **p. 171**
2. Kaysersberg: Christmas **p. 213**
3. Rouffach: witches' festival **p. 189**
4. Seebach: *Streisselhochzeit* (country wedding festival) **p. 103**
5. Sélestat: Corso festival of flowers **p. 155**
6. Artzenheim: Eldorado park **p. 233**

Parks

7. Morsbronn: *Fantasialand* **p. 109**
8. Mulhouse: zoological and botanical garden **p. 229**
9. Obernai: Les Naïades aquarium and park **p. 147**

Delicacies and sweets

10. Gertwiller: glazed gingerbread **p. 148**
11. Osenbach: snail race **p. 190**
12. Sigolsheim: bilberry picking **p. 210**

Walks

13. Bouxwiller: geological trail **p. 210**
14. Colmar: tourist train **p. 192**
15. Ferrette: dwarves' trail **p. 164**
16. Gunsbach: water trail **p. 205**
17. Huningue: planet trail **p. 162**
18. Metzeral: Festival of *transhumance* **p. 208**
19. Riquewihr: tourist train **p. 220**
20. Ste-Croix-aux-Mines: historic and botanical trail **p. 225**
21. Sentheim: tourist railway, Doller valley **p. 173**
22. Strasbourg: Parc de l'Orangerie, *Ceinture verte* (green belt) walk **pp. 127, 135**
23. Vogelsheim: Rhine tourist railway **p. 232**

Animals

24. Hunawihr: stork and otter sanctuary **p. 221**
25. Kintzheim: birds of prey and barbary ape sanctuary **p. 158**
26. Munchhausen: ornithological reserve **p. 105**
27. Orbey: visit to a fish farm **p. 215**
28. Westhalten: donkey festival **p. 191**

Museums

29. Colmar: interactive toy and tourist train museum **p. 194**
30. Mulhouse: national automobile museum and French railway museum **pp. 226, 227**
31. Riquewihr: stagecoach museum **p. 220**
32. Ste-Marie-aux-Mines: school museum **p. 224**
33. Soultz: La Nef des Jouets (toys) **p. 186**

Nature

34. Feldbach: St-Loup orchard **p. 169**
35. La Chapelle du Chêne: ecological paradise **p. 156**

Alsace in detail

The Upper Rhine (Haut-Rhin)   160

Alsace in detail

In the following pages you'll discover all the necessary clues to exploring the real Alsace. The *départements* are colour-coded to help you find relevant information more easily.

● Nancy

N4

① *The Lower Rhine (Bas-Rhin)*
pp.102-159

② *The Upper Rhine (Haut-Rhin)*
pp.160-233

LORRAINE

Épinal ●

N57

FRANCHE-COMTÉ

● Vésoul

0   5   10   15   20   25 km

0   10   20 miles

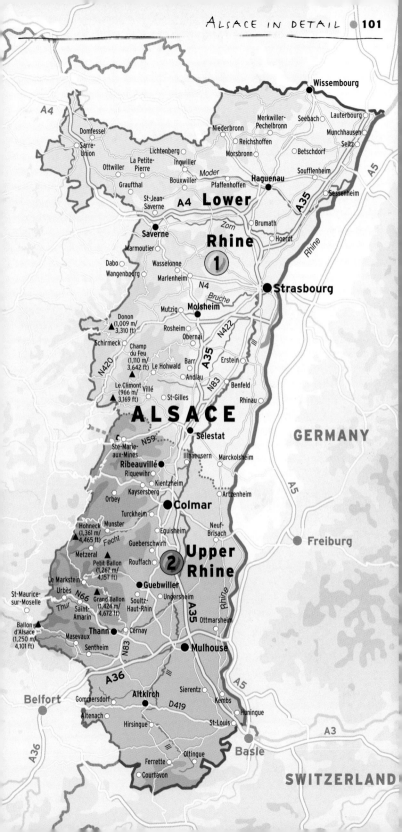

Wissembourg,
pearl of the north

Place de la République

W issembourg, or the 'white town', is a fascinating place, an ancient frontier town on the banks of the Lauter. A vibrant commercial and industrial centre, it boasts a wide variety of activities and an interesting history. Many visitors cross the Rhine to walk through its picturesque streets.

A stroll through the town

Musée Westercamp
3, Rue du Musée
☎ **03 88 54 28 14**
Open Mon., Wed., Thurs. 2-6pm, Fri. and Sat. 9am-noon, 2-6pm, Sun. 10am-noon, 2-6pm. *Admission charge.*
Start your tour at the small Musée Westercamp, housed in a 16thC. building with a lovely oriel window. It contains furniture, costumes and mementoes from the 1870 battlefield, as well as prehistoric and Roman exhibits.

Turn right as you leave the museum, passing the St-Jean church and head for the banks of the Lauter. Past the bridge is the St-Pierre-et-St-Paul church; its attractive square belfry is the only remains of an earlier Romanesque building. Inside, a 15thC. fresco depicting St Christopher holding Jesus, is the largest painted figure in France, reaching a height of 11 m/36 ft. As you pass Rue du Chapitre, visit the lovely half-cloister containing lapidary

(gemstone) relics. Return to the town hall, stopping to admire the Maison du Sel – a former hospital, slaughterhouse and salt warehouse dating from 1448. It has a remarkable undulating roof, balconied dormer windows and canopies. Finally, take a walk along the ramparts from the Stichaner roundabout, following Boulevard Clemenceau.

Cycle routes on the border

Information at the tourist office, Hôtel du Département
☎ **03 88 76 67 67,**
PAMINA
☎ **03 88 94 67 20**
Wissembourg is the start of many attractive cycle trails that straddle the French-German border. The first (shady and quite easy) goes to

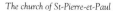
The church of St-Pierre-et-Paul

Radeln ohne Grenzen

Vélo sans frontière

... im Lautertal ... circuit de la Lauter

STREISSELHOCHZEIT

Traditional country wedding
☎ 03 88 94 70 94
(Union des associations)
in June & July;
☎ 03 88 94 74 06
(town hall) out of season.
Admission charge.
Streisselhochzeit is a wonderful festival, held in Seebach over 3 days in mid-July. You are cordially invited to attend a re-enactment of a Protestant rural wedding, with all players dressed in traditional costume. The programme is varied and includes an historic theatrical display, lighting, tastings of local specialities in the neighbouring farms, exhibitions, singing, dancing and, of course, the bridal procession, complete with horse and carriage.

Scheibenhard (15 km/9 miles to the east) along the left bank of the River Lauter. It returns via Schleithal, the longest village in Alsace (6 km/3¾ miles), and Bruchwald. The second, a more challenging circuit, explores the *Südwest-weinstrasse* (the German wine route), returning via several pretty villages. Two useful maps are available: one covers the Lower Rhine (from the Hôtel du Département), the other more specific map can be bought from the tourist office or from PAMINA (an association promoting cross-frontier co-operation).

The Outre-Forêt

3 km/2 miles
S of Wissembourg
Geisberg monument
Take the D264 to Riedseltz, then turn left on to D186
This monument to the Franco-Prussian war has a spectacular view of the Outre-Forêt, an area bordered by the Haguenau forest and Germany. Its landscape is a mixture of rolling fertile hills and the northern Vosges foothills.

Seebach

8 km/5 miles
S of Wissembourg
A trip into the past
Seebach is among the best-preserved villages of the Lower Rhine. Its half-timbered, flower-laden houses paint an accurate picture of an Alsatian village in the 1700s.

The churches of the north
Begin your tour in Altenstadt (3 km/2 miles E of

Spotcheck
D1

Things to do
Musêe Westercamp
Cycle routes on the French-German border

With children
Streisselhochzeit (traditional country wedding) in Seebach

Within easy reach
Lauterbourg (17 km/ 11 miles E), p.104
Fortified castles of northern Alsace (25 km/16 miles W), p.106

Tourist office
Wissembourg:
☎ 03 88 94 10 11

Wissembourg) with its lovely Romanesque church. The 11thC. belfry, decorated with Lombardy banding, was later given a third storey, and it has an unusual porch. Take the CD263 to Surbourg (20 km/ 12½ miles south) and admire its church. Founded in the 6thC., it is all that remains of the oldest abbey in Alsace. The building is typical of the Romanesque architecture of the Rhine, with its powerful square pillars and fine columns.

Altenstadt church

Lauterbourg and the Rhine,

explore the river and the spa region

L auterbourg is the county town of the canton of Lower Rhine, an active industrial hub and port of the Rhine. Take the opportunity to walk along the river and follow its course to Strasbourg, making some interesting excursions into Germany.

Lauterbourg

A Rhine town

Lauterbourg is an easy town to explore. Begin at the Renaissance doorway to the town hall, which features local coats of arms, and then make your way to the Porte de Landau gate (1708), fortified by the French military architect Sébastien Le Prestre de Vauban. A sculpted sun on the gate evokes the oath of allegiance sworn by the town to Louis XIV, the 'Sun King', in 1680. Stroll through the small streets to the Rue des Moulins, with its attractive inn

and lovely children's play area laid out on the ramparts.

Cycle routes and footpaths

Information from the tourist office

Lauterbourg is the departure point for several excursions by bike (see Wissembourg, p.120) or on foot. One of the most enjoyable

and beautiful is the Haut du Canton path, starting at the police station. It takes around 5 hours to complete and is signposted with a red circle.

Rastatt

16 km/10 miles S of Lauterbourg

Château de Sybilla

5 km/3 miles E

Schloss Favorite

☎ (00 49 for Germany) 72 22 41 207

Open Tues.-Sun. 9am-5pm. *Admission charge.*

Rastatt has one of the most romantic châteaux – the Baroque Schloss Favorite ('favourite castle'). Built in 1710 for Sybilla Augusta, a young widow, its magnificent interior features *scagliola* floors (imitation marble), a Florentine room and large porcelain collections.

Porte de Landau

Baden-Baden

*10 km/6 miles
E of Beinheim via the
Iffezheim dam bridge*

Cure your ills or roll the dice

Casino
Kaiserallee, 1
☎ (00 49) 72 21 21 060
Open daily 2pm-2am
(weekends to 3am).

FRANCO-GERMAN
TOURIST DETAILS

LES BORDS
DU RHIN
entre Culture et Détente

PASSEPORT
TOURISTIQUE

TOURISTIK-PASS

ALSACE

Information centre
Ehemaligetrinkhalle,
Kaiserallee, Baden-
Baden, Germany
☎ (00 49) 72 21 21
060
This is the place to
come for information
on German attractions
further along the
Rhine. Baden-Baden
itself and Rastatt are
both interesting, and
Karlsruhe is worth a
visit. It lies 21 km/13
miles from Lauterbour
and is home to the
Trifels Palace, a marble
splendour within a
medieval castle.

**Caracalla
Thermal Baths**
Römerplatz, 1
☎ (00 49) 72 21 27 592
Open daily 8am-10pm.
Admission charge.
Baden-Baden is not only a
spa town, but also home to
a very popular casino. After
a bit of a flutter, relax in the
Caracalla thermal baths,
named after a Roman
emperor who came here to
cure his rheumatism.
Stroll along
Lichtentalerallee,
following the
course of the
Oos. Finish
off your walk
with a visit
to Gönneranlage, an
attractive park.

Munchhausen

*8 km/5 miles
S of Lauterbourg*

Ornithological reserve

**Education and
information centre**
42, Rue du Rhin
☎ 03 88 86 51 67
Open Mon.-Fri. 9am-
noon, 2-6pm.
Free admission.
Munchhausen is a tranquil
village, very popular with
anglers and home to an
ornithological reserve that
regularly arranges courses and
meetings. The information
centre has details of all the
available activities.

The northern Rhine

Visit the
Ligne des Amers

Head up the Rhine from the
port of Lauterbourg, past
Munchhausen, Seltz and
Roeschwoog, where you turn
left towards Fort-Louis.
Several species of birds make
their home on the banks of
the river, so keep an eye out
for them. Follow the EDF
route to the Gambsheim dam.

Spotcheck

D1

Things to do

Cycle routes and footpaths
Schloss Favorite (Château de
Sybilla) at Rastatt
Casino and spa in Baden-
Baden
Stroll along the Rhine

With children

Lauterbourg park
Ornithological reserve in
Munchhausen

Within easy reach

*Wissembourg (17 km/
11 miles W), p.102
Pottery country (20 km/
13 miles S), p.120*

Tourist offices

Lauterbourg:
☎ 03 88 94 66 10
(Place du Château)
Rastatt:
☎ (00 49) 72 22 97 24 62
Baden-Baden:
☎ (00 49) 72 21 27 52 00

A 2-km/1-mile signposted
walk along the Rhine takes
you to the *Ligne des Amers*.
This contemporary work by
Alain Willaume features
wonderful photographs,
coated with enamel to protect
them from the weather, which
depict the great rivers and
capes of the world.

The fortified castles of northern Alsace,
a trail of discovery

Survivors of a turbulent history, Alsace's fortified castles were mostly dismantled on the command of Louis XIV, following the region's return to French control in 1748. Although little remains of their former defensive roles, they make splendid viewing points and perfect surroundings in which to unwind.

Château de Fleckenstein
22 km/ 14 miles W of Wissembourg
Information at the Lembach tourist office
Open daily
15 Mar.-30 Apr. 10am-5pm;
May-Oct. 10am-6pm.
Admission charge.
Built in the 12thC. and destroyed in 1680, the castle is perched on a spur of rock that stands more than 40 m/ 130 ft high, surrounded by a wood. The rooms inside are hewn out of the rock, including the spectacular Salle des Chevaliers (knights' hall) with its central pillar. The views are really magnificent.

Château de Hohenbourg
6 km/4 miles NE of Fleckenstein
Information at Lembach tourist office
Free admission.
The château has a beautiful and ornate Renaissance gate which leads into the main courtyard, a powerful artillery bastion and an impressive barbican. There's a wonderful view of the neighbouring German castle, Wegelnsburg.

Château de Wasigenstein

Château de Wasigenstein
10 km/6 miles W of Fleckenstein Parking at Klingenfels Access to the château is via a pleasant 10-min waymarked walk, or take the 4-hr signposted circuit from Niedersteinbach (6 km/3³/₄ miles) W of

Château de Fleckenstein

GIMBELHOF FARM-INN

At the Château de Hoehnbourg
Open Wed.-Sun. noon-2pm, 6.30-9pm. Refreshments available all day
☎ 03 88 94 43 58
This pleasant farm-inn makes a perfect pitstop on your travels. It serves a tasty Alsatian daily special at €10 or an à la carte menu that won't cost more than €12, including a selection of Alsatian specialities (try the *choucroute/sauerkraut*). Book ahead, if possible. Children are welcome and there's a lovely 'medieval' play area to keep them happy.

Fleckenstein via the Rocher des Tziganes (gypsy rock) and the Maimont (an ancient Druid stone).
Information at Lembach tourist office
Free admission.
Many a legend is attached to Wasigenstein castle, a romantic and enchanting place, with its irregular steps and lovely arched window. It was here that the epic tale of Walther d'Aquitaine unfolded. As told in the 10thC. *chanson de geste* (narrative poem), Walther was obliged to fight his friend Hagen, a Frankish

chief. Happily, they were finally to be reconciled over a jug of wine.

Château de Windstein

12 km/7¹/₂ miles S of Wasigenstein
Free admission.
Two very different castles, just 500 m/547 yd apart, bear the same name. Windstein and New Windstein are thought to date from the end of the 12thC. and the mid-14thC. respectively. The dilapidated ruins of Old Windstein consist of stairs, bedrooms, cells and a well, 340-m/1,115-ft deep. New Windstein's elegant ruins include lovely pointed windows with seats.

Château de Lichtenberg

25 km/16 miles SW of Windstein; take the RF to the right past Rothbach and the D28 to Ingwiller
☎ 03 88 89 98 72

Sculpted head from the dungeons of Lichtenberg

Open Apr., May, Sept. & Oct. Tues.-Sat. 10am-noon, 1.30-6pm; June-Aug. 10am-6pm (Sun. & pub. hols. to 7pm). Kiosk closes 30 mins. before final visit.
Admission charge.
Guided tours available.
Lichtenberg castle escaped dismantling due to its role as a garrison fort. It was fortified by Vauban using modifications

devised by the military architect from Strasbourg, Specklin (1580). It features a chapel with a Renaissance mausoleum for the Lichtenberg family, a clock tower, a 13thC. keep and sculpted heads in its dungeons. The castle was restored after damage caused by shelling during the Franco-Prussian war in 1870. A programme of current events is available at the castle.

The great architect Vauban

Spotcheck
C1

Things to do

Visit the fortified castles
Gimbelhof farm-inn
Climb the rock to the Château de Windstein

With children

'Medieval' play area at Gimbelhof farm-inn

Within easy reach

Niederbronn (10 km/ 6 miles S), p.108
Wissembourg (17 km/ 11 miles E), p.102

Tourist offices

Lembach: ☎ 03 88 94 43 16
La Petite-Pierre:
☎ 03 88 70 42 30

Niederbronn and the spa towns,
a region of oil and water

Niederbronn has two springs, one Roman (*Source Romaine*), one Celtic (*Source Celtic*). It has developed into a major spa town and is home to Alsace's only casino. Two neighbouring *communes*, Morsbronn and Merkwiller-Pechelbronn, are also endowed with hot springs, and Pechelbronn can even boast oil among its past resources.

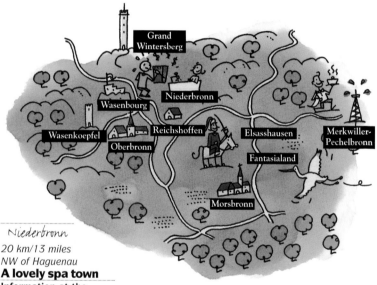

Niederbronn
20 km/13 miles
NW of Haguenau
A lovely spa town
Information at the tourist office

Niederbronn is an attractive spa town, as well as the ideal starting point for hikes and excursions. The Grand Wintersberg tour starts at the Celtic spring, at the western exit from the town. It's signposted and takes around 90 minutes. The ruins of the 13thC. Château de Wasenbourg can be reached on foot via a normal path or a botanical, historic discovery trail. Both are waymarked from the centre of town. The neighbouring village of Oberbronn (3.5 km/2 miles SE) is the starting point of a lovely signposted 7-km/4-mile circuit leading to the château via the Wasenkoepfel tower.

Celtic bottling plant, Niederbronn

Reichshoffen
1 km/¹/₂ mile
SE of Niederbronn
Mementoes of the Franco-Prussian war

Reichshoffen is known for its De Dietrich factories, its attractive lake and its *cuirassiers* – cavalrymen who were the heroes of the Franco-Prussian war. In fact, there was never a cavalry charge in Reichshoffen, nor did any actual combat take place here, although a communiqué of defeat was sent by General Mac-Mahon from the Château de

THE CASINO

10, Place des Thermes
☎ 03 88 80 84 88
Slot machines: Mon.-Thurs. 11am-2pm, Fri. & Sat. 11am-3pm, Sun. 11am-2pm; roulette: Mon.-Thurs. 4pm-2am, Fri. & Sat. 4pm-3am, Sun. 3pm-2am.
Website: www.casinodeniederbronn.com
The only casino in Alsace, its popularity has been boosted by the popular arrival of 135 slot machines. There is also a room for traditional games and three restaurants, including an Alsatian *winstub* serving excellent meals at reasonable prices. The casino is a pleasant spot with a friendly atmosphere.

Spotcheck

C1

Things to do

Walks around Niederbronn
The hamlet of Elsasshausen and its battlefield
Musée du Pétrole in Merkwiller-Pechelbronn

With children

Fantasialand in Morsbronn

Within easy reach

*Fortified castles in northern Alsace (10 km/ 6 miles N), p.106
Hanau region (16 km/ 10 miles S), p.116*

Tourist offices

Niederbronn:
☎ 03 88 80 89 70
Merkwiller-Pechelbronn:
☎ 03 88 80 72 36

Reichshoffen. If you want to see the field of battle, located 7 km/4 miles to the east in the hamlet of Elsasshausen, take the road first to Woerth and then on to Foreschwiller, and turn immediately right. A small track makes its way into the countryside between commemorative monuments and the many individual graves.

War memorial, 1870

A children's paradise

'Fantasialand'
1, Route de Gunstett
☎ 03 88 09 46 46
Open daily July-Aug. 10am-6pm; opening times vary Apr.-June & Sept. *Admission charge.*
Morsbronn, a small spa town, is also home to an imaginative leisure park with all kinds of attractions, including rafts, mine trains, pirate ships and a 180-degree cinema screen. Great fun for all the family.

General Mac-Mahon

Morsbronn

16 km/10 miles E of Reichshoffen

Merkwiller-Pechelbronn
18 km/11 miles E of Reichshoffen
Petrol galore!
Musée du Pétrole
4, Rue de l'Ecole
☎ 03 88 80 91 08
Open Sun. & pub. hols. 2.30-6pm (and Thurs. in July & Aug.). *Admission charge.*
Merkwiller-Pechelbronn was the site of France's first oil refinery, which closed in 1960

when extraction costs became prohibitive. Its history is recounted in the Musée du Pétrole. Merkwiller-Pechelbronn also has hot springs, known as the Source des Hélions (65°C/149°F), used to treat rheumatism. The spa is located near the town hall towards Woerth.

Unexpected pleasures

Auberge Le Puits VI
☎ 03 88 80 76 58
Open Wed. evening to Sun. evening. This is a good spot to have lunch or dinner, housed in the former canteen of an oil refinery. The cuisine is imaginative and light, based on fresh, local produce and no smell of petrol remains!

Northern Vosges regional nature reserve,
a delight for tourists

The northern Vosges regional nature reserve stretches from the German border in the north to Saverne. It encompasses the northern region of the Vosges massif, 102 *communes* and more than 120,000 ha/296,500 acres. It was created in 1976 and classified as a biosphere reserve by UNESCO in 1989.

Château in La Petite-Pierre

La Petite-Pierre

22 km/14 miles NW of Saverne
Park activities
Château de la Petite-Pierre
☎ 03 88 01 49 59

Open daily throughout the year 10am-noon, 2-6pm.
Free admission (charge for exhibitions).
The castle was built in the 12thC. and remodelled several times, most notably in the 16thC. It now houses the Maison du Parc, with six thematic multimedia rooms. A published guide covering all the events and activities in the park is available from the tourist office (and other outlets in the region). Options include instruction on flora and fauna, a visit to a mill, a wine-making cellar and a variety of shows.

The museums and the château

Musée du Sceau Alsacien (museum of Alsatian heraldry)
17, Rue du Château
☎ 03 88 70 48 65
Musée des Arts et Traditions Populaires (museum of folk art and traditions)
11, Rue des Remparts
☎ 03 88 70 41 41
Open daily (exc. Mon.) Mar.-Oct. 10am-noon, 2-6pm; same opening times Nov.-21 Dec. and weekends; 22 Dec.-5 Jan. daily, same opening times (closed 6 Jan.-Feb.).
Free admission.

The château is near the two museums. Fortified by Vauban, it has impressive ramparts, watchtower, water tank and defences.

Graufthal

10 km/6 miles S of La Petite-Pierre
The Troglodytes of Alsace

Troglodyte houses
Rue Principale
☎ 03 88 70 19 59
or 03 88 70 15 62
(out of season)
Open daily July & Aug. 2-6pm (plus Easter-June, Sept. & weekends).
Admission charge.
In this hamlet in the Zinsel

Hagenau coat of arms

THE ART OF THE CLOGMAKER

Musée du Sabotier (clogmaking museum and workshop)
Rue de la Fontaine, Soucht, Moselle
4 km/2¹/₂ miles
W of the Breitenstein
☎ 03 87 96 87 46
Open weekends and pub. hols. Easter-Oct. and daily July & Aug. 2-6pm.
Admission charge.
Clogs for sale
This museum and former workshop displays the traditional local craft of making clogs, which used to be worn by everyone in the countryside. Treat yourself to a pair – they're very comfortable.

valley you'll find troglodyte houses dug into red sandstone cliffs that are 70 m/230 ft high. They were inhabited until 1958, when the last person left, deterred by the damp. The houses have now been restored as a tourist attraction. Enjoy one of the many lovely walks from Graufthal, which are signposted. One of the most pleasant routes is the GR 53 to La Petite-Pierre (red triangular markers).

The Breitenstein

On the D12 between Wimmenau and Goetzenbruck
The *Breitenstein* (wide stone) is an authentic prehistoric menhir. Also known as the 'stone of the 12 apostles', the ancient standing stone, 4 m/2¹/₂ ft high, was decorated in 1787 by a peasant who sculpted a cross and the 12 apostles on the top of the stone to fulfil a vow. Each menhir has its own mystery and the *Breitenstein* is a popular spot for visitors.

Meisenthal

2 km/¹/₂ mile
W of the Breitenstein
Glass and crystal museum
Maison du Verre et du Cristal
Place Robert-Schuman, Moselle
☎ 03 87 96 91 51
Open daily (exc. Tues.) Easter-Oct. 2-6pm.

Admission charge.
Located in the centre of the village, the former glassworks now houses the glass and crystal museum. It contains lovely collections by Lalique, Daum and Gallé, and in the annexe you can see reconstructions of the art of glass-blowing. The workshop has displays of modern pieces from Italy, Germany and France, and contemporary exhibitions are sometimes held in the adjacent crystal factory, now disused.

Spotcheck
B2

Things to do

Walks around Troglodyte houses and the Breitenstein (stone of the 12 apostles)
Maison du Verre et du Cristal, Meisenthal

With children

Activities in the park in La Petite-Pierre
Musée du Sabotier

Within easy reach

Hanau region (1.5 km/ 1 mile E), p.116
Alsace Bossue (15 km/ 9 miles W), p.112

Tourist office

La Petite-Pierre:
☎ 03 88 70 42 30

Alsace Bossue,
abandoned and misunderstood

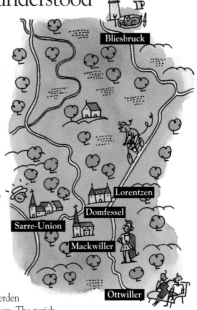

A lsace Bossue, also known as *Tortue* (from the Old French meaning 'deviating from the straight line'), is an often forgotten region, located in the extreme west of the *département*. Many are unaware of its historic treasures, such as the Roman ruins in Mackwiller, lost in the depths of the countryside, and the Empress's bench in Ottwiller, the only surviving one of its kind.

Sarre-Union

37 km/23 miles NW of Saverne
The straw hat town
Musée de L'Alsace Bossue
Parking area: Rue des Juifs, Jesuit college
☎ 03 88 00 13 83 or 03 88 00 28 08 (out of season)
Open daily (exc. Tues.) July & Aug. 2-6pm; out of season by appt. only for groups.
Admission charge.
Sarre-Union is the capital of Alsace Bossue and owes its name to the amalgamation of two neighbouring towns during the French Revolution,

Neu-Sarrewerden and Bouqenom. The parish church has lovely panelling and an interesting statue of St George, and there are several Renaissance houses with oriel windows. The Musée de L'Alsace Bossue has two highly individual and unusual features: an exhibition on the gas generator invented by Georges Imbert, a native

of the region, and another on straw hats. Until the start of the 20thC., 90 per cent of boaters, panamas and other styles of French headgear were made in Sarre-Union.

Bliesbruck-Reinheim

26 km/16 miles N of Sarre-Union in Moselle
Roman country
Franco-German archaeological park
Reception area
1, Rue Robert-Schuman
☎ 03 87 02 25 79

Open Apr.-Oct., Tues.-Sat. 10am-6pm, Sun. 10am-7pm (open Mon. hols.); Nov.-Mar., Tues.-Sun. 10am-5pm. *Free for under 16s.*

THE EMPRESS'S BENCHES
Ottwiller

17 km/11 miles SE of Sarre-Union

Alsace contains several 'Empress's benches', either in their original state or restored. The empress in question was the Empress Eugénie, wife of Napoleon III, and the benches were resting places for travellers, originally installed on the initiative of prefect Lezay-Marnésia and then his successor, August-César West. The existing benches date from the latter period (1854), except for the one in Ottwiller, the only survivor of the earlier 'King of Rome's Benches' of 1811. The Ottwiller bench, at the junction of the D9 towards Asswiller and the D13, is 4 m/13 ft long and 1.75 m/ 5³/₄ ft high. More ornate than other benches, it bears a Latin inscription from the *Aeneid*.

The park lies on both sides of the border and has proved an excellent example of successful cross-border co-operation. The site has been excavated by French and German archaeologists since 1978. Roman and Gallo-Roman finds are on display in appropriately majestic settings. You can visit the springs, public baths, artisans' quarter and the original heating system, as well as the grave of a princess from Reinheim (400 BC). A souvenir shop sells replicas of pottery and other items. Reinheim itself contains the remains of a vast villa from the same period. Le Silène restaurant serves honey-based Roman dishes (roast pork or pike-perch) at reasonable prices (☎ 03 87 02 22 11). Located in the middle of the park, among the ponds, it's open daily, except Monday, between April and October (Friday to Sunday from November to March).

Domfessel

8 km/5 miles E of Sarre-Union
Fortified church

Domfessel is the home of a beautiful 14thC. church that is well worth a detour. Pure Gothic in style, with a 15thC. tower-gate leading to the cemetery, it's a rare example of a semi-fortified church in Lower Alsace.

Spotcheck
A-B1

Things to do

Musée de L'Alsace Bossue in Sarre-Union
Roman dishes at Le Silène restaurant in Bliesbruck-Reinheim

With children

Archaeological park in Bliesbruck-Reinheim

Within easy reach

Northern Vosges regional natural park (15 km/ 9 miles E), p.110

Tourist office

Saverne: ☎ 03 88 91 80 47

Lorentzen

2 km/1 mile E of Domfessel
An agricultural château

Lorentzen has an 18thC. château built on the site of a medieval castle belonging to the Counts of Sarrewerden. Its current aspect dates from 1847, but as a working castle, involved in the agricultural industry, it does not admit visitors. You can admire its two impressive towers, however, and the ruins of an ancient mill, in the small garden in front of the huge building.

Saverne,
a castle, a cardinal and a scandal

The town's emblem, the unicorn fountain

Saverne, referred to as Tres Tabernae (three taverns) in early chronicles, stands on the Paris to Strasbourg axis. The settlement was founded by the Celts and developed by the Romans. It still has reminders of the era of Cardinal de Rohan, implicated in a scandal involving the necklace of Queen Marie-Antoinette, and is pleasantly situated on the Zorn and Marne-Rhine canal.

A stroll through the historic town
Musée du Château des Rohan
☎ 03 88 91 06 28
Open daily (exc. Tues.) 15 June-15 Sept. 10am-noon 2-6pm (rest of the year, 2-5pm). Closed Dec.-Feb. (exc. Sun. & pub. hols., 2-5pm).
Admission charge.

Renaissance doorway to the former bishops' residence

The imposing red-sandstone château, built in 1780, replaced its predecessor, which was destroyed by fire, on the commission of Louis-René de Rohan – the famous cardinal

involved in the Versailles necklace scandal of 1784. The façade facing the town is in the style of Napoleon III, whereas the one facing the canal is an elaborate affair with Corinthian-style columns, described as 'Versailles in Alsace'. The castle is set in lovely gardens, and houses impressive archaeological collections. Head back up the Grand-Rue to the Notre-Dame church, which has a Romanesque belfry porch dating from the 12thC. and a 15thC. nave with a pulpit by Hans Hammer. Behind the church is a beautiful Renaissance doorway belonging

to a former 17thC. bishops' residence, now used as an administrative building.

Culinary delights
Taverne Katz
80, Grand-Rue
☎ 03 88 71 16 56
Open daily 10am-10pm. This interesting inn is housed in a magnificent Renaissance

house (1603). Choose from a wide selection of Alsatian dishes, including *choucroute*, *grumbeereknepfle* (potato quenelles), *presskopf*

THE ALSATIAN KAMA SUTRA

Jacques Bockel's chocolate shop
77, Grand-Rue
☎ 03 88 91 29 49
Open Tues.-Sat.
9am-noon,
2-7pm.
Prepare to be surprised by this shop – it's a paradise for hedonists. The aphrodisiac qualities of chocolate are widely known, and Jacques Bockel combines gourmet pleasures with those of the flesh in his 'illustrated chocolates', depicting scenes from the Kama Sutra. There's something for more conventional chocoholics, including a trip around the world in eight different flavours. Children will love the cow and rabbit-shapes, and there's even a chocolate mobile phone!

Spotcheck
B2

Things to do

Musée du Château des Rohan
Gourmet delights at Taverne Katz
Romanesque church and walk to Mont St-Michel in St-Jean-Saverne

With children

Jacques Bockel's chocolate shop

Within easy reach

Switzerland in Alsace (10 km/6 miles S), p.138
Northern Vosges natural park (20 km/12 miles to N), p.110
Hanau region (20 km/12 miles N), p.116

Tourist office

☎ 03 88 91 80 47

(pork brawn) and fruit tart. It won't break the bank (set menu: €14; à la carte €23), and you couldn't hope for a warmer welcome.

Kings of the castle!
*2 km/1 mile
SW of Saverne
Free admission.*
Head towards Haegen and follow the signposted forest

the second rock. After a pitstop at the restaurant, have a look at the reconstruction of Claude Chappe's telegraph tower, which stands on the original site.

St-Jean-Saverne
*4 km/2¹⁄₂ miles
N of Saverne*
Making amends

The Devil's Bridge at Haut-Barr

path leading to the parking area for the Château de Haut-Barr. Built on three huge sandstone rocks overlooking the valley of the River Zorn and the Plaine d'Alsace, the château commands a stunning panoramic view – at its most impressive once you have crossed the Pont du Diable (devil's bridge) footbridge to

The pretty village church in St-Jean is all that remains of an abbey for Benedictine nuns founded in the early 12thC. and built by Pierre de Lutzelbourg in atonement for the sins of his wife Itta, reputed to be a witch. Start your tour in the gardens before entering the church with its interesting Romanesque doorway and fine cubic capitals, decorated

with foliage motifs. Itta was a frequent visitor to Mont St-Michel, one of the key witchcraft sites in northern Alsace. Enjoy an easy, signposted walk (15 mins) from the church to the enigmatic and mysterious spot. Its wide but shallow excavation is thought to be a Celtic cult site. A 16thC. chapel was built here, overlooking a cave known as 'witches' hole'.

The Hanau region,
a brew of religion and witchcraft

The Protestant church in Ingwiller

The Hanau region takes its name from the counts of Hanau-Lichtenberg, whose main residence was in Ingwiller. It embraces the northern part of the fertile Kochersberg area and the foothills of the Vosges, near La Petite-Pierre. The twin towns of Bouxwiller and Ingwiller are the main centres. You are now deep in Alsace, where a whiff of paganism still lingers in the air.

Bouxwiller

17 km/11 miles NE of Saverne
The town with a golden glow
Musée du Bouxwiller
1, Place du Château
☎ 03 88 70 70 16

Pulpit in the Protestant church in Bouxwiller

Open daily 2-6pm.
Admission charge.
Musée Judéo-Alsacien
62A, Grand-Rue
☎ 03 88 70 97 17
Open 15 Mar.-15 Sept., Tues.-Fri. 9am-noon, 2-5pm, Sun. 2-5pm; out of season by appt. for groups.
Admission charge.
Discovery trail: 1 hr
Start your visit in the square of the former château, where a school now stands on the site of the former baronial residence. The restored 17thC. Hôtel de Ville (town hall) houses the museum, with collections of painted furniture, glassware and reconstructions of interiors. Take a stroll through the streets of the old town, with their characteristic ochre-coloured and half-timbered houses. Immerse yourself in the history and culture of the Jewish community, once substantial in these parts, in the Musée Judéo-Alsacien and follow the museum's 30-minute discovery trail through the picturesque streets.

THE TAPESTRIES OF ST ADELPHUS

Originally made in Neuwiller, these magnificent tapestries are housed in the church of St-Pierre-et-St-Paul. They portray the legend of St Adelphus, Bishop of Metz and founder of the abbey in Neuwiller in the 8thC. The fabrics date from 1460, and are wonderful examples of the art of tapestry-making in Alsace (free admission to the church, viewing of tapestries by special request; ☎ 03 88 70 00 51/03 88 70 01 38).

The summit of Bastberg

Reached by car from Imbsheim, 5 km/ 3 miles SW of Bouxwiller, or on foot (2-hr signposted walk from Rue du Général- Bolgert in Bouxwiller).

Ingwiller

2 km/1 mile N of Bouxwiller

Capital of Hanau- Lichtenberg

More commercial and in some ways less attractive than its neighbour, Ingwiller still possesses some interesting sights, such as the impressive ramparts, the Romanesque tower belonging to the Protestant church and a synagogue with an unusual onion-shaped dome, all of which are worth seeing.

Spotcheck
B2

Things to do

Musée Judéo-Alsacien in Bouxwiller
Ramparts and Romanesque tower in Ingwiller
St-Pierre-et-St-Paul church in Neuwiller-lès-Saverne

With children

Geological trail in Bouxwiller

Within easy reach

*Northern Vosges regional nature reserve (15 km/ 9 miles W), p.110
Niederbronn (16 km/ 10 miles N), p.108*

Tourist office

Pays de Hanau, Ingwiller: ☎ 03 88 89 23 45

Bastberg was traditionally an important site for witchcraft, but don't expect to run into a witches' sabbath today. Instead, follow the geological trail, rich in fossils, that leads to the summit of Bastberg. A map is available from the Town Hall, 1, Place du Château (☎ 03 88 70 70 16). The walk takes you through meadows, pastures and vineyards and a wide variety of local flora, such as sloes, viburnum, hawthorn, dogwood and many more.

Ingwiller synagogue

Neuwiller-lès-Saverne

7 km/4 miles W of Bouxwiller

The church of St- Pierre-et-St-Paul

Don't be misled by the 'lès- Saverne' part of the town's name – you're actually quite a way from Saverne. The church of St-Pierre-et-St-Paul is Alsace's most important Romanesque building. St Catherine's chapel in the crypt dates from the beginning of the Romanesque era, while the double-storeyed choir-chapel is from the Carolingian period.

The chapel of St Sebastian, dating from the 11thC., is carved with beautiful motifs. The church itself is a harmonious mixture of styles from the Romanesque choir to the 18thC. towers and façade. Note the 13thC. tomb of St Adelphus at the west end of the south aisle, supported on its eight columns. The south transept contains a 15thC. statue of the seated Virgin, and don't forget the tapestries (see box). There is also a lovely 15thC. retable (a shelf enclosing decorative panels) and 18thC. panelling.

The Moder valley,
former shoemaking country

The Moder valley lies between two historic settlements, Haguenau and Saverne. The tranquil but frequently flooding river feeds an area made up of mostly agricultural land. One by one, the key industries of former days have departed, including shoemaking, which was once so important to the region.

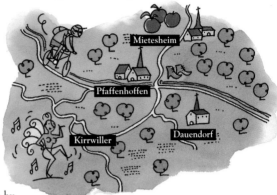

The refurbished brewery in Place des Brasseurs

Pfaffenhoffen, only Heckel and Lemaître (a specialist manufacturer) remain. Gone are Adidas and Salamander, former employers of a large workforce, leaving a fragile economy in their wake. Efforts are now being made to find alternative commercial enterprises.

Pfaffenhoffen
15 km/9 miles
W of Haguenau
Capital of Val de Moder
Pfaffenhoffen is a small and charming town, fortified in the 15thC. to guard the south bank of the river. It has retained part of its fortifications and has some beautiful timber-framed houses, an attractively renovated former brewery, an interesting museum of hand-painted pictures and a Catholic church with a 13thC. crypt.

The rise and fall of the shoe
Of the many shoe factories that once operated in

Dauendorf
5 km/3 miles
E of Pfaffenhoffen
Chapelle de la Croix-Noire
Access via the chapel's cul-de-sac
Dauendorf is a tranquil village when not busy serving

Former shoe factory

LOCAL ARTS AND CRAFTS

Musée de L'Image Populaire
24, Rue du Docteur-Schweitzer
☎ 03 88 07 80 05
Open Tues.-Sun. 2-6pm, Wed. 10am-noon, 2-6pm.
Admission charge.
This museum pays tribute to the long-standing Alsatian tradition of imagery and painting with an impressive and substantial collection of hand-painted pictures. Painted on paper, vellum, glass or decorative objects (all by local people), they depict the customs and culture of the region. The collection includes ex-votos, souvenirs, mats, postcards and religious items, and even an army of lead soldiers, each coloured by hand.

its culinary delights to eager visitors (their *flammekueche* is renowned). It's also home to one of Alsace's many isolated countryside chapels, the Croix-Noire (black cross) chapel, built because of a vow made by a prosperous rural family. Its substantial size is quite a surprise, given its setting. As its name suggests, the chapel boasts an impressive black ebony cross.

Mietesheim
6 km/4 miles
NE of Pfaffenhoffen
Horseradish and apple juice

This somewhat unusual combination really does work, at least in the tiny village of Mietesheim, which produces both locally, despite its rather isolated location, some distance from the main routes. CIDOU (not open to the public) produces fruit juice, and RAIFALSA (4, Rue de la Gare, ☎ 03 88 90 31 85; free tours by appt. through-out the year) makes horse-radish, much loved by the Alsatians. It's a cruciferous plant, grown for its peppery taste. Used as a condiment, horseradish is grated, either roughly or smoothly, depending on taste.

Kirrwiller
10 km/6 miles
SW of Pfaffenhoffen
The Moulin Rouge of Alsace
Adam-Meyer's music hall & restaurant
20, Rue de Hochfelden
☎ 03 88 70 71 81
Dinner dance Wed., Thurs., Sun. noon-6pm; dinner dance and show, Fri. & Sat. 8pm-3am.
Booking essential.

Spotcheck
C2

Things to do

Musée de l'Image Populaire in Pfaffenhoffen
Chapelle de la Croix-Noire in Dauendorf
Adam-Meyer's music hall and restaurant

With children

Horseradish and apple juice tasting

Within easy reach

*Hanau region (10 km/ 6 miles W), p.116
Niederbronn (15 km/ 9 miles N), p.108
Haguenau (15 km/9 miles E), p.122*

Tourist office

Haguenau: 03 88 93 70 00

Programme available.
It's certainly a surprise to find a Parisian-style cabaret show in the middle of the countryside. Adam-Meyer launched his immensely popular music hall shows several years ago, and he entertains coachloads of people with colourful shows full of dance and song as well as orchestral performances. His lunch/ dinner dances are, however, the key attraction. The establishment has featured on French television on a number of occasions and has therefore gained a certain notoriety. There seems to be no stopping its popularity and expansion.

Pottery country,
two friendly rivals

I n Alsace, the word 'pottery' is inextricably linked with Betschdorf and Soufflenheim – two towns whose potters employ the same techniques with different results. Betschdorf's ceramics are traditionally produced in shades of blue and green, whereas those from Soufflenheim feature deep rich hues, especially brown tones.

Soufflenheim
15 km/9 miles
E of Haguenau
Pottery city
This industrial town, famous for its pottery, holds an impressive Wednesday morning market. A former fortified cemetery overlooking the Grand'Rue has been converted into a park housing a life-size sculpture of the Last Supper. The Oelenberg park is open 7am-8pm in season (7am-5pm out of season) and admission is free. Enjoy cycling or walking through the beautiful neighbouring forests.

Marlene Schackis Pottery
20, Rue de Haguenau (at end of a long road)
☎ 03 88 86 65 14
Open daily 10am-noon, 2-6pm.
No visit to Soufflenheim would be complete without a quick visit to this pottery. Marlene Schackis is a ceramic designer and her husband, a potter and former history teacher, will happily enthuse about his wife's work and ceramics in general. Her creations feature delicate motifs in deep brown tones in the Soufflenheim tradition.

Gérard Lehmann pottery
7, Rue de Haguenau
☎ 03 88 86 60 02
Open daily 10am-noon, 2-6pm.
You'll receive a warm welcome at the Lehmann establishment, which contains an entire range of typical and classic Soufflenheim pottery. Prices for this quality, handthrown work are very reasonable.

ALSACE POTTERY
Making sandstone pottery is an ancient Alsatian tradition. In former times the stoneware containers were essential for preserving and cooking food, but today their purpose is more artistic than utilitarian. Plates, bowls, cooking pots, moulds and fondue-dishes are bought as decorative items, but no kitchen in Alsace is complete without the large vessel needed to prepare a *baeckeoffe* – the Alsatian hotpot made with different meats, potatoes and onions.

A round of golf
Soufflenheim golf complex
Allée du Golf (Route de Drusenheim)
☎ 03 88 05 77 00
Open daily 8am-8pm.
Admission charge.

You'll enjoy this 18-hole golf course, with its additional attractions such as deer, herons and storks. If you're new to the game, check the times of lessons at the club. Children can have a free lesson on Saturday from 2pm to 4pm. The complex also contains a hotel and a top quality restaurant, serving an excellent daily special at €12.

Betschdorf

10 km/6 miles
NW of Soufflenheim
Fortuné Schmitter pottery
47, Rue des Potiers
☎ 03 88 54 42 74
Open Mon.-Fri. 9am-noon, 1.30-6pm; weekends & pub. hols. 10am-noon, 2-6pm.

This lovely studio is located in a courtyard and sells traditional, beautiful pieces of Betschdorf pottery, at reasonable prices. The pottery has a grey back-ground with blue decoration in a characteristic Betschdorf style.

Pottery museum
Musée de la Poterie
2, Rue de Kuhlendorf
☎ 03 88 54 48 07
Open daily Apr.-Oct. 10am-noon, 1-5pm.
Admission charge.

Housed in an old farmhouse, this charming little museum traces the history and techniques of pottery, with an interesting collection starting in the Middle Ages, with some stunning pieces from the 17th and 18thC.

Sessenheim

4 km/2¹/₂ miles
S of Soufflenheim
Goethe museum
Auberge Au Boeuf
1, Rue de L'Église
☎ 03 88 86 97 14
Closed Mon., Tues., 2nd week Feb, last week July, 1st two weeks Aug.
Admission charge (except for guests of the auberge). Visits available by appt.
It was in Sessenheim that Friederike Brion, the younger daughter of a clergyman, and the German poet Goethe enjoyed a romance in 1770-1771. He visited her often

and 'Goethe's oak tree', allegedly a favourite spot for the couple, still stands in the forest to the southwest of the village (signposted). The small Goethe

Spotcheck
D1-2

Things to do

Market, pottery and golf in Soufflenheim
Musée de la Poterie in Betschdorf
Goethe museum at the Auberge Au Boeuf in Sessenheim

With children

Walking or cycling in the Oelenberg park in Soufflenheim

Within easy reach

Lauterbourg (20 km/ 12¹/₂ miles N), p.104
Haguenau (15 km/9 miles W), p.122

Tourist office

Soufflenheim:
☎ 03 88 86 74 90

museum is housed in a typical Alsatian inn, the Auberge Au Boeuf, and displays letters, prints and portraits relating to the great man, who returned to Frankfurt in 1771, leaving a distraught Friederike behind.

Haguenau,
the city of Barbarossa

Frederick I (Barbarossa)

This small town flourished under Frederick I of the House of Hohenstaufen, known as Barbarossa, ruler of the Holy Roman Empire between 1152 and 1190. One of his favourite residences was the castle in Haguenau, built in 1115. Today it's a busy commercial and industrial centre, surrounded by a number of attractive villages.

St-Georges church
Rue St-Georges
☎ 03 88 93 90 03

A good start to a tour of Haguenau is the St-Georges church, originally built in 1137 by the emperor Conrad II. A harmonious mix of Romanesque and Gothic styles, the church's unusual layout is a result of successive additions that catered for increases in population and the number of canons. Enter via the south door to admire the ribbed vaulting and consoles, and then make for the St-Jacques chapel with its baptismal fonts, followed by the sculpted and painted altarpiece representing the Last Judgement and the 15thC. wooden crucifix.

A stroll through the town
Musée Historique
9, Rue du Maréchal-Foch
☎ 03 88 93 79 22

Open Mon. & Wed.-Fri. 9am-noon, 2-6pm, Sat. & Sun. 3-5.30pm.
Admission charge.
From St-Georges church, head to the town centre via the house of the bailiff, Hoffman (57, Grand'Rue) and its 18thC. neighbour. Turn left to admire the Customs building with its

Roman collection (Dieu Medru) in the Musée Historique

Gothic wall and keep going to the car park, where you'll find the remains of a watermill. Further on stands the Tour des Chevaliers (knights' tower), the most impressive remnant of the surrounding defensive wall built in 1230. Head back to the centre of town on Rue de la Moder, which covers the underground river, and take a look at the Tour des Pêcheurs (fishermen's tower). Finish your circuit at the

Tour des Pêcheurs

Musée Historique, housed in an imposing early 20thC. building, part neo-Gothic, part neo-Renaissance in style. The museum contains sculptures, ceramics, books and archaeological finds, as well as some beautiful gold and silver plate.

PHILIPPE JEGO
La Cassolette Restaurant
27, Rue du Général-de-Gaulle
Schweighouse-sur-Moder
4 km/2¹/₂ miles W of Haguenau
☎ 03 88 72 61 12
Closed Mon. evening, Tues. evening & Wed.

Philippe Jego, a Breton by birth but an adopted Alsatian, has managed to achieve something that no native chef of Alsace has ever done, despite their numerous talents. He has earned the title of 'best worker in France' (MOF or *meilleur ouvrier de France*). His cuisine is both mouth-watering and awe-inspiring and star dishes include snail *baeckoffe* cooked in Riesling, tartare of tuna with spices, smoked salmon in a lentil vinaigrette and magret of duck with maple syrup. Just the names set your taste buds tingling...

Haguenau forest
The most substantial forest in Alsace covers 200 sq. km/ 77 sq. miles. It stretches west as far as Niedermodern, east to Soufflenheim, and from Surbourg in the north to

Bischwiller in the south. The forest contains several tumuli (burial mounds), which are often hard to locate. The huge oak (Le Gros Chêne), however, is clearly signposted (on the Route de Soufflenheim, turn left at the Maison Forestière information office). The site of the oak is a pilgrim destination dedicated to St Arbogast. The tree itself was damaged by a fire and is

Musée Alsacien

not a thing of great beauty. However, it stands in an attractive and tranquil clearing, perfect for picnics, and is the departure point for some splendid forest walks.

Kaltenhouse
5 km/3 miles SE of Haguenau
Damien Spatara and his *kacheloffen*

Spotcheck
C2

Things to do
Walk and picnic in the forest
Ceramic stove workshop at Kaltenhouse

With children
Walks in the Haguenau forest

Within easy reach
Pottery country (15 km/ 9 miles E), p.120
Val de Moder (15 km/ 9 miles W), p.118
Brumath (10 km/6 miles S), p.124

Tourist office
Haguenau:
☎ 03 88 93 70 00

Ceramic stove workshop
6, Rue des Prés
☎ 03 88 63 78 55
Damien Spatara is a skilled restorer of *kacheloffen* (ceramic stoves), loved so dearly by all Alsatians. His workshop is crammed with stoves, each more attractive than the next, and his own collection includes antique ovens and wonderfully decorated tiles.

From Brumath to Strasbourg,

onions, asparagus, forests and thriving industry

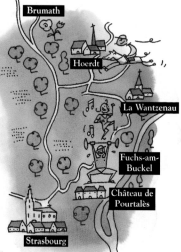

B rumath is a dynamic, medium-sized town, worth visiting en route to Strasbourg. The region's landscapes are as varied as the activities it offers.

Brumath

*11 km/7 miles
SW of Haguenau*
Brocomagus

Few vestiges of the important Gallo-Roman past of Brumath (*Brocomagus* in Latin) remain. It's an interesting town historically, however – the ancient capital of the Triboques clan. The town's floral arrangements and the Hostellerie à l'Écrevisse (crayfish) are well worth a look (4, Avenue de Strasbourg, ☎ 03 88 51 11 08; closed Mon. evening, Tues. & for a fortnight end July/beg. Aug.), and every year, at the end of September, the onion festival attracts many visitors. Enjoy a relaxing stroll in the former hospital park (access via the Route de Bilwisheim, turn left after the bridge over the railway and follow signs for the tennis club). It's a huge area, full of different species of trees (with helpful informative signs) and a lovely pond full of fish in which to gaze and reflect.

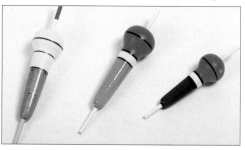

Hoerdt

*7 km/4 miles
SE of Brumath*
Queen of asparagus
À la Charrue
restaurant
30, Rue de la
République
☎ **03 88 51 31 11**
Open daily for lunch (exc. Mon.) & dinner Fri.-Sun. Hoerdt is the region's asparagus capital, challenged only by its neighbour Lampertheim. In season, people come for miles to enjoy vast quantities of asparagus *aux trois sauces* in À La Charrue, the town's restaurant. The racecourse also draws large crowds during the racing season. Information on dates and meets is available on a large signpost on the D37.

Le Fuchs-am-Buckel

*4 km/2½ miles
N of Strasbourg*
Relaxing
in the forest
The Fuchs-am–Buckel ('fox on the bump') forest is located between La Wantzenau and Strasbourg. This large green space is

much appreciated by the inhabitants of Strasbourg, who enjoy walking along the paths that lead as far as the Rhine. It's also home to a fitness trail and a health club, La Cour de Honau, where you can benefit from such facilities as body building equipment, a sauna, a swimming pool and excellent childcare. It's located in Allée de Hanau, on the road from Strasbourg

(one retro, one modern), a huge karaoke room, four bars and a pizzeria, as well as three thematic restaurants: Villa Cuba, El Pueblo and El Rancho (open Tues.-Sat. 7pm-1am, Sun. to 11pm, with terraces for warmer nights). The disco has won a number of awards, including best regional disco, 'Golden Disco', a French award for tourism and 'Trophy of the Night'. The accolades are justified and big names, such as Céline Dion, have been on the guest list.

Château de Pourtalès
La Robertsau, 5 km/ 3 miles N of Strasbourg
A magnificent park
Free admission.
At the gates of Strasbourg, the Château de Portalès (not open to visitors) is not

to La Wantzenau (open daily 9am-11pm, weekends to 9pm; ☎ 03 88 96 33 44).

Dancing the night away
Jean-Claude Helmer dance complex
376, Route de La Wantzenau
☎ **03 88 31 18 31**
Night owls in Fuchs-am-Buckel can dance till they drop – or until dawn breaks – in a wonderful complex, offering a range of nocturnal activities and complete with refreshment facilities. Le Chalet (open 9pm-4am, ticket prices vary according to time of entry) has two discos

particularly remarkable in itself but is set in wonderful grounds. Several attractive walks wind among works of contemporary art, including the *Nains* (dwarves) by J.-M. Krauth.

Spotcheck
C2-3

Things to do
Onion festival in Brumath
The grounds of Château de Pourtalès
Jean-Claude Helmer dance complex in Fuchs-am-Buckel

With children
Fitness trail in Fuchs-am-Buckel forest

Within easy reach
Haguenau (15 km/9 miles N), p.122
Strasbourg, p.126

Tourist offices
Strasbourg:
☎ **03 88 52 28 28**
Haguenau:
☎ **03 88 93 70 00**

ASPARAGUS
In 1873, a pastor by the name of Heyer, who had mastered the art of asparagus growing in Algeria, brought his skills home to Hoerdt and established the annual celebration of the short asparagus season (lasting only from May to June). It's the custom in Alsace to serve large portions of asparagus with a selection of three sauces – vinaigrette, mayonnaise and mousseline. If this is not filling enough, you can add a portion of local ham, and wash it down with a large glass of white wine.

Strasbourg,
capital of Europe and heart of Alsace

With a population of 500,000, Strasbourg is Alsace's largest conurbation. Strategically located, it's not only the 'capital' of Europe, but also the historic, economic and artistic pulse of Alsace. Its historic centre has been on UNESCO's World Heritage List since 1988.

The Ponts Couverts

A short history of Strasbourg

Argentoratum

Strasbourg's origins lie in a Celtic fishing settlement which was fortified by the Romans and named *Argentoratum*. The town soon became prosperous, located on an important crossroads

European Council

Strasbourg Cathedral

Rapid growth

Strasbourg's expansion began again in 1015, when the first cathedral was constructed. The town's commercial and trade activities developed swiftly, and it was accorded the enviable status of a 'free town' at the heart of the Holy Roman Empire. The Reformation did little to disrupt the town, and with the outbreak of the Thirty

between eastern and western Europe. Abandoned by the Romans in 407 AD and destroyed by Attila in 451, Strasbourg was subsequently rebuilt by the Franks, who named it *Strateburgum* (city of roads), due to its position near the main road between Gaul and Germany. Here in 842 the Strasbourg oaths were sworn, the first official text to be written both in a Romance and a Germanic language.

Years War, Strasbourg began to make political moves towards the French kingdom, spurred on by its fear of a Swedish advance.

From France to Europe

The treaty of Westphalia (1648) awarded Strasbourg to France, and the town continued to expand under the French régime. However, it came under German rule between 1870 and 1918, following capitulation after a 50-day siege in the Franco-Prussian war. At the end of World War II, it was decided that Strasbourg should become the heart of the new Europe, and it is now the seat of the European Council and other European institutions.

The Capital of Europe

European Parliament
Allée du Printemps
☎ 03 88 17 52 85
Free admission (booking essential one month ahead for individuals, four months for groups). Identification required.
European Council
Free admission (booking essential).
Palais des Droits de l'Homme (home to the European Court of Human Rights)
☎ 03 88 41 20 18
Avenue de l'Europe
Visits outside parliamentary session, Mon.-Fri. (booking essential, at least one month ahead).

Strasbourg shares with Geneva and New York the privilege of housing international institutions without being the state capital. The European Council was created in 1949 (with 41 member countries) and focuses on matters of education, culture, the environment and human rights. The European Parliament is the legislative arm of the European Union, and its 625 members are elected by the 15 countries of the European Union (Maastricht, 1992). The Palais des Droits de l'Homme was designed by Richard Rogers and houses the European Court of Human Rights.

Parc de l'Orangerie

Opposite the European Council
☎ 03 88 61 62 88
24-hr free admission for park and zoo.
This park, designed in 1692

Spotcheck
C3

Things to do
Explore Strasbourg by bike, taxi, tram or boat
Christmas markets

With children
Parc de l'Orangerie
Ceinture verte (green belt) walk
The Babel festival

Within easy reach
Brumath (15 km/9 miles N), p.124
Molsheim (20 km/12½ miles E), p.140
Marlenheim (20 km/12½ miles Et), p.136
Erstein (20 km/12½ miles S), p.150

Tourist office
Strasbourg:
☎ 03 88 52 28 28

Palais des Droits des Hommes

by André Le Nôtre, is Strasbourg's largest green space, complete with artificial lake, waterfall and zoo. It's home to a number of different tree species, floral displays, a rose garden and various statues. You can enjoy pleasant strolls or let the children loose in the organised play areas. The excellent Buerehiesel restaurant in the park boasts three Michelin stars, and chef Antoine Westermann offers a mouth-watering menu (around €60 per person).

LE TIRE-BOUCHON

5, Rue des Tailleurs-de-Pierre
☎ 03 88 23 10 73
Open daily
If you're feeling peckish after a visit to the cathedral, head for Le Tire-Bouchon (the corkscrew), a pleasant *winstub* with an authentic traditional atmosphere, although it is part of a German chain. It serves typical dishes from Strasbourg and its surrounding region, in particular the Kochersberg. Try the *lewerknaepfles* (liver meatballs), washed down with a glass of Riesling or a Pinot Noir. The wine list is excellent and you'll spend around €12 per head.

Notre-Dame cathedral

Place de la Cathédrale
☎ 03 88 21 43 34
Open daily 7am-7pm (closed noon-1pm).
Notre-Dame is one of the finest and most original Gothic cathedrals, destroyed over the centuries by fire and war but always rebuilt. Enter via the beautiful 13thC. south portal (the 'Portail de l'Horloge' or clock doorway). Note the statues of Solomon, the Church Triumphant on the left and the Synagogue Defeated on the right.

South portal

The façade

The right-hand portal is remarkable for its allegorical statues, although some were mutilated during the Revolution and have been replaced with replicas. Most notable is the parable of the Wise and Foolish Virgins. The Wise Virgins carry

Statue on the right-hand portal

full oil lamps, symbols of purity, and receive the divine spouse, while the Foolish Virgins are tempted by a handsome man holding an apple, another obvious symbolic reference. The Foolish Virgins have upturned their lamps and the first of them is already undoing her robe. The central and left side portals are just as impressive but more classical in approach. Now make your way to the magnificent St-Lawrence doorway, in High Gothic style.

The interior

Before you enter the cathedral, take time to admire the wonderful façade (142 m/ 466 ft high) and have a look at the Maison Kammerzell (1467) on the square, with its ornate half-timbers (☎ 03 88 32 42 14; restaurant open daily noon-3.30pm, 7-11pm). The beautiful stained glass windows date from the 12th and 14thC.

Maison Kammerzell

and delicacy. Sculptors from Chartres created its three levels of finely worked statues.

The astronomical clock
Behind the pillar is the astronomical clock, the cathedral's most popular feature. It was made in 1838 by Schwilgué, a native of Strasbourg, and features the

Hans Hammer's pulpit

Exploring the cathedral
For a modest sum you can light up the intricately carved hexagonal pulpit, designed by Hans Hammer in an elaborate Gothic style. Head to the St-Laurent chapel and admire the magnificent baptismal fonts (1443) and a stone group depicting Christ on the Mount of Olives (1498). A magnificent, coloured 14thC. organ-case over the nave beneath the triforium contains an organ dating from 1716 by J. Andreas Silbermann, restored in 1893. The 15-m/ 50-ft rose window of 1340 is equally beautiful.

The angels' pillar
Also known as the pillar of the Last Judgement, this structure was erected in the 13thC. Best appreciated when illuminated, it's a splendid example of Gothic art – a wonderful mixture of strength

oldest known portrait of Copernicus. The clock runs half an hour behind normal time, and when midday chimes (at 12.30pm!), a great parade takes place at the top of the clock. The apostles pass in front of Christ, bowing as he blesses them, while the cock crows three times, a reminder of Peter's denial of Christ. To your left on the balustrade stands a mysterious stone figure, gazing at the pillar, thought to be a self-portrait of the sculptor Nicolas de Leyde.

THE TRAM
In 1960, when petrol was cheaper than electricity, the authorities consigned the tram to history. Forty years later, however, Strasbourg once again relies on this restored form of transport. Travelling by tram is certainly the best way to get around town, avoiding the traffic and parking problems. It's an efficient system; contact the CTS – *Compagnie Strasbourgeoise des Transports* – 14, Rue de la Gare-aux-Marchandises, ☎ 03 88 77 70 70 for more information on the network.

Musée de l'Oeuvre Notre-Dame
3, Place du Château
☎ **03 88 52 50 00**
Open daily (exc. Mon.) 10-6pm.
Admission charge (exc. for under 18s).
After visiting the cathedral, head to this museum, which is dedicated to medieval and Renaissance art. It contains a number of impressive collections, together with statues rescued from

destruction during the Revolution. Several of the cathedral's original statues are featured, among them the Church and the Synagogue, as well as paintings, gold and silver plate, ivories, furniture and tapestries. The Gothic wing of the building was built in 1347 and has a crenellated gable, while the German Renaissance wing of the late 16thC. is equally impressive. There is also a small medieval garden.

A stroll through the town centre

Set off from the cathedral and make for Place Gutenberg, which has a statue of Gutenberg by David d'Angers. Here you'll find the Hôtel de la Chambre de Commerce (chamber of commerce) of 1582, a fine Renaissance building with a portal adorned with the bust

Place Gutenberg

HOW TO GET AROUND

The best ways of exploring Strasbourg are by foot, bus and tram.

Hiring a bicycle

Daily hire is available at three pick-up points (closed noon-2pm at weekends):
4, Rue du Maire Kuss, near the railway station (☎ 03 88 52 01 01);
10, Rue des Bouchers, near the Musée Alsacien (☎ 03 88 22 59 19);
Ponts Couverts tower (☎ 03 88 22 59 19).
€5 for a full day, €3 for half-day.

Travelling by taxi

Taxi 13 (☎ 03 88 36 13 13) arranges tours with a commentary (€28 for 1-4 passengers)

Taking the mini-tram

Departs from Place du Château, near the cathedral, and in 50 minutes takes you to La Petite-France, Ponts Couverts and Finkwiller. Leaves every half hour between 9.30am and 8pm during the summer (July-18 Sept.).
Tickets: €5 for adults and €3 for children aged 4-12 (☎ 03 88 77 70 03).

By boat

A trip down the River Ill with commentary departs daily from Strasbourg, lasting 70 minutes and costing €7 (half-price for children and students). It leaves from the Château des Rohan pier (evening trips leave at 9.30pm and 10pm May-Sept. Tickets: €7). Bookings at Strasbourg Fluvial: ☎ 03 88 32 75 25/03 88 84 13 13.

Trips down the Rhine, leave from the Dauphine pier (opposite the Centre Administratif in Place de l'Étoile) 10.30am-2.30pm in July & Aug., lasting $2^1/_2$ hours and costing €8 (€4 for children). Bookings at port ☎ 03 88 44 34 27.

The Strasbourg tourist office (17, Place de la Cathédrale, ☎ 03 88 52 28 28) sells a 'Strasbourg-Pass' that includes admission to various places and bicycle hire for one day. It's valid for 3 days and costs €9.

of Hermes. Head down the Rue des Grandes-Arcades until you reach Place Kléber, Strasbourg's most famous square, with its statue of Jean-Baptiste Kléber erected in 1840. A brilliant general of the Revolutionary period, he

Place Kléber

La Petite-France

was born in Strasbourg in 1753 and murdered in Cairo on 14 June 1800. Continue to the Place de l'Homme-de-Fer (man of iron), the name deriving from the *lansquenet* (German mercenary) whose statue adorns the pharmacy. Return to Place Kléber and head up Rue des Francs-Bourgeois, full of shops. Turn left into Rue Gutenberg and make your way back to the starting point.

Gourmands' delight

Strasbourg's culinary highlights include two particularly good places near Place Kléber. The patisserie-chocolatier, Christian (12, Rue de l'Outre, ☎ 03 88 32 04 41; open Mon.-Fri. 7.15am-6.30pm, Sat. 7am-6pm, Sun. in Dec. 9am-6pm), with its simply irresistible chocolates. Hard on its heels is Crocodile (10, Rue de l'Outre, ☎ 03 88 32 13 02; closed Sun. & Mon. exc. Sun. pm at Easter, Whit Sunday, Mother's Day, 2nd Sun. in Dec.).

La Petite-France and the Ponts Couverts

Begin your tour at Place Gutenberg and take Rue des Serruriers (locksmiths) leading to Place St-Thomas.

Mausoleum of Maréchal de Saxe

St-Thomas church

This five-naved Protestant church has an impressive pure Gothic façade and an elaborate interior containing Adeloch's tomb, the Chapelle des Évangélistes and the famous 18thC. mausoleum of the Maréchal de Saxe (Moritz von Sachsen, Marshal of France). The church is open daily from May to Sept., (exc. for services) 10am-noon, and 2pm-6pm (to 5pm out of season). It is closed in January.

In the heart of La Petite-France

Stroll along Rue des Dentelles with its fine buildings and picturesque Rathsamhausen courtyard (at number 9). You'll come to the charming

Maison des Tanneurs (tanners' house), built in 1572. Not far away, take the Rue du Bain-aux-Plantes and turn left into Rue des Moulins. Beyond the swing bridge, pass under a porch to your right, leading into a small square. Here you'll find

Maison des Tanneurs

the Ponts Couverts (covered bridges) – three bridges spanning the River Ill, each guarded by a large square tower. The three towers used to be linked by covered wooden bridges. Behind them is the impressive Barrage Vauban, a casemate bridge that formed part of Vauban's fortifications. It has a viewing terrace (free admission, open

Open Tues.-Sun. 11am-7pm, Thurs. noon-10pm. *Admission charge (exc. under 18s).* Strasbourg's new museum of modern art opened in November 1998, containing works by Monet, Sisley and Doré, as well as more contemporary artists such as Picasso, Arp, Klimt and Sarkis. There's also a restaurant, Art

Finkwiller

Return to Rue de la Glacière and turn right on to Rue des Greniers to reach Finkwiller quay via Rue St-Marc. Admiring its elegant houses, continue to the St-Thomas bridge, with its fabulous view of the locks of La Petite-France. With the Choucrouterie on your right, continue along the quay to the

daily 9am-8pm) with a stunning panorama of the Ponts Couverts and La Petite-France.

Musée d'Art Moderne et Contemporain

1, Place Hans-Arp
☎ 03 88 23 31 31

Café (☎ 03 88 22 18 88), offering reasonably priced meals and a panoramic terrace with views of the Vauban dam and Ponts Couverts.

On the banks of the River Ill

The Haras Nationaux

1, Rue Ste-Élisabeth
☎ 03 88 36 10 13
Open Mon.-Sat. 9am-11.30pm, 2-4.30pm (end March to mid July). *Free admission.*
Head up Rue de la Glacière, towards the Old Hospital, and turn left to the national stud farm, housed in a former medieval hospital for travellers, dating from the 18thC. The stables house various breeds of stallion, including thorough-breds, French saddle ponies and draught horses.

Musée Alsacien (see below). On the other side of the river is the former customs house, the *Kaufhüs* or Ancienne Douane, dating from 1356 but reconstructed after its destruction during the bombing of World War II. It was here that the citizens of Strasbourg traditionally came to pay their taxes and unload their merchandise.

Roger Siffer and La Choucrouterie

La Choucrouterie
20, Rue St-Louis
☎ 03 88 36 07 28
www.choucrouterie.com
Open every evening from 6.30pm (exc. Sun & for 3 weeks in summer).
For the last 15 years, this former coaching inn has housed a restaurant-theatre of typically Alsatian character. Created by Roger Siffer, a

Gustav Klimt's Accomplishment

singer, entertainer and now cabaret performer, it offers the opportunity to enjoy a spot of dinner, accompanied by the satirical humour and lively performance (in French and Alsatian) of some of the region's greatest comic talents and singers.

Musée Alsacien
23-25, Quai St-Nicolas
☎ **03 88 52 50 00**
Open daily (exc. Tues.) throughout the year 10am-6pm.
Admission charge (exc. under 18s).
This museum of popular art is housed in three buildings

I. Pils, Rouget de Lisle chantant La Marseillaise (*Musée Historique*)

from the 16th and 17thC. and is among the most charming of its kind in France. The museum tour leads through a maze of stairs and wooden galleries, over-looking a lovely internal courtyard. It has a remark-able collect-ion of Alsatian furniture, much of it painted, as well as tiled stoves, chests, butter churns, household utensils and costumes. Individual rooms focus on different themes, such as agriculture, wine-growing and local arts and crafts.

Le Chemin des Bateliers

Start at Place du Corbeau, near the Musée Alsacien
Follow the Quai des Bateliers (boat-men's quay) to the Pont du Corbeau. Formerly known as Pont des Supplices, it was the site of duckings meted out to adulterous women and brigands. On the opposite side of the River Ill stands the Musée Historique, housed in the former Grande Boucherie of 1587, now renovated. The nearby 18thC.

PLACE DU MARCHÉ-GAYOT
Free from traffic, this lovely square is dotted with restaurants, shady terraces and young, energetic people. It is a stone's throw from the cathedral, and the area surrounding it is full of tempting boutiques, located along the natural extensions of Rue des Juifs and Rue des Hallebardes. Both streets are pedestrianised and full of lovely places in which to spend your holiday money.

Château des Rohan

Château des Rohan was built according to plans by Robert de Cotte, the royal architect, for the dynasty of eponymous bishops. The façade which overlooks the River Ill is quite beautiful, featuring Corinthian columns and a courtyard. A number of museums are housed here, including decorative arts, fine arts and archaeology, ☎ 03 88 52 50 00; open daily (exc. Tues.) 10am-6pm; admission charge (except for under 18s). Whatever you do, don't miss *La Belle Strasbourgeoise*, attributed to Nicolas de Largillière.

CHRISTMAS WONDERLAND

Strasbourg really comes into its own at Christmas. From the first Sunday in Advent, the traditional *Christkindelmärik* (Christ Child market) is held in Place Broglie, providing a focus for all kinds of festive activities, lights and lively spectacles. Visitors come from far and wide and the shops are full of colour and Christmas surprises, so have your wallets at the ready...

On the way to the old University

Follow the River Ill past St-Guillaume church (early 1300s), with its beautiful stained glass windows and 14thC. two-storey tomb. Heading towards the old university, pause to watch the swans gliding where the waters of the Faux-Remparts canal and the Ill meet. At the university a statue of Goethe, stands near a lovely botanical garden (entrance via the Rue de l'Université, ☎ 03 88 3583 67; free admission Sun. at 3pm). St-Paul church, built in 1892, is also worth a visit.

The *Port Autonome*

The Mannheim Convention of 1868 created the oldest European organisation, the Central Commission of the Rhine. As a result, the Rhine has 800 km/497 miles of excellent navigable waters. In 1924 the *Port Autonome* (Port Authority) was established in Strasbourg, charged with maintaining the docks and warehouses, and today the city is one of the key ports on the River Rhine. To understand the importance of the river, travel its length by boat or car, following the Quai des Alpes, passing the pleasure piers and then driving up Rue du Port-du-Rhin before reaching the Rue de Dunkerque towards the north lock.

The *Ceinture Verte* (green belt) walk
Information at Club Vosgien
16, Rue Ste-Hélène
☎ 03 88 32 57 96
The *Ceinture Verte* is a lovely 17-km/11-mile walk, encompassing green open spaces, urban areas and waterways. It's well marked

(red circles) by the Club Vosgien and can be joined at a number of places including Place Kléber. The walk offers fabulous views and unexpected delights, and appeals to children and adults alike.

Young town, old traditions

Strasbourg has a wide range of activities for young people. The Babel Festival is held every summer, around 14 July, when local musicians join Bretons, Provençals, Africans and others to celebrate (information ☎ 03 88 34 02 34). The Laiterie music venue, 20, Rue du Hohwald, is a popular spot, and everyone is welcome to attend the free concerts in Place des Tripiers (Mon. evening), Place Benjamin-Zix (Tues.) and Place du Marché-aux-Cochons-de-Lait (Wed.). Folk festivals take place in the courtyard of Palais Rohan (daily at 8pm, 15 July-6 Aug.).

Winstube

Winstube are inviting, atmospheric taverns and very much an Alsatian institution. You can enjoy a jug of *win* (wine) and a number of traditional dishes, such as *bibeleskäs* (fromage blanc served with fried apples), *knaepfle* (meatballs), *presskopf* (pork brawn), *waedele* (knuckle of pork) and onion tart. Not ideal fare for those on a strict diet, but delicious nevertheless. A popular spot is Chez Yvonne (10, Rue du Sanglier, ☎ 03 88 32 84 15, closed Sun., Mon. lunchtime, 14 July & 15 Aug.). Hailich Graab, in the tiny Rue des Orfèvres (no. 15, ☎ 03 88 32 39 97, closed Sun. & Mon.), is an authentic *winstub* with

an unusual 1950s-1960s décor and welcoming atmosphere. The more elaborate Muensterstuewel (8, Place du Marché-aux-Cochons-de-Lait, ☎ 03 88 32 17 63, closed Sun. exc. lunchtimes in Dec., Mon. except for last two in Dec., 18-28 Feb. & 19 Aug.-12 Sept.) is an excellent spot. Also worth a try is Le Clou (3, Rue du Chaudron, ☎ 03 88 32 11 67, closed Wed. lunchtime & Sun.), a small wine bar in a street near the cathedral, with a typical décor, friendly atmosphere and good Alsatian cuisine.

The Kochersberg region, a fertile land

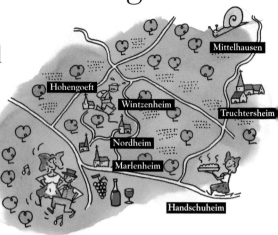

This vast, immensely fertile plain, dotted with valleys, is an important agricultural centre in Alsace. The land is rich in *loess*, black alluvium, deposited at the end of the Ice Age.

Alsatian agriculture

The Kochersberg is a typical Alsatian agricultural region, with few large fields but a series of small parcels of land, each around 100 sq metres/ 1076 sq ft) in size. Sometimes these plots of land are distributed unevenly around an area, which is an inconvenience to farmers but creates a patchwork of colours in the landscape. Bright yellow fields of rape lie next to the golden tones of sunflowers, interspersed with tall hop-fields and small country hamlets.

Marlenheim
20 km/12½ miles
W of Strasbourg
The *Route du Vin*
Marlenheim has many lovely houses, a small château, ancient wells and an interesting church with a Louis-XV altar

and pulpit and Renaissance baptismal fonts. It marks the start of the *Route du Vin* (wine route), an 180-km/112-mile trail that winds through the vineyards to Thann. The wines of the Lower Rhine were traditionally considered inferior to those of the Upper Rhine, but they are certainly catching up now. You can sample an excellent Riesling or a Pinot Noir at the Mosbach cellar,

10, Place du Kaufhaus,
☎ 03 88 87 50 13).

The wedding of *L'Ami Fritz*

During the weekend of 15 August, the famous wedding from the novel by Erckmann and Chatrian is recreated in Marlenheim (see pp. 41 and 87). An evening of folk song and fireworks takes place, followed by a bridal procession and the wedding of Fritz and Suzel itself.

The three chapels trail

Departs from behind Marlenheim town hall
Information at Marlenheim tourist office
The popular *Trois Chapelles* itinerary begins at the chapel

Marlenheim church

FLAMMEKUECHE

Auberge à l'Espérance
5, Rue Principale, Handschuheim
8 km/5 miles E of Marlenheim
☎ 03 88 69 00 52
Open for dinner Wed.-Sun.

This is the place to come for a truly fabulous *flammekueche*, a *tarte flambée* (still flaming, to be strictly accurate). Tuck into this famous Alsatian speciality (p.60), and try it *au naturel* like the locals generally do, without the addition of cheese. The inn also has a range of house specialities, all freshly prepared and tasty, including *bibeleskäs* (fromage blanc), pâté in pastry and *presskopf* (pork brawn). The average bill of €10 won't break the bank, though it may expand the waistline. Book ahead to avoid disappointment.

in Marlenberg, making its way to the chapel in Goeftberg via the TDF (Télédiffusion de France) transmitter in Stephansberg. Once you reach Hohengoeft, head towards Wintzenheim and take the path to Kuttolsheim, home to the Ste-Barbe chapel, before returning to Marlenheim via Nordheim. This is a fairly challenging 15-km/9-mile walk which takes a good half-day to complete. It's worth the effort, however, and it winds its way through fields, vineyards and hills with some really glorious views.

Truchtersheim

13 km/8 miles NE of Marlenheim
Maison du Kochersberg
4, Place du Marché
☎ 03 88 69 85 84

Open Sun. 2.30-6.30pm. *Admission charge.* Truchtersheim, the centre of the Kochersberg area, has an attractive museum dedicated to the region and its rural life, the Maison du Kochersberg. Temporary exhibitions

Spotcheck
B3

Things to do
Wine tasting in Marlenheim
The three chapels trail

With children
Wedding of *L'Ami Fritz* in Marlenheim

Within easy reach
Switzerland in Alsace (5km/3 miles E), p.138
Molsheim (15 km/9 miles S), p.140
Strasbourg (20 km/ 12½ miles E), p.126

Tourist office
Marlenheim:
☎ 03 88 87 75 80

of remarkable quality are often held here – drop in and take a look.

Mittelhausen

6 km/4 miles N of Truchtersheim
Snail country
Bernard Kolb
3, Rue des Roses
☎ 03 88 51 40 33
This is Alsace's only snail farm. It operates on a relatively small scale, producing around 3 to 4 tonnes a year – only 10 per cent of the annual consumption of snails in Alsace. You can buy them direct or enjoy them in the farm-inn on site. Go on, be brave and give them a try!

Switzerland in Alsace,
chalets, mountains and legends

The tourist association, *La Suisse d'Alsace* (Alsatian Switzerland), is made up of 17 *communes*, administrative areas bordered by Oberhaslach and Marmoutier. The forest is quite beautiful and the mountains are a true haven of peace.

Marmoutier

Dabo

Wangenbourg

Wasselonne

Château and waterfall of Nideck

Wasselonne
25 km/16 miles W of Strasbourg
A thriving country town

A tower is all that remains of the castle overlooking this former stronghold. Today, it's a dynamic commercial hub that plays annual host to a traditional fair (last Sun. and Mon. in Aug.), complete with an impressive floral float.

Villagers from as far as 20 km/ 13 miles away come to enjoy the Wasselone fair.

Wasselonne château

Marmoutier
8 km/5 miles NW of Wasselone
The abbey-church
8, Place du Général-de-Gaulle
Open daily.
Admission charge.

Marmoutier is home to the wonderful Benedictine abbey-church of St-Étienne. Dating from 1140, it features a splendid Romanesque façade, an impressive porch and a charming 'parish priest's garden' (not open to visitors). Built in local red sandstone with a heavy square belfry and two octagonal towers, it has a Gothic interior (except

for the Romanesque narthex), containing beautiful carved stalls and an organ built by Silbermann in 1710. Concerts are held regularly (ask the tourist office for information).

On your bike
Mountain bike trail
Information at tourist office in Marmoutier
A pleasant, clearly marked mountain bike trail begins at

SILBERMANN, THE ORGAN-MAKER

André Silbermann (1678-1734) was by far the most famous Alsatian organ-maker. His instruments were known for their exceptional sound quality, but sadly not many of his creations have survived. A few, such as the one in Strasbourg Cathedral, have been restored, and two beautiful organ cases can be found at Marmoutier and Ebersmunster. Silbermann's brother Geoffroy is believed to have invented the first pianoforte, precursor to the modern piano.

Marmoutier. It's an easy route, with few hills, ideal for a family outing in the forest of Tannenwald. Covering 12.7 km/8 miles, it departs from the old railway station.

Wangenbourg-Engenthal

11 km/7 miles SW of Marmoutier
A touch of Switzerland
Wangenbourg and the small neighbouring towns of Engenthal and Obersteigen lie at the foot of the Schneeberg mountain. Wangenbourg itself is a charming summer resort,

home to a centuries-old linden tree and the ruins of a castle, dating from the 13th and 14thC., complete with pentagonal keep. Admission is free and the ruins, with their wonderful views, are accessible on foot.

Nideck's château and waterfall
A pretty walk leads to the romantic château and impressive waterfall of Nideck (free admission), providing a magnificent view of the glacial valley and wooded chasm into which the waterfall cascades. It's here that the giants of Nideck are said to live – apparently

benign and obliging creatures, they live in harmony with the locals. Legend also has it that the water nymph of Nideck, a young girl seduced and then abandoned by a rich lord, was saved by a fairy, who then gave her the task of keeping the waters pure for ever.

Dabo

14 km/9 miles W of Wangenbourg, in Moselle
Le Rocher de Dabo
The Dabo rock is a fabulous site, best appreciated from the road between La Hoube and Haselbourg. It requires a detour, but is well worth the effort. Dabo itself is steeped in history, and was once believed to be the birthplace of

Spotcheck
B2

Things to do

Annual Wasselonne fair
Walk to the château and waterfall at Nideck

With children

Mountain biking in Marmoutier

Within easy reach

*Korchesberg (5 km/ 3 miles W), p.136
Saverne (15 km/9 miles N), p.114*

Tourist office

Marmoutier:
☎ 03 88 71 46 84

Bruno (who became Leo IX, the only Alsatian pope), although he was actually born at Eguisheim, near Colmar. The 'impregnable rock' (664 m/2,178 ft) was of vital strategic importance and it once was the site of a castle, destroyed on the orders of Louis XIV. Today the sandstone rock is crowned with two viewing platforms and a chapel, built in 1830 and rebuilt in Neo-Romanesque style in 1899. The view from the chapel's tower includes the Vosges mountains and the 'X'-shaped village of Dabo below.

Leo IX

Molsheim and Mutzig,
close-knit towns

Molsheim and Mutzig are neighbours, but they are also linked historically and economically. Mutzig suffered a blow in 1990, when its brewery closed down, but it still hosts a beer festival in September.

Molsheim

25 km/16 miles SW of Strasbourg

Molsheim, from past to present

Molsheim is a charming town, surrounded by ancient ramparts, and home to the impressive Église des Jésuites. It contains a lovely pulpit, finely carved doorways, original stuccowork and an organ by Silbermann. The Tour des Forgerons (1412), a fortified gate in Rue de Strasbourg, is worth a look, as is the Metzig, a graceful Renaissance building erected by the butchers' guild. The Musée du Prieuré des Chartreux (4, Cour des Chartreux, ☎ 03 88 9 25 10, open daily exc. Tues. 15 June-15 Sept. 10am-noon, 2-6pm, weekends 2-5pm; €3 entrance charge), recounts the history of Molsheim. The museum is housed in the priory an old Carthusian monastery, which is also home to the Bugatti Foundation

Bugatti

Ettore Bugatti was born in Milan in 1881. He founded his

automobile factory in Molsheim in 1909, where he produced his prestigious range of cars. Among the magnificent models in the Molsheim collection is the famous yellow and black 1936 convertible, along with a display of family memorabilia.

Mutzig

3 km/2 miles W of Molsheim

Choose your weapon

Mutzig is a charming little town with ancient houses, fine doorways and small streets in which to wander. The château (1673), renovated by Cardinal Rohan just

Mutzig's fortified gate

before the French Revolution, passed to the Coulaux brothers, who used it as an armaments factory. Today, the château is a cultural centre and home to the Musée Régional des Armes (open 2 May-15 Oct. Wed.-Sun. 2-5.30pm, Sun. to 6.30pm; admission charge) housing a collection of firearms and charting the history of the Chassepot rifle (see box).

The Jacobin

On the belfry of Mutzig's Hôtel de Ville is a strange bearded head, sporting a cap,

WEAPONS MANUFACTURE

Mutzig was the birthplace of Antoine Chassepot, inventor in 1870 of a rifle that bears his name. It was far superior to its German counterpart, but a shortage of munitions in the Franco-Prussian war made it redundant. Chassepot worked for the Coulaux brothers, major weapons manufacturers who even constructed a special canal to supply Strasbourg with arms. When the factory closed, the business was divided into a number of companies, of which Manufrance is the most famous today.

Spotcheck
B3

Things to do
Visit Feste Kaiser Wilhelm II

With children
See the Bugatti collection in Molsheim

Within easy reach
Switzerland in Alsace (15 km/9 miles N), p.138
Obernai (10 km/6 miles S), p.146

Tourist office
Molsheim: ☎ 03 88 38 11 61

the west. Built by the German ruler in 1893, it features a number of technical and strategic innovations.

Avolsheim
3 km/2 miles N of Molsheim

who sticks his tongue out and wiggles his ears every hour. This is Le Jacobin, said to commemorate Euloge Schneider, an executioner during the French Revolution, who caused carnage in Mutzig with his portable guillotine.

The Kaiser's fortress
☎ 06 08 84 17 42
Open Sun. 2-6pm.
Admission charge.
(2-hr tour)
Mutzig's fort, Feste Kaiser Wilhelm II, is signposted from Dinsheim, 1 km/¹/₂ mile to

Avolsheim's famous church, St-Pierre or the Dompeter (a truncation of *ad Dominum Petrum*), was founded by the Frankish King Dagobert. Thought to be the oldest sanctuary in Alsace, it is a splendid example of Early Renaissance architecture.

The Chapelle St-Ulrich in the centre of the village was built around 1000 AD and is decorated with fine 13thC. frescoes, uncovered in 1967.

Niederhaslach
13 km/8 miles W of Mutzig
The Benedictine abbey-church
Open daily.
Free admission.
Built in the 13thC., this church is a wonderful example of Gothic architecture, with a beautiful façade and a large doorway framed by statues. It has attractive stained glass, baptismal fonts, fine stalls and a 14thC. Holy Sepulchre.

The Bruche valley,
enjoying life by the river

Between Saales and Strasbourg, the lovely River Bruche flows through a range of landscapes, feeding the large towns of Schirmeck, Mutzig and Molsheim. The area offers a number of enjoyable walks.

Le Donon
Grandfontaine
Schirmeck
Étang du coucou
Grendelbruch
Château d Guirbader
Struthof
La Bruche
Natzwiller
Saales

first, Schirmeck, has now disappeared, but the ruins of the second, Struthof, remain. The double fence of barbed wire, the main gate, the

Schirmeck
50 km/31 miles SW of Strasbourg
The heart of the valley
Schirmeck, a lively industrial town and holiday resort, is the epicentre of the valley. Sited along the Bruche, it makes a good base for a variety of excursions. Visit the church (1757) with its ornate tower framed by four Baroque statues, the medieval château that has been partially

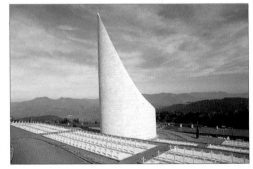

restored, and the viewing point with its lovely panorama over the valley.

crematorium, a few prison cells and two huts bear witness to the atrocities of the past.

Struthof
9 km/6 miles SE of Schirmeck
Struthof concentration camp
Musée de la Déportation
☎ 03 88 97 04 49
Open daily Mar.-24 Dec. 10-11.30am, 2-4.30pm; July & Aug. 10am-5pm.
Admission charge (free for under 18s).
Alsace has the tragic legacy of being the site of two concentration camps. The

Grendelbruch
12 km/7½ miles NE of Schirmeck
Château fort de Guirbaden
Free admission.
The 11thC. château in this friendly little village is impressively large and has retained many of its original features. Take the Rue du Quartier-Guibaden (about 30-45 mins walk), past a number of attractive doorways. First into view is the castle, with its main supporting arch, followed

A DREAM DESTINATION
Auberge Metzger
55, Rue Principale
Natzwiller
*8 km/5 miles
SE of Schirmeck*
☎ 03 88 97 02 42
Closed Sun. pm, Mon., 3 wks Jan., last wk June & Christmas wk.
A delightful inn stands in the heart of Natzwiller, combining a lovely setting and a charming building with top quality cuisine. The chef, Yves Metzger, serves delicious food at reasonable prices. The rooms are very pretty and cost around €46 for half-board and between €54 and €69 for full board. The small village also has some great walks that include the waterfalls of Serva and Belmont – two more reasons to spend a night at this interesting spot.

Spotcheck
B3

Things to do
Musée de la Déportation in Struthof
Château fort de Guirbaden
Market of country produce in Saales

With children
Picnic by Coucou lake

Within easy reach
Mont Ste-Odile (25 km/ 16 miles E), p.147

Tourist office
Tourist association from Haute-Bruche to Schirmeck:
☎ 03 88 47 18 51

by the Romanesque ruins of the great house, then the *Hungerturm* (hunger tower – a former prison), and the St-Valentin chapel.

The Donon
*10 km/6 miles
NW of Schirmeck*
Celts and Romans
The Donon (1,009 m/3,310 ft) takes its name from the Celtic word *dunum*, or mountain, and its two-tier summit marks the boundary between Alsace and Lorraine. It's thought that the Roman god Mercury was worshipped on the mountain, and a reconstruction of the original Temple

of Mercury was built in 1869 on the site of the Gallo-Roman ruins. Nearby is a sacrificial altar and the remains of a Roman villa. The panorama is magnificent and the surrounding countryside emerges as a patchwork of blues and greens.

Étang du Coucou
*5 km/3 miles
NW of Schirmeck*
Pastoral peace and picnics
Just before you reach Grandfontaine, take the small road to the left
Coucou lake was created by the Germans in the 20thC. to feed Grandfontaine's steel industry and provide water for the mining vehicle engines. Despite its past, it's now a lovely, tranquil spot. Above it lies the peat bog of La Maxe, the remnant of an ancient glacial lake, used strategically during World War I.

Saales
*20 km/12¹/₂ miles
SW of Schirmeck*
Market of country produce
☎ 03 88 47 18 51
Fri., June-Sept. 3-7pm.
This is the valley's last village before the Vosges mountains. Its lively market, established in 1966, is held in the halls under the Hôtel de Ville. The stalls are loaded with delicious local produce,

including Munster cheese, *bleu des Vosges*, farm butter, eggs, *foie gras*, duck, trout, carp sausages, snails, gentian syrup, honey, gingerbread, dried sausage and fruit. You'll find them all very hard to resist!

Around Mont Ste-Odile,
Obernai, Rosheim, Barr…

Mont Ste-Odile's summit stands at 764 m/2,507 ft and is one of Alsace's most significant religious sites. It was a magical and mysterious place long before the arrival of Christianity, as witnessed by some of the ancient remains. Today it's a popular spot for tourists, drawn by the small towns surrounding the mountain that welcome them warmly.

Rosheim

28 km/18 miles SW of Strasbourg
A town of towers
Rosheim is a small, wine-growing town with ruined ramparts and some of Alsace's oldest buildings, including half-timbered houses, impressive towers and a Renaissance well (1605), located near the town hall. Two of the most remarkable buildings include the Maison Romane, thought to be the most ancient building in Alsace (1160), situated between nos. 21 and 23 on Rue du Général-de-Gaulle, and the 12thC. St-Pierre-et-St-Paul church, a Romanesque basilica with three naves. It has several sculptures on its exterior (note St Peter trampling a lion underfoot). The interior is both dark and sober, full of square pillars and columns.

The Rosenmeer Inn
45, Avenue de la Gare Rosheim
☎ 03 88 50 43 29
Closed Sun. pm, Mon., 3 wks in winter & 2 weeks in summer.

Hubert Maetz, a former pupil of Antoine Westermann (chef at the Buerehiesel restaurant in Strasbourg), opened this inn in 1985, next door to his father's *winstub*. The cuisine is a successful and subtle mix of local produce and traditional recipes, and the hotel, with its glorious wooden panelling (even in the lift), is worth a detour. The talented young chef is still in his thirties and describes himself simply as an *aubergiste* (innkeeper). An average bill is usually around €38 per head, but those wanting to spend less can tuck into delicious dishes next door in the *winstub* at around €15.

St-Pierre-et-Paul church

THE ART OF MARQUETRY

The Spindler workshop

St-Léonard
2 km/1 mile from Boersch, towards Ottrott
☎ 03 88 95 80 17
Open Fri. & Sat. 9am-noon, 2-6pm (by appt. on other days).
Free admission.

The art of marquetry, or inlaid work, involves the delicate layering of thin pieces of different woods to form a complete image. Alsace has a long history of the craft, but it was Charles Spindler (1865-1938) who played a key role in revolutionising the technique, transforming it into an art form in itself, rather than simply a decoration. Spindler and his successors were not the only practitioners in Alsace – there were several craftsmen and

talented amateurs operating in the region. The landscapes and scenes depicted in this establishment are typically Alsatian, and the different woods used form harmonious images with subtle shades and textures.

Boersch/St-Léonard

3 km/2 miles SW of Rosheim

A beautiful village

The small and picturesque village of Boersch has retained its surrounding wall, together with three ancient gates.

Boersch

Its town hall is Renaissance in style as is the magnificent well on the square (1617). On the Ottrott road you'll pass St-Léonard, an unusual hamlet reached via a doorway leading to a courtyard, a relic of its past status as a Benedictine convent.

Ottrott

2.5 km/1½ miles S of Boersch

Wine and food

Ottrott is a charming village, known for its excellent *Rouge d'Ottrott* – a rosé wine very close to a Pinot Noir – and its quality restaurants. It makes a good base for a number of walks, including the classic climb up to Mont Ste-Odile (signposted).

Two castles

Accessible from the car park on the left after the crossing in the centre of Klingenthal.

Spotcheck

B3

Things to do

Walk along the Mur Païen
Walk to the Châteaux of Andlau and Spesbourg
Ski resort in Champ-du-Feu

With children

Les Naïades aquarium in Ottrott
Glacé gingerbread in Gertwiller

Within easy reach

Vallée de la Bruche (25 km/16 miles W), p.142
Molsheim (12 km/7½ miles N), p.140
Val de Villé (15 km/9 miles S), p.152

Tourist offices

Barr: ☎ 03 88 50 75 38
Obernai: ☎ 03 88 95 64 13
Rosheim: ☎ 03 88 50 75 38

Head towards Résidence Fichwaedel Entry charge: €1 (free for under 14s). Free guided tours 2nd & 4th Sun. in month. Accommodation available.

Ottrott has two neighbouring castles, the 13thC. Château de Rathsamhausen, with its magnificent *palas* (palace), and the smaller 12thC. Château de Lutzelbourg. Both are maintained by the Centre for Medieval Studies in Strasbourg (4, Rue du Tonnelet-Rouge, Strasbourg, ☎ 03 88 37 17 20).

Ottrott by Hansi

Klingenthal
2 km/1 mile
NW of Ottrott
Historic weapons factory in Klingenthal
2, Rue de l'École
☎ 03 88 95 95 28
Open Sun. & pub. hols.
May-Dec. 2-6pm.
Free admission (guided tours for groups).
The small resort village of Klingenthal is home to a former weapons factory, established in 1730 to manufacture fine swords and bayonets (the name Klingenthal translates from German as 'valley of swords').

After 1838, control of the factory passed to the Coulaux brothers (see Mutzig, p.140) and until 1962 it made tools and farming equipment.

Obernai
4 km/2½ miles
E of Ottrott
The Alsatian ideal
A pleasant holiday resort, Obernai is an attractive village full of local colour and character. It has a thriving economy thanks to various dynamic industries, not least the Kronenbourg brewery, known locally as 'K2'. The *Kappelturm*, a 13thC. belfry, was originally the tower of a chapel, but is now reduced just to the chancel. The old

Obernai market

covered market in the Ancienne Halle aux Blés dates from 1554, and the building now houses a pleasant restaurant. Don't miss the Puits à six Seaux, an elegant Renaissance well crowned by a weather cock.

The ramparts
Head for the church (via the reconstruction of a Renaissance well), which houses a reliquary containing the heart of the bishop of Angers, Charles Freppel, a native of Obernai. To your right is a tower that once served as a prison. Turn to the right to enjoy a pleasant stroll on the ramparts, lined with a

double row of trees, and make for the white cross that stands above the town. Head on up the road, taking the car if you're not feeling energetic), turning right after the church and then left, climbing all the while. The view over Obernai is magnificent, enhanced by the pretty roofs with their polished tiles. The morning light is best for photography.

Heaven and earth

Mont Ste-Odile is a sacred and holy site, open to all (free admission daily). Enter via the 18thC. porch of the convent, destroyed by fire in 1546 but rebuilt half a century later. Enjoy a tour of the ramparts with their wonderful views and visit the lovely neighbouring chapels, Chapelle des Larmes and

LES NAÏADES

Aquarium Park
On the D426 between Ottrott and Klingenthal
Open daily throughout the year 9.30am-6.30pm.
Admission charge.
This large aquarium, known as Les Naïades, houses more than 3,000 fish from all over the world. A specific natural environment from a wide variety of continents, such as mountain stream, river, lake, estuary, sea and ocean, has been recreated in each of the aquarium's tanks. You can watch exotic fish, such as piranhas, electric eels and sharks, and keep a wary eye out for the crocodiles. Children will be fascinated.

Mont Ste-Odile convent

Mont Ste-Odile

8 km/5 miles SW of Ottrott

The garden of delights

After the death of St Odile (see p.88), she was succeeded by a number of abbesses, the most famous being Herrade de Landsberg, author of *Hortus Deliciarum* (garden of delights). The book was a medieval poetic encyclopedia, illustrated with lovely illuminations and dating from c.1170. Sadly, it was destroyed in 1870 in a fire that ravaged Strasbourg library.

Chapelle des Anges. The monastery church, rebuilt in 1692, is adorned with fine woodwork. From there you can reach the Chapelle de la Croix, the oldest part of the convent, and then pass through a low doorway to the small Chapelle Ste-Odile, which contains the relics of St Odile in an 8thC. sarcophagus. There is also a lovely sundial from the 17thC. The Auberge des Pèlerins (pilgrims' inn) is on site to satisfy the visitor's hunger or thirst.

Sundial

The *Mur Païen*

5-hr walk, signposted by Club Vosgien; can be shorter if desired. Leaves from the foot of the stairs at the Chapelle du Rocher

The exact origins of the *Mur Païen* ('pagan wall'), a mysterious structure which runs through forests and screes for a distance of more than 10 km/6 miles are unknown. Its average thickness is 1.5 m/5 ft and the wall reaches a height of between 1 and 3.5 m/3 and 11 ft. The prehistoric or Celtic work is made from huge blocks of unhewn stone, which the Romans reused to create the *castrum* of Altitona (the ancient name for Mont Ste-Odile). The walk is enjoyable and takes you to the Rocher

Barr

*11 km/7 miles
S of Mont Ste-Odile*

Musée de la Folie Marco

30, Rue du Docteur-Sulzer
☎ 03 88 08 94 72
Open daily (exc. Tues.) June-Sept. 10am-noon, 2-6pm.
Admission charge (free for under 15s).

A busy industrial town, Barr is involved in a number of activities, including tanning and wine-growing (Sylvaner, Riesling and Gewürztraminer). Visit the Folie Marco, an 18thC. merchant's house that contains an

GINGERBREAD

Lips
110, Rue Principale, Gertwiller
2 km (1 mile) E of Barr
☎ 03 88 08 93 52
Open daily 8am (10am Sun.)-noon, 1.30pm (2pm Sun.)-5pm (6pm Sat. & Sun).

Gertwiller is the gingerbread capital of Alsace. The glazed spiced bread made in this village (also famous for its wine) is highly prized, particularly at Christmas, when people come for miles around to buy it. It's available throughout the year, however, and is particularly delicious in Lips, where the staff enthuse noisily about their own recipe.

Andlau

2 km/1 mile S of Barr

Ste-Richarde church

Andlau is a charming village, lying at the heart of Riesling country. St Richarde (see p.89) is buried in the 12thC. church, a relic of a famous convent that she founded. The doorway is a fine example of Romanesque sculpture – Italian in inspiration, with outstanding carvings such as the figures of Adam and Eve on the lintel. The lower part of the tower is decorated with a frieze of animals, monsters and a mixture of realistic and allegorical scenes. The interior has fine 15thC. stalls, an 11thC. crypt and a pulpit

du Panorama, or *Wachstein* (a huge 1-m/3-ft high block), the Druid cave, a number of tumuli and – having crossed the Hohwald road – the medieval castles of Dreistein and Hagelschloss.

attractive museum. Antique furniture, porcelain, pewter and documentation on local history are on display, and one section is devoted to the *schlitte* or sledge, used to transport logs down steep slopes.

supported by the figure of Samson. The cavity in the crypt is said to have been dug by the bear found by St Richarde, and outside a 15thC. well bears the statue of the saint and her bear.

Andlau and Spesbourg châteaux

Access (free) via the CD854 from Barr to Mont Ste-Odile, and then on a surfaced path to the left leading to the Hungerplatz forest lodge. Car park.

The château of Andlau is very imposing, with two huge towers and Gothic windows. The interior is more sober, with fine chimneys. The neighbouring château of

Château d'Andlau

Spesbourg, designed on more military lines, was built in the 13thC. and destroyed in the 14thC.. Many of its features remain, however, including fine twinned windows and seats. From here it is only a 3-minute walk to the Andlau château and a 10-minute stroll to Spesbourg.

Le Hohwald

8 km/5 miles NW of Andlau

A secluded resort

Surrounded by spruce and beech woods and a landscape dotted with farms, chalets and hotels, this resort is the starting point for a number of excursions, on foot or by car. The routes are signposted with helpful information.

Le Champ du Feu

11 km/7 miles SW of Hohwald

A mountain ski resort

From the observation tower of Champ du Feu, the panorama is glorious – on a clear day

you can even see the Swiss Alps. It's a lovely ski resort (mainly cross-country), with a 40-km/25-mile pisted area (Téléski in La Serva, ☎ 03 88 97 30 53).

Erstein and Benfeld,
sugar and tobacco

E rstein and Benfeld both lie in the plain. The towns have similar economies and commercial activities, with tranquil lifestyles and regular celebrations of local produce, in particular sugar and tobacco. The sugar comes from the beetroot grown all around the area, especially in Kochersberg, while Benfeld is an important warehousing and manufacturing centre for tobacco, used mostly in Strasbourg cigars.

Limersheim

Erstein

Osthouse

Benfeld

Diebolsheim

Rhinau Island

sucre morceaux

Sugar lumps · Würfelzucker

erstein

4

Erstein

22 km/14 miles
S of Strasbourg
Sugar festival
Last Sun. in Aug.
Erstein is home to an important eponymous sugar refinery, Sucre Erstein. Huge lorries laden with beetroot arrive from all over the region, and the town celebrates its close bond with sugar in a traditional festival. The lively events include a procession with floral floats, an arts and crafts market, music and folk traditions, and the festival attracts thousands of people.

The outdoor life on Erstein lake
Municipal campsite
Rue de la Sucrerie
☎ **03 88 98 09 88**
Erstein has a very pleasant campsite, situated near a lake. Its range of activities include swimming (a lifeguard is in attendance), canoeing and kayaking, diving, fishing and rowing. Not surprisingly, it's one of Alsace's most popular campsites.

Osthouse

3 km/2 miles
S of Erstein
A fairytale castle
Osthouse contains a quite charming Renaissance castle, dating from 1558. Unfortunately, visitors are not allowed into the château, which is owned by the great Alsatian Zorn de Bulach family, but even its exterior is very impressive. It's one of the few remaining Wasserburg-style

Benfeld town hall

castles, surrounded by moats full of water and fed by a tributary of the River Ill. The roof tiles are also worth a careful look.

THE KIEFFER
TOBACCO
PLANTATION
**2, Rue Haute,
Limersheim**
*5 km/3 miles
N of Erstein*
☎ **03 88 64 01 97**
Open Mon.-Sat. July & Aug.
Explore a day in the life of a tobacco farmer with a visit to Xavier Kieffer's plantation and he'll answer any questions you may have on the subject. The farm also features an exhibition on New World plants (corn, tomatoes, beans etc.), which have become key ingredients in our modern diet. The *Alsatabac* organisa-tion arranges regular tobacco-related events and excursions (☎ 03 88 19 17 60).

Benfeld
*6 km/4 miles
S of Osthouse*
Tobacco country
Benfeld holds its tobacco festival in August (for information on exact dates contact the tourist office, 10, Place de la République ☎ 03 88 74 04 02). The most spectacular monument in the town is undoubtedly the Renaissance town hall, with its lovely carved doorway and Jacquemart-style clock, with three figures that strike the hours: Death, a Knight and Stubenhansel, a sinister but legendary figure who sold the city to its enemies in 1311. In his hand is a purse full of gold, the price of betrayal.

Rhinau and its island
*13 km/8 miles
SE of Benfeld*
A jungle in Alsace
The landscape changes dramatically as you enter the alluvial forest of the Rhine, accessed from Diebolsheim (5 km/3 miles to the south). Make for the dam and park

Spotcheck
C3-4

Things to do

Sugar festival in Erstein
Water sports on Erstein lake
Tobacco festival and visit to Kieffer tobacco farm in Benfeld

With children

Explore the alluvial forest in Rhinau

Within easy reach

*Obernai, Barr (15 km/ 9 miles W), p.146, p.148
Sélestat (20 km/ 12¹/₂ miles S), p.154*

Tourist office

Erstein: ☎ 03 88 98 14 33

the car just beyond the lock. A pleasant and easy sign-posted walk makes its way round an island between the Old Rhine and the Grand Canal. The forest is lush and green, almost jungle-like, but serious work has been under-taken to make it accessible to walkers. Enjoy a quiet stroll through the sloes, vines, wild hops, dogwood, clematis and Himalayan balsam, keeping an eye out for birds such as the nuthatch, woodpecker, black kite, egret and tufted duck. Deer are numerous too. You can also visit the island by boat (for more information contact the tourist office in Rhinau, ☎ 03 88 74 68 96).

Val de Villé,
the forgotten valley

This green and pleasant valley is often forgotten. It leads to the Col d'Urbeis (602 m/1,974 ft), the only pass in the Vosges that is still negotiable, and is essentially an agricultural area. Tourism is developing slowly, with visitors attracted by the splendid walks on offer in the region.

Dambach-la-Ville

Carving from Villé church

By car and on foot

From Villé, take the D424 to Thanvillé (4 km/2½ miles SE), where you'll find an attractive 17thC. Renaissance manor house (privately owned). Next, head for St-Pierre-Bois (1.5 km/1 mile NE) and Blienschwiller (6 km/4 miles NE). Just after the road meets the Route de Nothalten, park on the right and take the GR 5 trail to the beautiful ruined Château de Bernstein (12th-13thC.), commanding a fine view of the Plaine d'Alsace. Return via the pretty wine-growing towns of Blienschwiller and Epfig

(4 km/2½ miles NE), home to the Chapelle Ste-Marguerite, a lovely church in the shape of a Latin cross. You end up in Dambach-la-Ville (8.5 km/5 miles S), a renowned wine-growing centre with a fortified wall, tower-gates, town hall and pretty timber-framed houses. From Dambach a signposted path climbs to the Chapelle St-Sébastien, with its late-17thC. Baroque altar and retable.

St-Gilles

4 km/2½ miles E of Villé
A Midsummer Night's Dream
Booking essential (not possible by phone)
For information:
☎ **03 88 58 99 11**
By Minitel: 3615
RESALSACE
End of July.
Admission charge.

Villé

30 km/19 miles NW of Colmar
In the heart of the Val de Villé
Villé, at the centre of the valley, is the birthplace of a number of famous people, such as Roger Siffer (owner of La Choucrouterie in Strasbourg, see p.132) and religious artist René Kuder. Visit the church with its Renaissance statue of the Virgin and keep an eye out for the lovely house with an oriel window nearby.

Blienschwiller

VILLÉ'S DISTILLERIES
Les Délices du Val de Villé
2A, Quai du Glessen
☎ 03 88 57 14 39
By appt.
Jean-Paul Vonderscher
13, Rue de l'Abbatoir
☎ 03 88 57 11 48
Open daily (exc. Tues.) 9am-noon,
2-7pm.
The Val de Villé is still home to a
few distilleries. As the profession
is becoming more and more strictly
controlled, the number of amateur
distillers is gradually declining.
However, these larger outlets are
no less interesting. You'll come
across *eaux de vie* made from
mirabelles, pears, plums and
even eggs (this odd liqueur can
be obtained from Les Délices du
Val de Villé).

At the end of July, the lovely
village of St-Gilles comes alive
with a fairytale spectacle,
different in content each year
and enjoyed immensely by
locals and visitors alike. Events
start at 10pm with a fabulous
son et lumière show, complete
with special effects. Wurzel, a
goblin from the woods,
narrates the colourful history
of the Val de Villé in 50
successive scenes (tickets: €14
for adults, €6 for children).
Booking by phone is not
possible, so unless you have
the option of booking on the
French Minitel system, you
should apply in writing to
Association St-Gilles, Place du

Marché, 67220 Villé. It's well
worth the effort, but you must
book ahead to get a seat.

Albé

2 km/1 mile N of Villé
A seductive village
Lost among the vines, Albé is
the starting point for two
excellent waymarked paths,
the first of which leads to
Breitenbach (1 hr)
across the *Chemin
des Ânes* (donkey
path). The second
walk takes around
3 hours and leads to
Le Hohwald along
the same path.

Spotcheck
B4

Things to do
Excursion by foot and car to
Villé
Walks from Albé
Val de Villé distilleries
Panoramic view from Climont
tower

With children
Summer performance and
spectacle in St-Gilles

Within easy reach
*Le Hohwald (10 km/
6 miles N), p.149
Sélestat (15 km/9 miles
SW), p.154*

Tourist office
Villé: ☎ 03 88 57 11 69

Le Climont

*13 km/8 miles W of
Albé via Col d'Urbeis
mountain pass*
**You won't believe
your eyes!**
The panoramic view from the
Climont tower (966 m/
3,169 ft) is really quite
breathtaking. Also known
as *Tour Euting* (after the
President of the hiking club
that constructed the path in
1897), it has 78 steps and
overlooks a stunning wooded
landscape and the Champ-
du-Feu tower. It is also the
starting point for a number of
excursions along marked trails
that lead to the Bruche valley.
St-Blaise-la-Roche, Bourg-
Bruche and Saales are all
around 3 hours from here on
foot.

Sélestat,
linking Upper and Lower Alsace

Sélestat is often compared with Saverne, in terms of size, history, heritage and commercial activity. Both towns have strategic locations, with Sélestat lying between Upper and Lower Alsace.

The church of Saint-Georges

An historic town

Sélestat (*Schlestadt* in German) was the birthplace of many key figures, particularly in the Humanist era when its university flourished. It was occupied by the Swedes during the Thirty Years War and fortified by Vauban in 1675.

An artistic town

Art is everywhere in Sélestat. The imposing St-Georges church has magnificent Gothic architecture, 14thC. vaults, lovely stained glass, a rose window and Renaissance pulpit. Nearby stands the fine Romanesque church of Ste-Foy, built from red sandstone and granite from the Vosges. It has a fine porch, decorated with arcades, cornices and capitals (featuring remarkably benign lions) and a central, polygonal tower with arcades on each face (43 m/141 ft high as opposed to the 60 m-/197 ft- high tower of St-Georges).

Journey from the Romanesque to the contemporary by viewing the original work of Sarkis near the ramparts and in the nearby FRAC building (a contemporary regional art organisation), where exhibitions, meetings and conferences are held. All the sights are sign-posted and located within a small area near the bridge over the River Ill.

Ste-Foy church capital

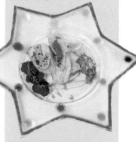

Bibliothèque Humaniste

1, Rue de la Bibliothèque
☎ 03 88 58 07 20
Open daily exc. Sat. pm & Sun. 9am-noon, 2-5pm.
Admission charge.
The great Dutch scholar Erasmus, founder of

Humanist Library. Over 500 works from his *Beat Bild* collection are housed here, along with 450 manuscripts, 500 incunabula and around 2,000 printed books from the 16thC. Admire the 15thC. retables and the intriguing cast of a female head, taken from a body found buried in the Ste-Foy church.

Spotcheck
B4

Things to do
Contemporary art
Ebersmunster church

With children
Corso Fleuri street festival

Within easy reach
*Haut-Koenigsbourg
(10 km/6 miles W), p.158*

Tourist office
Sélestat: ☎ 03 88 58 87 20

Humanism, had a number of disciples in Alsace, in particular Beatus Rhenatus (1485-1547). A native of Sélestat, Rhenatus was an author and publisher, and founded the

Floral floats

2nd Sun. in Aug.
Séléstat's Corso Fleuri festival was first held in 1929 and has become one of the most popular in Alsace. Musical ensembles, folk groups, acrobats and floral

floats take part, and festivities continue well into the evening. A huge firework display takes place at dusk (€6 adults, free for children under 12; information from the Cultural office, Cour des Prélas, ☎ 03 88 58 85 75).

Ebersmunster

*8 km/5 miles
NE of Sélestat*
A miracle of Baroque
The Austrian architect, Peter Thumb, built the church in Ebersmunster between 1719 and 1727. Built on the site of a 7thC. Benedictine abbey, thought to have been founded by Duc Adalric of Hohenbourg, father of St Odile, the abbey-church is arguably the finest example of 18thC. Alsatian Baroque art. Its two bulb-shaped steeples can be seen from afar (the third is set back), and the interior is decorated with stucco work and paintings, restored in the 19th C. Look out for the wooden statue of Samson under the altar, the attractive stalls and the imposing high altar. The Silbermann organ has an extraordinary quality of sound.

From the Ried to the Rhine,
a land of water, plants and wildlife

The term '*ried*' is used to describe the marshy area between the Rivers Ill and Rhine. The Ried, however, designates the region lying between Sélestat and the Rhine.

The Ried

La Chapelle du Chêne
4 km/2½ miles
S of Sélestat
The waters of the Ried
The ground water in the Ried, which mixes with the water from the Rhine, is actually quite shallow, and even the slightest excess of water can cause a flood. This ecological paradise for both flora and fauna also faces the constant danger of drying out, a recurrent problem in marshland areas. In 1962, the Ried was classified as a 'zone of exceptional scientific value' and in its shifting, unstable landscape, you can appreciate the variety of colours and the flora and fauna (such as deer, rabbits, partridges and pheasants) that thrive in the area. Above all, it's a place to experience perfect calm and tranquillity.

Muttersholtz
7 km/4 miles
E of Sélestat
Koelsch, the fabric of Alsace
Tissus Gander
Rue de l'Étang
☎ 03 88 85 15 32
Open daily (exc. Sun.) 2-5pm.
Gander is one of the few manufacturers of *koelsch*, a typically Alsatian linen fabric with a checked pattern (see p.47). People come from far and wide to buy tablecloths, mats and napkins. Simple in design, they are hardwearing and have an individual, rustic charm. Don't go home without buying a souvenir from this shop.

Diebolsheim

13 km/8 miles
NE of Muttersholz
A floral village
Diebolsheim is one of the many charming floral villages which are the pride of Alsace. Take a look at the Château du Comte de Beaumont (unfortunately, not open to visitors) and visit the charming Lourdes grotto at the northern exit to the village.

Marckolsheim

13 km/8 miles
SE of Sélestat
Hydro-electric power station
4 km/2¹/₂ miles E on D424 on the Alsace canal
Exterior only accessible.

Stretch of the Alsace canal at Marckolsheim

When travelling through Marckolsheim, take the opportunity to have a look at the hydroelectric power station, one of many on the Rhine – or, to be more precise, on the Alsace canal. Alsace receives its electricity not only from power stations such as this one, but also from the nuclear power station in Fessenheim, the first one in France to use a high-water-pressure reactor.

THE MAGINOT LINE

This famous line of defensive fortifications was devised by War Minister Paul Painlevé and his successor, André Maginot (1877-1932). The Line was planned as a defence running the length of the frontier, from the north to the east, but in the event only the east and northeast parts were fortified. A range of structures from the Maginot Line have been preserved, of varying sizes and uses. Many of them are open to visitors, including the lime kiln in Lembach, the fort at Schoenenbourg (the most important of the series), the Musée de l'Abri in Hatten and the Heidenbuckel in Leutenheim. Admission charges vary (in Leutenheim, for example, admission is free).

André Maginot

Spotcheck
C4

Things to do

Hydroelectric power station in Marckholsheim
André Maginot memorial museum

With children

La Chapelle du Chêne

Within easy reach

Sélestat (15 km/9 miles W), p.154
Illhausern (15 km/9 miles W), p.233

Tourist office

Sélestat: 03 88 58 87 20

André Maginot memorial museum

1 km/¹/₂ mile E of Marckolsheim on the road running parallel with the D424 (signposted)
☎ **03 88 92 57 79**
Open Sun. & pub. hols. 15 Mar.-14 June & 16 Sept.-15 Nov. 9am-noon, 2-6pm (daily 15 June-15 Sept.).
Admission charge.
Tour: 1 hr
The museum was founded in 1971 to commemorate the Maginot Line and the liberation of France. Many weapons and military artefacts are displayed, including objects connected with the battle of 15-17 June 1940, when the Line was defended by only 30 men.

Around Haut-Koenigsbourg,
castles and vineyards

The Château du Haut-Koenigsbourg is one of the most popular tourist sites in France. It stands proudly on a sharp promontory, overlooking the pretty wine-growing villages and the Plaine d'Alsace below.

Kintzheim

*4 km/2¹/₂ miles
W of Sélestat*
The castle of eagles
Kintzheim boasts two castles, the Château Willemin, dating from the 18thC., and a medieval castle whose courtyard houses an aviary for

Open Apr.-Oct. 10am-noon, 1-5pm (to 6pm in May, Jun. & Sept.); July & Aug. 10am-6pm. *Admission charge.*

Haut-Koenigsbourg

*6 km/4 miles
W of Kintzheim*
A brief history
Haut-Koenigsbourg was built in the 11thC. and destroyed during the Thirty Years War. In 1899, the town of Sélestat, owners of the ruins, offered the château to Kaiser William II as a token of their loyalty. He had it restored by Bodo Ebhardt, an architect from Berlin, and it was returned to France 10 years later.

birds of prey. They take part in the *Volerie des Aigles*, a spectacular training flight (see box). The castle ruins include a strange cylindrical keep connected to the surrounding wall by a rectangular tower.

Monkey mountain
4 km/2¹/₂ miles along the Route du Haut-Koenigsbourg
☎ 03 88 92 11 09

In 1969 150 Barbary apes were brought from the upper reaches of the Atlas Mountains. They spend their time in total freedom in the large 20 ha/50 acre park of the Kintzheim forest. The *Montagne aux Singes* (monkey mountain) has proved to be such a successful breeding ground that some of the apes have even been reintroduced into Morocco. Children will adore this place.

Haut-Koenigsbourg castle

TRAINING OF BIRDS OF PREY

Château de Kintzheim (signposted)
☎ 03 88 92 84 83
Open Apr.-Oct. 2-5pm;
14 July-20 Aug. 10-11.15am.
Demonstrations (unless poor
weather): at 3pm & 4pm (plus
5pm Sun. & pub. hols.) and
14 July-20 Aug. at 11.15am,
2.30pm, 3.45pm and 5pm.
Admission charge.
The main courtyard is the
site of a fabulous spectacle,
the *Volerie des Aigles*, during which birds of prey,
including eagles, condors,
kites and secretary birds,

fly freely. It's fascinating for adults and children
alike. The birds swoop and dive, and then return to
the protective gloves of their trainers.

Spotcheck
B4

Things to do

Château du Haut
Koenigsbourg
Walk to Château
d'Ortenbourg

With children

Volerie des Aigles and
Monkey mountain in
Kintzheim

Within easy reach

*Sélestat (10 km/6 miles
E), p.154
Route du Vin (10 km/
6 miles E), p.218*

Tourist offices

Kintzheim:
☎ 03 88 82 09 90
Scherwiller:
☎ 03 88 92 25 62

Exploring Haut-Koenigsbourg
☎ 03 88 82 45 82
Open daily March, Apr.
& Oct. 9.30am-noon,
1-4pm; May, June &
Sept. 9am-noon, 1-5pm;
July & Aug. 9am-6pm.

Coat of arms on the south gate

*Admission charge (free
for under 18s). No extra
charge for commentary.
Restaurant and
bookshop*
Enter the château via the
main gate bearing the coat of
arms of Count Oswald de
Thierstein. Pass through
another gate, which carries
those of Charles V, and then
follow a cobblestone path.

Cross the drawbridge that
leads to the Porte des
Lions (lions' gate) and
look for the fortified well
just inside the gates. Enter
into the main courtyard,
and then head for the
baronial residence, with its
armoury and banqueting
hall. Leave via the garden,
rounding off your tour
with a visit to the large
artillery bastion.

scherwiller

*3 km/2 miles
NW of Sélestat*
A peasant revolt
The last battle in the war
of the Rustauds took
place in Scherwiller in
1525, when the rebels were
crushed by Duc Antoine
de Lorraine. A discreet
cross on the CD35
commemorates an ossuary
erected on the battlefield.

Château d'Ortenbourg
*Accessible by foot from
the Huhlenmuhl farm
(2 km/1 mile W of
Scherwiller).*
This attractive walk takes

about 90 minutes. The
Château of Ortenbourg
extends over an area 130 m/
426 ft in length,
hugging the line of the
rock. It contains a
32-m/105-ft
pentagonal keep
and a massive
surrounding
wall in the
form of a
shield.
The
building
proved
so difficult
to capture
that
Othon
d'Ochsenstein
installed a
redoubt
(defensive
structure) that
was eventually
to become the
Château of
Ramstein.

Armoury

The three-frontier region,

France, Switzerland and Germany

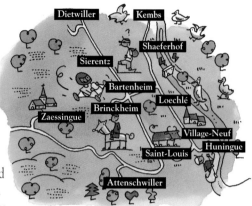

Dietwiller
Kembs
Shaeferhof
Sierentz
Bartenheim
Loechlé
Brinckheim
Zaessingue
Village-Neuf
Huningue
Saint-Louis
Attenschwiller

This area is an intricate jigsaw formed by the political boundaries imposed by three different countries. Although the trio of cultures have similarities, they also differ hugely and the area is defined by one of Europe's greatest rivers, the majestic 'Father Rhine'.

SENTIERS DE DÉCOUVERTE
DU PAYS DE SIERENTZ

Bartenheim

14 km/9 miles
S of Mulhouse
The Sierentz region
8, Place du Général-de-Gaulle
Information at Sierentz region tourist office
The Sierentz region stretches from the Rhine to Sundgau. Signposted trails from Bartenheim allow you to discover the area on foot or by bike. The Hochkirch route (blue markers) starts at Sierentz (3 km/2 miles N), and is best appreciated by walkers, with its range of aquatic flora. The Gutzwiller circuit (orange markers) from Zaessingue (9 km/6 miles SE) is also a delight. The Muhlgraben trail (yellow markers) crosses fields and forests. For a tour around

architectural treasures, follow the red markers from Dietwiller (11 km/ 7 miles NE).

Eco-karting
Euro Arena
Oarc 3, A35 exit
☎ 03 89 70 77 70
Open Mon.-Thurs.
11am-midnight;
Fri. 11am-1.30pm;
Sat. 10am-1.30pm,
Sun. 10am-midnight.
Admission charge.
Climb aboard these electric hi-tech go-karts and tackle the 400 m/440 yd track. Other facilities at the complex

include a games room, with simulators that allow you to enjoy virtual car and bike races, skiing, aquaski, archery, football and billiards. A special section is designed for young children.

Kembs

11 km/7 miles
NE of Bartenheim
The Corbusier lock
Twin canal trail
This signposted trail, the *Circuit des Deux Canaux*, is both easy and enjoyable. It leads from the Canal de Huningue to the Grand Canal d'Alsace (around

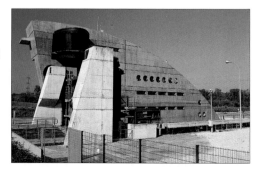

THE GRAND CANAL D'ALSACE

The canal was developed in the 1930s and completed in 1970. It's 51 km/ 32 miles long and was built to allow boats to travel from Strasbourg to Basle without having to navigate the fast-flowing Rhine. Wider than the Suez Canal (110-140 m/360-460 ft), each of its reaches comprises a double lock and a hydroelectric power station producing millions of kilowatts of electricity.

Kembs marina

5 km/3 miles, 90 mins, departing from Place de la Mairie). On the trail you'll encounter the only lock designed by the celebrated architect Le Corbusier, who also designed the church at Ronchamp near Belfort.

A canal drawbridge

The marked path that weaves its way around the Canal de Huningue rejoins Kembs further south, at Shaeferhof (8 km/5 miles, 2½ hrs). It passess a magnificent drawbridge on the canal,

dating back to 1835. Take the opportunity to enjoy the abundant flora and fauna, including several species of birds.

Boat hire

Marina
Rue P. Bader
☎ 03 89 48 38 10
Open Mon., Tues. & Thurs. 3-6pm; Sat. 9am-noon, 2-6pm; Sun. 10am-7pm.
Kembs is located on the banks of the Rhine between Huningue and Mulhouse. You can hire boats by the hour, half day or full day, with or without a river permit (which you can obtain after 16 hours of theory and practice on the Rhine, should you so wish).

Hydraulic power station

6 km/4 miles S of Kembs
By appt.
☎ 03 89 32 48 23
The first hydraulic power station on the Rhine was built at Kembs between 1928 and 1932. A dam feeds the network of four power stations installed on the Grand Canal d'Alsace and regulates the flow of the Rhine. Near the dam a fish ladder enables the migrating fish to navigate the 12 m/40 ft difference in water level between the Rhine and the Grand Canal.

Spotcheck

C7

Things to do

Discovery trails of the Sierentz region
The Petite Camargue
Parc des Eaux-vives in Huningue

With children

Eco-karting in Bartenheim
Planet trail in Huningue

Within easy reach

Sundgau (15 km/9 miles S), p.168-169
Basle and Swiss Jura (20 km/12½ miles E), p.164-167
Mulhouse, city of museums (30 km/19 miles S), p.230-231

Tourist offices

St-Louis-Huningue:
☎ 03 89 70 04 49
Pays de Sierentz:
☎ 03 89 68 28 58

Loechlé

5 km/3 miles S of Kembs
Île du Rhin trail

Departs from Place du Colonel-Gauvin
The marked trail crosses two canals before reaching the Île du Rhin. Here, you have a choice of two paths, one which loops to the Rhine and back, crossing a nature reserve (6 km/4 miles, 105 mins, on foot); the other a 17-km/11-mile tour of the island to the dam, between the Vieux Rhin (old Rhine) and the Grand Canal, taking about 5½ hrs on foot or 1½ hrs by bike.

Village-Neuf

10 km/6 miles S of Kembs
A living nativity

In the church
☎ 03 89 89 76 16
This is one of Alsace's oldest and most beautiful nativity

From Water to Wheels

A 5-hour circuit departs from the hire centre in Huningue (in the marina) and heads to Île Napoléon near Mulhouse. The outward journey is made in a three-seater canoe on the canal that links the Rhône to the Rhine. The return trip is completed in the saddle along the canal towpath (where mountain bikes are permitted). Information and details on how to hire the canoes and bikes (for adults and children), prices for individuals and groups, and how to return the canoes can be obtained from Cardinale East, ID (Rue du Mal Foch, Kembs, ☎ 03 89 48 38 10/06 80 10 64 58. Open Mon.-Thurs. 3-6pm, Sat. 9am-noon, 2-6pm).

scenes, held throughout Christmas Eve and Christmas Day. The villagers create a wonderful performance which charms thousands of visitors.

Huningue

2 km/1 mile
S of Village-Neuf
Musée d'Histoire
Rue des Boulangers
☎ 03 89 44 65 67
Open 1st & 3rd Sun. in month 2.30-5.30pm. Closed Aug.
This history and military museum includes a remarkable model of the town in 1724 which reveals the strength of Vauban's fortifications, and shows how closely the civilian and military buildings were interwoven.

Huningue, a former fortress, was bravely defended in 1799 and 1815.

Vauban

Historic trail
Information at tourist office
☎ 03 89 70 04 49
The historical society of Huningue and its region

devised this interesting trail (free leaflet available from the information office at 6, Rue des Boulangers). Discover the colourful past of this frontier town through a number of buildings, including the small houses on Place de la Victoire and the house in which Louis XVI's daughter, Madame Royale, stayed in Rue Abbatucci.

Madame Royale, daughter of Louis XV

Parc des Eaux Vives (whitewater course)
3, Quai du Maroc
☎ 03 89 89 70 20
Open daily 9.30am-8.30pm (check opening times out of season).
This artificial whitewater course, originally built for slalom racers, is the only one of its kind in France. The 350-km/1,150-ft course (class II–III) is suitable for all levels, including beginners, experts and children, and is remarkably well equipped. Surf- and rodeo-wave, flatspin, cartwheel or pirouette – you can attempt them all (or learn how to, at least).

Planet trail
☎ 03 89 70 04 49

The Galileo School of St-Louis dreamt up the 6-km/3³/₄-mile *Chemin des Planètes,* which runs between Huningue and Rosenau (starts 200 m/ 200 yds N of the bridge over the canal, near Parc des Eaux Vives). Both adults and children will enjoy discovering the stars on this astronomical trail. A leaflet is available from the tourist office (6, Rue des Boulangers).

St-Louis
2 km/1 mile
S of Huningue
La Petite Camargue Alsacienne
Marked trail (3 hrs) from car park at Au stadium
☎ 03 89 89 78 59
Guided tour (admission charge) throughout year by request.

This nature reserve (120 ha/ 297 acres) was home to a fish farm in the days of Napoleon III. Known as the 'miniature Camargue of Alsace', a marked footpath leads you through the marshland, with its wide variety of flora and fauna. The information centre has a video show, library, exhibition room and shop (open Sun. & pub. hols. 1.30-5.30pm).

Book fair
☎ 03 89 69 52 00
Open mid-May, Fri., Sat. & Sun.

Thousands of literary enthusiasts and professionals flock to this book fair, which has a different theme each year. It attracts local, national and international publishers, as well as famous authors.

Attenschwiller
9 km/6 miles
SW of St-Louis
Arboretum
Bruckmatt-Muhlematt
☎ 03 89 69 79 41
Guided tours Thurs. 3-5pm & by appt.
Free admission.
Take the D419 from Hésingue, then the D473, turning right on to the D21 after 500 m/ 550 yds. Before you reach the village (400 m/440 yds), take the left-hand path and at the end, to the left of an old willow tree, you'll find a path leading to the arboretum. It's a tranquil spot with plenty of fresh air and some unusual scents and plant species.

Brinckheim
10 km/6 miles
N of Attenschwiller
The Koer equestrian centre
Ginder Gérard
10, Rue des Fleurs
☎ 03 89 68 29 15
Open 10am-6pm in high season.
If you or your children are interested in horses, this is the place to come. You can visit the stables, exercise in the ring and enjoy equestrian excursions of all levels.

Alsatian Jura,
a unique region

Alsatian Jura, formed by two parallel mountain ranges, covers an area of over 25 km (16 miles) along the Swiss frontier, from Courtavon to Basle. The highest point, Raemelsberg, reaches 832 m (2,730 ft). Above the village of Winkel is the source of the Ill, the river that feeds the whole of Alsace before thundering into the Rhine in Strasbourg.

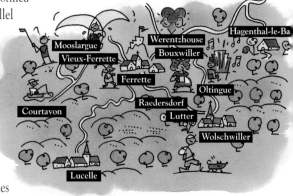

Ferrette

40 km/25 miles
S of Mulhouse

Jewel in the crown
☎ 03 89 40 40 01
Ferrette, a medieval city lying close to the Swiss border, clings to the slope of an impressive limestone promontory, overlooked by the ruins of two castles. Historically, it was the seat of independent and powerful counts (*comtes de Ferrette*) whose name survives even today, since the Prince of Monaco lists 'count of Ferrette' among his many titles.

The château
☎ 03 89 40 40 01
Free admission.
Climb the pretty and steep slope (15 per cent gradient) leading to the château, taking time to admire the half-timbered and Jura-style façades. You'll find a chapel, the Mazarin boundary marker, high and low gates, the palace and the impressive inner façade of the château, built into the rock itself. The view is lovely and free guided tours start at the town hall.

The 'dwarves' trail'
Leaves from opposite the old court building
46, Rue du Château
☎ 03 89 08 23 88
2-hr walk of average difficulty.
Wear walking shoes.

THE BREAD OVENS OF ALSACE

The houses in Alsatian Jura are typical of 19thC. rural life. Grey and roughcast with white architectural features and half-timbering, the buildings often have bread ovens that jut out from the main structure. For several years now the renovated buildings have been painted in colours similar to those used in the Middle Ages.

Spotcheck

B7

Things to do

Folk museum in Oltingue
Visit to Ferrette
La Largue golf course

With children

The 'dwarves' trail'
From Baignade to Courtavon

Within easy reach

Ballon d'Alsace (30 km/ 19 miles W), p.172, 182 Mulhouse, city of museums (20 km/12½ miles S), pp. 230-231

Tourist office

Ferrette: ☎ 03 89 08 24 00

This trail explores the Gorge aux Loups (wolves) as it plunges deeply into the mountains, between the rocks of the Heidenflüh. A leaflet available from the tourist office explains the legend of the gorge, in which dwarves possessing eternal youth lived in harmony with local people.

Oltingue

*9 km/6 miles
E of Ferrette*
Two religious buildings

Visit the historic 13thC. St-Martin-des-Champs church in Oltingue. Excavations here unearthed a sarcophagus and tombs from the 7th and 8thC., as well as a collection of frescoes. The parish church contains some historic organs, the work of J. and C. Callinet, dating from 1843, and don't miss the St-Brice chapel, which houses a lovely colourful altar.

Sarcophagus from St-Martin-des-Champs church

3-6pm, & Sun. 11am-noon, 3-6pm.
Admission charge.
This folk museum lies in the heart of a charming village. The Musée Paysan houses a unique collection of rural tools and household objects,

shapes for different occasions. Traditional rural life of the past is reconstructed in artisan workshops and living rooms, and the bakery has an impressively large bread oven.

Vieux-Ferrette

*1 km/½ mile
W of Ferrette*
Take to the skies
Vieux-Ferrette centre
☎ 03 89 08 21 23/
06 80 02 79 51
Admission charge by appt.
Take advantage of an original, accessible way of exploring the region – by microlite! Beginners, experts and those wanting to learn the craft

Musée Paysan
10, Rue Principale
☎ 03 89 40 79 24
Open 15 Jun.-30 Sept.
Tues., Thurs., Sat.,

including furniture, crockery and kitchen utensils. It even includes a fascinating array of *kugelhopf* moulds, used to make the traditional Alsatian bun, produced in different

are all welcome. Without being an 'extreme' sport, it will offer you an unforgettable experience.

Cheese platter
Sundgauer Käs Keller
☎ 03 89 40 42 22
Open daily 11am-10pm
(closed Sun.).
Bernard Antony's inspiration
was to open a cheese-tasting
restaurant in an old building,
where cheeses from all over
France could be sampled.
The cheeses have become
famous and Bernard himself
supplies the best French and
European restaurants. It's well
worth a visit, but do book in
advance, as there are only a
few tables.

Hagenthal-le-Bas

14.5 km/9 miles
E of Ferrette
A great place to eat
Chez Jenny
84, Rue d'Hégenheim
☎ 03 89 68 50 09
Open all year. Closed
Sun. evening & Mon.
In this flower-laden
establishment, a meal will cost
you between €12 and €54,
for a remarkable gastronomic
experience. Regional flavours
and imaginative cuisine
combine with a sophisticated
décor and pleasant atmosphere
to make your meal a
memorable occasion.

Lucelle

11 km/7 miles
S of Ferrette
A frontier town
Lucelle is a lakeside village at
the southernmost end of the

Alsace region. It was once
home to an important
Cistercian abbey and enjoys a
lovely wooded setting. You can
visit the remains of a former
traditional hostelry (free
admission), complete with
stables, barns and sheds.

Mooslargue

6 km/4 miles
W of Ferrette
International
golf complex
at La Largue
Rue du Golf
Tourist office:
☎ 03 89 07 67 67
Open all year from
10am to dusk.
*Admission
charge.*
Take the opportunity
to improve your
golf on this 9-hole
course, set in a truly
idyllic location. You can
work on your technique on

the driving range, or boldly
tackle the complete 18-hole
course.

Courtavon

11 km/7 miles
S of Ferrette
International
watersports
complex
☎ 03 89 08 12 50
Free admission.
This important leisure
complex, developed by
14 *communes* and the Swiss
Jura canton, is open all year.
There's a large campsite
(open 1 May-30 Sept.) and
dedicated areas for swimming,
fishing, rowing and sailing,
as well as a miniature port.
There are seven marked
walking trails, encompassing
an area of 135 km/84 miles.
Facilities in the complex also
include a bar and restaurant.

Werentzhouse

5 km/3 miles
NE of Ferrette
The smallest museum in France
Musée des Amoureux
Rue Principale
☎ 03 89 08 23 88
France's tiniest museum, dedicated to lovers, is located in a delightful corner of Alsace. It's home to a wonderful collection of postcards, the work of a devoted collector, tastefully and well presented.

Bouxwiller

3 km/2 miles
E of Ferrette
Work on a farm
Luppachhof educational farm
☎ 03 89 40 39 87
Admission charge.
Learn about living and working on a farm, and gain a new understanding of its produce. Luppachhof has an interesting mix of activities on offer, varying according to the time of year.

Raedersdorf

6 km/4 miles
S of Ferrette
A botanical trail
Departs from the Sontag warehouse
☎ 03 89 48 11 37
Park at the start of walk.
The village of Raedersdorf has an interesting discovery trail,

dotted with informative signs about the plant life. Choose between walks of 2 km/ 1 mile or 3 km/2 miles.

Wolschwiller

10 km/6 miles
E of Ferrette
Cross from France to Switzerland
Leaves from Place de la Mairie
Reasonably difficult walk (3 hr 45 mins, 10 km/ 6 miles, steep over 380 m/416 yds)

On this marked trail (yellow diamond-shaped and blue triangular markers) you'll cross the border into

Switzerland at Burg-Raemelsberg. In the centre of the

Swiss village of Burg, turn right towards the Schlosberg convent and make for Rittimatte. Cross the fields to the edge of the ridge, or cross the woods, where views over the Sundgau are magnificent. Make sure you take the Club-Vosgien IGN map, Top 25, no. 3721.

THE LILY FESTIVAL

Fête des Trois-Lys
Courtavon
☎ 03 89 40 80 37
1st Sun. in Sept.
The emblem of Courtavon, the lily is celebrated every year in the town. Festivities include a flea market, exhibitions of the work of local artists and artisans, open-air cafés (selling *flammekueche*, fried carp and suckling pig), organ concerts and folklore events.

Lutter

8 km/5 miles
SE of Ferrette
L'Auberge Paysanne
24, Rue de Wolschwiller
☎ 03 89 40 71 67
Open all year (exc. Mon.).
This inn positively creaks under the weight of flowers. In this idyllic, bucolic setting you can enjoy a gastronomic treat, such as a salmon crêpe with an oyster mushroom sauce. A meal should cost between €10 and €38. The neighbouring inn has three lovely rooms and is an authentic 17thC. farm from Sundgau.

The Sundgau region,
visual and culinary delights

Feldbach church

Sundgau is the southernmost area of Alsace, along with Alsatian Jura and the three-frontier zone. Its hills, limestone cliffs, beech and pine forests, valleys, lakes, meadows and flower-decked traditional villages make it a haven of natural beauty and tranquillity.

Altkirch
20 km/12¹/₂ miles SW of Mulhouse
Musée Sundgauvien
Hôtel de Ville (town hall)
Rue de l'Hôtel-de-Ville
Open daily (exc. Mon.) July & Aug. only 2.30-5pm.
Admission charge.
The Sundgau museum is devoted to the region's history, archaeology and folklore, and also houses a collection of sculptures and statues, paintings by local artists, including Henner and Lihrmann, and a model of Altkirch in former times.

Notre-Dame church
38, Rue Ferrette
This 19thC. church contains an impressive polychrome Mount of Olives group and a copy of Prud'hon's *Christ*. The crypt houses the sarcophagus of St Morand, patron saint of Sundgau, who was an important figure in the region during the Middle Ages.

Carspach
4 km/2¹/₂ miles SW of Altkirch
Route de la Carpe frite
☎ 03 89 40 94 38
The Sundgau area is famous for its carp, and the *Route de la Carpe frite* (fried carp trail) was created in 1975 to

LE SUNDGAU, ROUTES DE LA CARPE FRITE

promote this local speciality. Informative signs are dotted along the route and one of the best places to try the dish is at La Couronne restaurant (9, Rue Steinsoultz,

☎ 03 89 40 93 09, open daily, 10am-10pm, closed Tues. & Sun. evening).

Hôtel du Tisserand, Gommersdorf

Gommersdorf
12 km/7¹/₂ miles W of Altkirch
A living museum
Gommersdorf is a one-street village (1 km/¹/₂ mile long), restored by an organisation which takes care of rural houses in Alsace. You'll come across old but still working farms, most of them half-timbered

THE FISH HARVEST

Traditionally, the ponds were drained around mid-September in order to remove the silt, leaving only a small amount of water in which the fish sought refuge. Men wearing huge boots that came up to their hips waded into the water to push the fish back to the overflow. A mesh there would capture the fish, and the men could transfer them to the newly cleaned waters using a landing net.

and laden with flowers. The village of Oberdorf lies 10 km/6 miles south of Altkirch and has similar local characteristics.

Feldbach
14 km/9 miles
S of Altkirch
The village church
This tiny village, located on the D452, has a 12thC. Romanesque church. Its barrel-vaulted apse has alternate round and square pillars, and thick walls separate off the section of the nave reserved for nuns.

Fruit in abundance
St-Loup orchard
13 km/8 miles
S of Altkirch
☎ 03 89 83 53 45
Open 15 Apr.-30 Oct. 10am-5pm.
Admission charge (includes tastings in season).
This 5-ha/12-acre park is planted with boxwood, a rose

garden, ornamental trees and an amazing 150 species of fruit trees. You can buy the jams and preserves and there's an archery range and pony-rides.

Altenach
14 km/9 mile
SW of Altkirch
Maison de la Nature
Rue Ste-Barbe
☎ 03 89 08 07 50

Open all year 9am-noon, 2-6pm.
Free admission.
Educational activities are organised for children over 8 and adults on a variety of environmental themes, such as forest, lake, river and meadow habitats, energy sources, conservation and recycling.

Zillisheim
11 km/7 miles
NE of Altkirch
The 'forgotten trades' trail
☎ 03 89 06 25 22
This historic trail is an unusual but interesting way of

discovering more about the village, which lies between Mulhouse and Altkirch. Cycling enthusiasts can follow the cycle path from the Rhône canal to the Rhine, leaving from the town hall. The trades of past centuries are recalled on enamelled signs attached to the houses.

Spotcheck
B7

Things to do
Route de la Carpe frite
Maison de la Nature, Altenach

With children
St-Loup orchard

Within easy reach
Alsatian Jura (15 km/ 9 miles S), pp.164-167
Mulhouse, city of museums (20 km/12½ miles N), pp.230-231
St-Louis and the three-frontier region (30 km/ 19 miles E), p.163

Tourist office
Altkirch: ☎ 03 89 40 02 90

The potash basin,
an industrial legacy

The Eco-museum at Ungersheim

Southern Alsace was a very active industrial region at the end of the 19th and beginning of the 20thC., and potash was extensively mined in the area between Mulhouse and the Vosges. These mines are now a thing of the past, but the wonderful Eco-museum in Ungersheim attracts thousands of visitors, eager to learn about the heritage of the region.

Ensisheim
12 km/7½ miles
N of Mulhouse
A meteoric museum
Musée de la Régence
Place de l'Église
☎ 03 89 26 49 54
Admission charge.
Housed in the former Palais de la Régence, a fine Gothic edifice dating from 1535, the museum charts the rural and mining history of the region, and includes some of the oldest ceramics in Alsace. It also contains archaeological finds and a meteorite that fell on Ensisheim on 7 November 1492. It originally weighed in at an impressive 150 kg/ 331 lb, but today's remnant is only about one-third the size, as much of the unusual exhibit was given away to famous visitors.

Ungersheim
7 km/4 miles
SW of Ensisheim
Eco-museum of Haute Alsace
☎ 03 89 74 44 74/44
Open daily throughout year; July & Aug. 9am-7pm; Apr.-June & Sept. 9.30am-6pm; March & Oct. 10am-5pm; Nov. & Feb. 10.30am-4.30pm.
Admission charge.
This open-air museum contains an entire village covering an area of 25 ha/ 62 acres. Its 70 half-timbered houses were brought from all over Alsace and reconstructed in their new location. You'll need a day to appreciate all that's on offer, including blacksmiths, cartwrights and potters in their workshops, historic spectacles, a tour of the village in an oxcart, boat and fishing trips, four restaurants and shops selling local produce and crafts.

Cernay
17 km/11 miles
SW of Ensisheim
A picturesque city
Musée de la Porte de Thann
Rue de Thann
☎ 03 89 75 50 35
Admission charge.
Housed in an 18thC. tower, the museum focuses on the Franco-Prussian war and the two World Wars. There are also displays of local arts and mining archaeology.

ALSATIAN POTASH

Potash has been mined in Alsace since the 19thC. Thousands worked in the industry in the northwest of Mulhouse, in Wittenheim and Wittelsheim, but it had an impact on the salinity of the Rhine. Competition, pricing and restructuring are all ongoing concerns and the mines are gradually closing as the resource is depleted. The final closure is planned for 2005.

Blodelsheim
14 km/9 miles
E of Ensisheim
Harvest festival
Last weekend in July, even years only
The festival features a procession of church figures dressed in traditional period costumes which makes its way

to the place where a harvest festival meal is held. Historic farm machinery is also brought out for the occasion. Various scenes are enacted during the festival, some secular and others drawing on a religious theme. In one of the latter, Mary and Joseph have a son called Jangalé who grows up, is baptised and takes holy communion.

Vieil-Armand
18 km/11 miles)
W of Ensisheim
The sacred mountain
National monument and necropolis, ossuary
Silberlock
☎ **03 89 23 12 03**
Crypt open Apr.-Oct.
8.30am-noon, 2-6.30pm.
Admission charge.
Vieil Armand (Hartmannswillerkopf) was the site of a ferocious battle during World War I, in which an estimated 30,000 German and French soldiers were killed. A national monument stands above the crypt that contains the remains of 12,000

Spotcheck
B6

Things to do
Eco-museum of Haute-Alsace at Ungersheim
Musée de la Régence in Ensisheim

With children
Harvest festival in Blodelsheim

Within easy reach
Vallée de Guebwiller (10 km/ 6 miles W), pp.186-187
Vallée de Thann (25 km/ 16 miles SW), pp.174-175
Mulhouse, city of museums (20 km/12¹/₂ miles S), pp.230-231
Route des Crêtes (20 km/ 12¹/₂ miles W), pp.178-181

Tourist office
Cernay: ☎ **03 89 75 50 35**

unknown soldiers. There is a military cemetery, together with a 22 m/72 ft-high cross marking the French front, in homage to the volunteers from Alsace-Lorraine. You'll also come across monuments to the *Diables Rouges* (red devils) of the 152nd Regiment and the *Chasseurs* (mountain troops) of the Prussian Guard. A number of trenches and shelters have been restored.

The southern Vosges,
at the foot of the Ballon d'Alsace

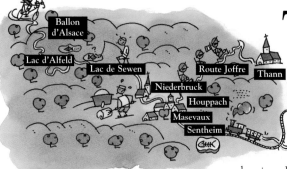

Ballon d'Alsace

Lac d'Alfeld

Lac de Sewen

Niederbruck

Houppach

Masevaux

Sentheim

Route Joffre

Thann

This valley with a thousand aspects is a wonderful green and fertile area, dotted with lakes, pastures and ravines. It's also home to the Ballon d'Alsace (1,250 m/4,101 ft), the highest peak of the Massif du Ballon d'Alsace at the southern end of the Vosges mountain range.

Masevaux

25 km/16 miles
W of Mulhouse
Houppach, place of pilgrimage
☎ 03 89 82 41 99
Masevaux is a small industrial and commercial town, which grew up round an abbey founded in 720 AD. It has retained all its charm with pretty squares adorned with fountains and lined with lovely 16th- and 17thC. houses. However, it's the hamlet of Houppach, lying higher up, that draws the most visitors. Home to Notre-Dame chapel, it's a well established pilgrimage site.

Route Joffre
In Masevaux, head towards Thann.
The *Route Joffre* was built by General Joffre's troops during World War I to establish communications between the Doller (Masevaux) and Thur (Thann) valleys, by way of the Hundsruck Pass (788 m/ 2,585 ft). During the winter of 1944-1945 it resumed its military role, becoming the only route by which French troops could approach Thann. Today, it makes an attractive tourist trail.

Ballon d'Alsace
Access via D466 from Masevaux and Sewen (Alsatian side)
Monument aux Démineurs
☎ 03 84 28 12 01
This powerful monument to bomb-disposal experts, by Rivière and Deschler, is dedicated to those who died in action during

the two World Wars. You'll also find statues of Jeanne d'Arc and Notre-Dame-du-Ballon, overlooking the Belfort depression.

Lac de Sewen and Lac d'Alfeld

10 km/6 miles
W of Masevaux
Paradise for anglers
The dam, built at the end of the 19thC., regulates the flow of the Doller, particularly during times of flood and snow melt. It created an artificial lake, Lac d'Alfeld, covering an area of 10 ha/ 25 acres and reaching a depth of 22 m/

Lac d'Alfeld

Lac Sewen

72 ft. Anglers can fish in Lac d'Alfeld for trout, perch or roach, but a permit is required (information from the Masevaux tourist office). The banks of the nearby Lac de Sewen are home to a number of Alpine and Nordic plants.

Niederbruck
2 km/1¼ miles
W of Masevaux
A day on the Entzenbach farm
Rue Entzenbach
☎ 03 89 82 45 49
Open Jun.-Oct.
11am-5pm
Signposted from village
Free activities.
This is a working farm, but visitors can lend a helping hand with the milking,

harvest and other daily tasks. Wellingtons are advised!

Sentheim
6 km/4 miles
SE of Masevaux
All aboard...
Tourist railway in the Doller valley
10, Rue de la Gare
☎ 03 89 82 88 48
Wed.-Sun. July & Aug.: diesel leaves Sentheim at 4.45pm, Cernay (St-André) at 3pm; Sun. & pub. hols. Jun.-Sept.; diesel/steam trains leave Sentheim at 2pm, Cernay at 11am; steam train leaves Sentheim at 3.30pm, Cernay at 5.30pm. Climb on board the steam or diesel train for a leisurely trip

Law village in the Doller valley

– bikes go free. The train passes through 14 km/9 miles of forests and meadows at a pleasant, relaxed speed.

Spotcheck
A6

Things to do
Visit the Ballon d'Alsace
Fishing in Lac d'Alfeld
Maison de la Géologie in Sentheim

With children
Tourist railway in the Doller valley

Within easy reach
The Sundgau region (15 km/9 miles E), pp.168-169
Vallée de Thann (10 km/ 6 miles N), pp.174-177

Tourist office
Masevaux: ☎ 03 89 82 41 99

Record of the rocks
Maison de la Géologie
35, Grand-Rue
☎ 03 89 82 55 55
Admission charge.
The tour is in two parts, and the first involves a visit to the Maison de la Géologie to admire its impressive collection of fossils and minerals. Then take the D466 to the geological trail (*sentier géologique*) in Wolfloch, which takes around 2 hours, covering a distance of 5 km/3 miles and including 12 geological sites. You'll return full of new insights into the region's geology, from millions of years ago to the present day.

IN MEMORY OF RENÉ POTTIER
In 1906 a key stage in the famous French cycle race, the Tour de France was established in the Ballon d'Alsace. A monument crowns the summit erected in memory of René Pottier, that year's eventual winner. The race has passed through this famous spot many times, and it was here in the 1970s that Eddy Merckx had his amazing victory in front of 200,000 spectators.

The Thann valley,
southern entrance to the *Route du Vin*

Thann is a large market town nestling at the foot of the Rangen vineyard. It marks the southern end of the famous *Route du Vin* (wine route). Don't be in too much of a hurry to set off, however. Located beneath the summit of the Vosges massif, the Grand Ballon, Thann is a beautiful place worth spending some time in.

Thann

16 km/10 miles
W of Mulhouse
St-Thiébaut collegiate church
Place Joffre
☎ 03 89 37 96 20
Open daily Oct.-May
8am-noon, 2-5pm;
Jun.-Sept. 8am-7pm.
*Free admission
(exc. during services).
Guided tours for groups
(admission charge).*
The splendid Gothic collegiate church dates principally from 1380-1516. It has a beautifully sculpted portal on the west front, with three tympana. The only one of its kind in France, it features 150 scenes and 500 figures. The elegant interior houses notable 15thC. stained glass windows and oak choir stalls. The spire, over 70 m/ 230 ft in height, was completed in 1516.

Oeil de la Sorcière

The Château d'Engelbourg
Park in the Bungert car park in the centre of Thann and follow the signposted route.
☎ 03 89 37 96 20
*Free admission.
Pedestrian access only.*
The ruins of the 13thC. Château d'Engelbourg will soon house a medieval-style garden. The ruined keep, nicknamed *Oeil de la Sorcière* ('witch's eye'), maintains its careful watch over Thann, the Plaine d'Alsace and, in the distance, the Black Forest.

Musée des Amis de Thann
24, Rue St-Thiébaut
☎ 03 89 37 03 93
Open daily (exc. Mon.),
mid-May to mid-Oct.
Admission charge.
The highlights of this small but fascinating museum include a model of the *Napoléon* locomotive that travelled on the first railway line from Alsace in 1839, a wonderful 18thC. ceramic stove, a 13thC. Virgin and Child, and a splendid Renaissance closet dating from 1677.

THE BURNING OF THE FIR TREES

Legend has it that the servant of the Italian bishop, St Thiébaut, native of Gubbio in Umbria, carried his master's relics in his staff. These included his thumb complete with episcopal ring. One day the servant stopped in Thann, planted his staff under a fir tree and fell asleep. When he awoke he was unable to pull the staff out of the ground. Three lights then appeared above three fir trees, a heavenly sign spotted by the Comte de Ferrette, who was inspired to build a chapel on the site. Only then was the staff released. A popular religious festival is held on 30 June in Thann, which includes vespers at the abbey church, a torch-lit retreat, a procession led by the statue of St Thiébaut, the burning of three fir trees and impressive fireworks. It is one of the most popular traditional festivals in Alsace.

Spotcheck
A-B6

Things to do
Walking tours
Haute Alsace museum of textiles and costumes
Urbès lake
Kruth-Wildenstein dam

With children
Storkensohn oil mill
Watersports at Kruth-Wildenstein dam

Within easy reach
Route des Crêtes (10 km/6 miles N), p.178-181
Ballon d'Alsace (40 km/ 25 miles W), p.172, 182
Grand Ballon (10 km/ 6 miles N), p.178, 183

Tourist office
Thann:
☎ 03 89 37 96 20

Decorated egg market
Regional cultural centre
5 Rue Kléber
☎ 03 89 37 92 52
Annually, Easter weekend.
Free admission.
This is the largest market selling decorated eggs in Alsace. Each stall seeks to outdo the next in terms of skill and imagination, with some very artistic results.

Walking trails
☎ 03 89 37 96 20
Seven walking trails leave from Thann, ranging from 1-4¹/₂ hours in duration. The Club Vosgien (see p.28) ensures they are all clearly marked and maintained, and maps and topographical guides are on sale at the tourist office (7, Rue de la 1ère Armée).

Christmas in Thann
☎ 03 86 37 96 20
Christmas events in the southern Vosges include the Christmas and New Year markets, exhibitions and concerts. Christmas lights are switched on, decorations go up and Thann is transformed into a fairytale setting.

Reconstruction of a classroom in the Musée Serret

St-Amarin

6 km/4 miles NW of Thann

Musée Serret
7, Rue Clemenceau
☎ 03 89 38 24 66
Open daily (exc. Tues.) May-Sept. 2-6pm.
Admission charge.
Named after the general in command of the battles of Hartmannswillerkopf, this small museum is housed in a

The banks of the Thur

former court that as used as a military hospital in 1914. It displays a collection of objects relating to the history of the valley and its commercial activities (textiles and glass), as well as religious artworks, paintings, coins, old tools and instruments.

Route de la Truite
☎ 03 89 82 13 90

Alsace has a number of thematic trails, and the *Route de la Truite* (trout trail) is one of the most unusual. It sets off from Remiremont in the Vosges and passes through the Col d'Oderen, stopping en route in Kruth, Oderen, St-Amarin and Thann before finishing in Ufhotz via Cernay. Ufhotz stands at the crossroads of the *Route des Crêtes* (ridge route) and the *Route du Vin*. Most of the restaurants serve fresh trout in a variety of ways.

Husseren-Wesserling

3 km/2 miles
NW of St-Amarin
Musée du Textile et des Costumes de Haute Alsace

On the RN66 past St-Amarin
☎ 03 89 38 28 08

Open daily (exc. Mon. & Sat. am, Apr.-Sept.,

2-6pm; Oct.-Mar. 10am-noon, 2-5pm *Admission charge.*

The museum of textiles and costumes is housed in a former factory and focuses on the valley's important textile industry, taking visitors through all the processes involved in transforming raw cotton into finished fabric. There's an exhibition of costumes and reconstructed scenes illustrating 19th-C. fashion and its evolution.

A delightful park
Free admission daily

Near the museum is a 10-ha/ 25-acre park containing four lovely gardens and a collection of 19th-C. industrial buildings. There are French, Italian and English gardens, a kitchen garden and even an old farm. This charming spot also hosts concerts, plays, festivals and markets of local produce.

Storkensohn

3 km/2 miles SW of Husseren-Wesserling
Oil mill

20, Rue de la Mairie
☎ 03 89 39 14 00

Open July & Aug. Tues.-Sun. 2-6pm; May-Jun. & Sept.-Oct, Wed., Fri. & weekends, 2-6pm; school hols. Thurs.-Sun. 2-6pm. *Admission charge.*

Built in 1732, this water mill was used to press nuts, rapeseed, sunflowers, apples and pears. It closed in 1960, but was restored in 1991 and once more water from the Runtzbach turns the reconstructed wheel.

Maison Munch, a taste of history
Same opening times as the mill.

A stone's throw from the mill, Maison Munch is a living memorial to the region's rural economy and traditional way of life. It recreates the typical atmosphere of the old buildings of the Upper Thur valley, including the living conditions of their inhabitants. You can also order lunch or dinner.

A HUNDRED WAYS TO SERVE TROUT

Trout is a delicacy in these parts, and a great favourite with the locals. Since the *Route de la Truite* was established in the Thann valley, restaurant owners vie with each other to find the most inventive and delicious ways of serving the fish. You'll find it cooked in Riesling, served with a horseradish sauce, with almonds or prawns, or eaten alone. Several farms keep the restaurants supplied, but wild trout is only available to expert flyfishers, equipped with a permit.

Urbès

N of Storckensohn
Hiking to Rouge-Gazon
Leaves from Place de l'Église, signposted
☎ 03 89 82 60 01
This 13 km/8 mile trail is quite challenging and takes around 6¹/₂ hours. Crossing the wild area known as La Cuisine du Diable (the devil's kitchen) is a wonderful experience, followed by the site of the Tête du Rouge-Gazon. Enjoy a meal at the Rouge-Gazon farm-inn, lying at an altitude of 1,086 m/ 3,563 ft (☎ 03 29 25 12 80).

A glacial legacy
See d'Urbès
☎ 03 89 82 20 12
Guided tours available.
The Urbès lake is a peat-bog and one of only three natural lakes on the Alsatian side of the Vosges. It fills a depression created by the glacier that formed the Thur valley and covers an area of 40 ha/ 99 acres. It's of significant botanical interest, featuring over 300 species of plants and 20 ha/50 acres of meadow-sweet. It's also the only site where the teals nest in winter, just one of the 40 species of birds found in the area. The signposted path is full of interesing information.

Kruth-Wildenstein

7 km/4 miles NW of Husseren-Wesserling

Watersoprts on the lake
This artificial lake is a great place for watersports enthusiasts. Diving, sailing, windsurfing, canoeing, kayaking and fishing (permit required, ☎ 03 89 37 06 85) are all available, and if none of these take your fancy, you can try a spot of swimming or mountain biking (to hire mountain bikes ☎ 03 89 82 27 05). The area also includes 70 km/44 miles of cycle paths (to hire cycles ☎ 03 89 38 72 48).

The *Route des Crêtes* in summer, on foot, on horseback or by car

The decision to create a strategic route along the ridge of the Vosges was made in World War I. Linking Cernay with Ste-Marie-aux-Mines, the route ensured north-south communications between the valleys along the front line of the mountains. It's now a wonderful way to see the beautiful features of the Vosges mountain chain.

The ridge shuttle
Information at park office
☎ 03 89 77 90 34
Free service on country bus July-Sept. Sun. & pub. hols. 10am-6pm.
A shuttle service operates every hour covering 15 points on the Vosges ridge between the Col du Calvaire and the Grand Ballon. It follows the GR 5 trail, sharing its red rectangular markers, and offers some fabulous views. Climb on board and enjoy the ride.

The farm-inns of the Vosges
The tradition of dairy farming and cheese-making in the mountains dates from the 9thC. The *marcaires* take their herds to the high pastures (*chaumes*) in May, returning in September. Today, with the development of tourism, many of the farms become *fermes-auberges* (inns), in the tourist season, serving regional country fare and combining an agricultural role with hospitality. Those belonging to the association of farm-inns are the best to try, their distinctive signs a guarantee of quality.

Hot-air balloon rides
Aérovision
☎ 03 89 77 22 81
Admission charge.
If a bird's eye view of the Vosges captures your imagination, this Munster-based company offers a very different way of exploring the *Route des Crêtes*. The best times for hot-air balloon rides are during spring and summer, but the privilege doesn't come cheap.

Diables Bleus monument

Grand Ballon
From Mulhouse, access via Thann, Cernay, Wattwiller, Soultz (climb the Col Amic) or Willer-sur-Thur

The Grand Ballon
The highest point of the Vosges massif (1,424 m/ 4,672 ft) is also known as the Ballon de Guebwiller. It's the site of a monument to the *Diables Bleus* (blue devils) by Vermare and Moreau-Vauthier, erected in memory of the celebrated French *chasseurs*

(mountain troops) who were active in World War I. The fabulous view from the monument encompasses the line of the mountain ridge, the Plaine d'Alsace and the Black Forest.

Le Markstein

7 km/4 miles
N of the Grand Ballon
A family resort
Le Markstein, at an altitude of 1,200 m/3,937 ft, is well equipped with accommodation and a range of walking trails.

MOUNTAIN BIKE TRAILS
Subject to constant erosion by water, rain, air and wind, the unstable mountain soil is made worse by the number of bicycles that cross it. The high pastures are particularly vulnerable and mountain bikers should take great care to stick to the firm ground and the signposted routes and avoid disturbing the animals. Responsible cycling is the order of the day.

Hikers can leave their cars and enjoy a meal in one of the two hotel-restaurants, or farm-inns in Haag, heading towards the Grand Ballon, or in Salzbach, as they make for Schnepfenried. Pony rides are organised in summer.

Benji Trampoline
☎ 03 89 82 14 46
Admission charge.
A company called Evasions 2000 is responsible for the ski lifts in Le Markstein and has now installed a new attraction – the Benji Trampoline. A cross between a trampoline and a bungee jump, it allows the intrepid participant to leap to a height of 5 m/16 ft, attached to a harness and elastic ropes, and then perform a series of aerobatics.

A pitstop at Salzbach farm-inn
Near the Route des Cretes, on the D27 towards La Schlucht pass, signposted.
☎ 03 89 77 63 66.
Françoise Spenlé is the niece of 'Tant'Cath', who is famous in these parts. She has now taken over at this farm-inn and cooks a delicious *Tarte Cathérine* (€10 for a slice accompanied by salad). The Alsace Academy has rewarded her the *Bretzel d'Or* (golden pretzel) for her culinary skills. There's also a great view of Hohneck massif from the inn, giving the gastronomy a whole new perspective.

Spotcheck
A5-6

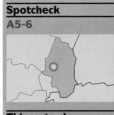

Things to do
Various walks
Country fare at a farm-inn
The chamois of Hohneck

With children
Benji trampolining in Le Markstein
Family mountain bike excursions

Within easy reach
La Bresse (15 km/9 miles SW), p.184
Le Vieil Armand (3 km/ 2 miles E), p.171
Guebwiller (10 km/6 miles E), p.186

Tourist office
Ballons des Vosges nature reserve office:
☎ 03 89 77 90 20

Col du Platzerwasel-Schnepfenried

15 km/9 miles N of Le Markstein, towards Munster
Uff Rain farm-inn
☎ 03 89 77 67 68
Signposted from the D27 before you reach the Platzerwasel pass
Enjoy a fabulous view of the ridge, from Hohneck to Spitzköpfe. Before tucking into your splendid meal here, visit the cheese dairy with its enormous copper cauldron and wooden moulds. This is one of

the most typical and traditional farms along the *Route des Crêtes*, and on late summer evenings, when there is a little less work to be done on the farm, the owner or one of his regulars will treat you to a few tunes on the accordion.

BILBERRY PICKING

The *Route des Crêtes* is laden with bilberries between the later part of July and the end of August. This is the time to pick the delicious fruit, available free of charge, but make sure you treat the fruit gently or you can cause damage. In under an hour, with two fellow pickers and without too much effort, you can collect enough bilberries to make a tasty tart. Served with a simple sprinkling of sugar, it should go down very well with a glass of Muscat.

Schnepfenried

At the summit of the Platzerwasel Pass, before the descent to Schnepfenried
'I' is for Icarus
Hang-gliding
Take-off site in Schnepfenried.
Free admission.
For experienced hang-gliders only.
Information at the Munster park office.
☎ **03 89 77 90 34**

Schnepfenried is a popular winter sports resort and provides an ideal launch spot for experienced hang-gliders. Brave beginners can arrange suitable classes by contacting the on-site instructors.

Le Hohneck
17 km/11 miles
N of Le Markstein
The wild mountain
The third and famous summit of the Vosges (1,363 m/ 4,472 ft) is accessible via a winding route that detours from the *Route des Crêtes*. The panorama from the viewpoint is marvellous.
The ridge marked the border between France and Germany before World War I. Le Hohneck is the

starting point for some wonderful walks, the most attractive of which heads down to Metzeral (a 2½-hr signposted trail).

Chamois
in the Vosges

Chamois live happily among the rocks of the Hautes Vosges in the Hohneck massif. They were first released in 1956, when 11 chamois from the Black

Forest joined five others from Haute Savoie in their new environment. Today they live in small groups totalling about a thousand in number. If you want to observe their

antics, do your chamois spotting at dawn and in total silence, between the Grand Ballon and Hohneck. You could stay the night near the Col de la Schlucht and be up with the larks. Camping and caravanning are prohibited.

Col de la Schlucht

5 km/3 miles
N of Hohneck
Strategic crossroads
This is the highest and one of the busiest of the Vosges passes at 1,139 m/3,735 ft, and is accessible from Munster (18 km/11 miles) along an easy route

lined with fir trees. Just before you reach the summit, take in the wonderful view (before the tunnel). Located at the intersection of the *Route des Crêtes* and the Gérardmer to Colmar road, Schlucht is linked to the Montabey summit by a chair-lift. If you head down the Alsatian side you'll be greeted by an equally wonderful view.

Jardin d'Altitude du Haut-Chitelet
☎ 03 29 63 31 46
Open daily Jun. 10am-noon, 2-6pm; July & Aug. 10am-6pm
Admission charge.
These botanical gardens are dedicated to the cultivation of Alpine plants from mountain ranges all over the world. The rockeries are spread over a 1-ha/2½-acre area and are home to some 2,700 species.

Col du Calvaire

18 km/11 miles
N of La Schlucht
A walk with a view
The Tête des Faux summit (1,220 m/4,002 ft) stands near the Calvaire Pass (1,144 m/ 3,753 ft). A signposted path (GR 5), marked in red and white, leads to a fantastic view over the Vosges massif, from north to south, and the two slopes, one in Alsace, the other in Lorraine.

Col du Bonhomme

3 km/2 miles
N of Col du Calvaire
The final stretch of the *Route des Crêtes*

This is the easiest pass to traverse (949 m/3,114 ft), even in the winter months (with special equipment). There are two lovely restaurants and you can park your car here before walking to the Col du Calvaire or Col des Bagenelles. The trails are relatively easy and make perfect family outings. The beautiful views go without saying.

The Vosges range in winter,
snow and ski runs

The Vosges massif is a paradise for skiers, whether cross-country or downhill, and it's a perfect destination for families. There are 170 lifts in a total of 36 ski resorts, and cross-country skiers can choose from over 1,000 km/ 621 miles of marked and well-maintained runs. You're also in the right place for a spot of night skiing, should this appeal.

Ballon d'Alsace
950-1,250 m/
3,117-4,101 ft
Access via Giromagny or Masevaux
☎ 03 29 25 20 38
There are 45 km/28 miles of Nordic ski runs in this area. Downhill ski runs range from green to black (via blue and red) and there are 11 chairlifts to the Ballon d'Alsace, together with two tows and three additional runs at Dolleren-Le Schlumpf. Accommodation includes hotel-restaurants, holiday houses, rural *gîtes* and *caravaneiges* (snow caravans).

St-Maurice-sur-Moselle
550-1,250 m/
1,804-4,101 ft
5 km/3 miles from Bussang (Vosges side)
☎ 03 29 61 50 37
Cross-country skiers can enjoy 11 km/7 miles of trails in Rouge-Gazon. La Jumenterie, with its three tows, has downhill runs (green and red). You can also connect to the Ballon d'Alsace ski resort, where facilities include a ski school and accommodation.

Bussang
600-1,200 m/
1,969-3,937 ft
Access via Thann and St-Amarin
☎ 03 29 61 50 37
Bussang has 60 km/37 miles of marked Nordic ski runs. Downhill skiers can choose between green, blue and red runs in La Bouloie (three tows) and L'Arcenaire (15 ha/37 acres of runs, four tows and snow machines). The French ski school (ESF) arranges private and group

classes and ski-jumping lessons (in L'Arcenaire). La Bouloie has six hotel-restaurants and a bar-restaurant-pizzeria.

Le Ventron

630-1,200 m/
2,067-3,937 ft
Past Le Bussang and Cornimont, head for La Bresse
☎ 03 29 24 07 02

This family resort has a ski area of 16 km/10 miles and three cross-country trails. The St Joseph's Hermitage area has eight downhill runs (green, blue and red), seven tows and a chair lift. The French ski school (ESF) runs individual and group classes. Accommodation includes seven hotels, apartments, farm-inns, rural *gîtes*, chalets and B&Bs.

Le Grand Ballon

1,100-1,340 m/
3,609-4,396 ft
Access via Soultz, Thann and Willer-sur-Thursday
☎ 03 89 83 13 25

This is the highest summit in the Vosges chain – on a fine day, views stretch over the Plaine d'Alsace, the Black Forest and the Vosges. It's a downhill resort with five tows

and six runs, covering an area of 30 ha/74 acres. It also has 22 km/14 miles of cross-country trails, a 400-seat restaurant and a farm-inn.

Le Markstein

770-1,267 m/
2,525-4,155 ft
Access via Guebwiller
☎ 03 89 82 74 98

Host to some of the Alpine World Championships in 1983 and 1987, Le Markstein offers 50 km/31 miles of Nordic ski runs, as well as an international standard

ski-jump (60 m/197 ft). The downhill ski area covers 6 ha/15 acres and is equipped with nine runs and tows together with a slalom run. Snow machines are poised for action if required. The French ski school (ESF) operates here alongside the cross-country ski school (from 1 Feb.-21 Mar.), and skiers can organise excursions and long-distance treks. The two hotels have a total of 70 rooms, the restaurant has seating for 70,

and accommodation includes chalets, huts, farm-inns and hostels.

Le Frenz

770-1,100 m/
2,526-3,609 ft
Between Le Markstein and Hohneck
☎ 03 89 72 25 78

This resort boasts 15 ha/37 acres of runs, a selection of tows, 10 km/6 miles of marked trails for cross-country skiers and a 25-m/82-ft ski-jump.

La Bresse-Hohneck
630-1,367 m/
2,066-4,482 ft
Access via La Schlucht
☎ 03 29 25 41 29
This is the largest ski area in the Vosges region with 50 km/31 miles of Nordic ski runs. There are green, blue, red and black downhill runs, 38 lifts and 38 runs in La Vologne-Hohneck, five tows and seven runs in Lispach, and three tows and five runs in Brabant. The French ski school (ESF) arranges individual and group classes plus instruction for beginners and in skiing and sledging. Accommodation ranges from hotel restaurants and holiday houses to rural *gîtes* and *caravaneiges* (snow caravans). Voted the most active sporting town in France, Bresse has produced a number of downhill champions from its population of 5,400; it's the most important winter resort in eastern France. The world championships of cross-country skiing have been held here, and night skiing is organised between 5 and 10pm on Tuesday, Friday and Saturday. Early risers can also enjoy dawn runs from 5.30am on Saturday and Sunday.

Gérardmer
Access via La Schlucht
☎ 03 29 27 27 27
Gérardmer boasts some 40 km/25 miles of cross-country ski runs, with 29 km/18 miles in Valtin. There are 20 lifts and 20 downhill slopes (green, blue, red and black) in Gérardmer as well as five tows and eight downhill runs in Valtin. Accommodation is in hotels, holiday houses, rural *gîtes* and *caravaneiges* (snow caravans). Gérardmer, voted the best French winter

resort, features some of the largest, as well as the most beautiful, runs in the Vosges massif. Le Valtin is not far away, and cross-country skiers can enjoy trails of differing degrees of difficulty in Gazon du Faing and Xonrupt-Longemer.

La Schlucht
1,258-1,346 m/
4,126-4,414 ft
Access via Munster
☎ 03 29 63 05 27
This resort is aimed mostly at beginners, with a blue downhill run complete with tow. In the Trois Fours resort there's a ski area of 16 km/10 miles with four signposted and properly packed runs. The ski school operates both individual and group classes, and the four restaurants can cater for 1,000 diners.

Le Schnepfenried
1,030-1,250 m/
3,379-4,101 ft
Access via Metzeral
☎ 03 89 77 72 92
Enjoy six downhill runs, eight tows, 30 km/19 miles of ski runs and five cross-country trails. Accommodation ranges from self-catering to hotels, farm-inns and apartments.

Le Gaschney
990-1,280 m/
3,248-4,200 ft)
Access from Muhlbach-sur-Munster
☎ 03 89 77 66 53

skiing and a piste link with La Schlucht, as well as eight downhill runs and four lifts. Lessons and long-distance treks are organised by the French ski school. Accommodation and a large restaurant are available.

downhill skiing, with 9 lifts and 11 runs of varying complexity. The Nordic ski area covers 40 km/25 miles, and include sledging and a ski school. Accommodation is available in the Auberge de

The Vosges

This resort, aimed at good skiers, has 16 downhill runs, a chairlift and four tows. It covers an area of 22 km/14 miles, and has well maintained, signposted cross-country trails. Lessons and long-distance treks (by appt.) can be arranged. There's a hotel-restaurant, farm-inn and apartments.

Le Tanet
1,000-1,288 m/
3,281-4,226 ft
Take the Lac Vert route from the top of La Schlucht lift
☎ 03 89 79 21 04
Le Tanet has 3 runs over 25 km/16 miles of Nordic

Le Petit Ballon
1,267 m/4,157 ft
Above Munster, access via Metzeral and Sondernach or via Luttenbach
☎ 03 89 77 32 49
If you're looking for wide open spaces for Nordic skiing, the routes here cover an area of 25 km/16 miles. The trails are signposted and well maintained and accommodation is available in a farm-inn.

Le Bonhomme-Lac Blanc
850-1,230 m/
2,788-4,034 ft)
☎ 03 89 71 33 11
This resort has artificial snow and arranges night and

Vallon, in one of two refuges or a *gîte*, and there's also a mountain restaurant.

Les Bagenelles
880-1.060 m/
2,887-3,478 ft
Access via Sainte-Marie-aux-Mines
☎ 03 89 58 70 01/
03 89 47 51 55
Open Wed., Sat., Sun. and school hols., 9am-5pm.
This resort has 44 km/27 miles of cross-country trails and two tows. Snowshoes are available for hire (☎ 03 89 58 56 40) and there's a 350-seat restaurant, three refuge chalets and six hotels, all within 6 km/4 miles.

The Guebwiller valley,
at the foot of the Grand Ballon

The Guebwiller valley is also known as Florival ('valley of flowers'), due to its colourful and attractive appearance. Once an industrial town, the number of factories in Guebwiller is now in decline, but its popularity as a tourist destination continues to rise.

Guebwiller

23 km/14 miles
NE of Mulhouse
Musée du Florival
1, Rue du 4-Février
☎ 03 89 74 22 89
Open daily (exc. Tues.) 2-6pm.
Admission charge.
This museum, complete with panoramic lift, houses a collection of pottery and ceramics by local artist Théodore Deck (1823-1891). Deck is famous as the creator of the Persian blue glaze, *bleu de Deck*.

Soultz

4 km/2¹/₂ miles
S of Guebwiller
Musée Historique du Château Bucheneck
Rue Kageneck
☎ 03 89 76 02 22
Open daily (exc. Tues.) May-Sept. 2-6pm.
Admission charge.
This moated château has been successfully restored and now contains various collections of portraits, archaeology, costumes, traditions and crafts as well as a model of the city in 1838.

La Nef des Jouets
12, Rue Jean-Jaurès
☎ 03 89 74 30 92
Open Mon. & Wed.-Sat. 2-6pm, Sun. 10am-noon, 2-6pm.
Admission charge.
This wonderful collection of toys is attractuively displayed. Exhibits include dolls, bears, games, lead soldiers, toy cars, planes, boats and more, made from such diverse materials as paper, cardboard, clay, wood and plastic. The styles range from simple to sophisticated.

Mountain bike excursions
Tourist office:
☎ 03 89 76 83 60
Meyer Cycle Hire
27-29, Rue du Mal-de-Lattre
☎ 03 89 76 87 60
Open daily (exc. Sun. & Mon.), 9am-noon, 2-6.30pm.

Discover the delights of the Soultz region, its forest and vineyards, via mountain bike. A professional guide will lead you through the area.

Lautenbach-Zell

7.5 km/5 miles
NW of Guebwiller
Vivarium (insect house) at the mill
Moulin de Lautenbach-Zell
6, Rue du Moulin
☎ 03 89 74 02 48
Open Apr.-June, Tues.-Sun. 2-6pm; July & Aug. daily 10am-7pm.
Admission charge.
As you drive along the Route du Markstein, you'll come across a restored flourmill, with a large paddle wheel

THE ART AND CRAFT OF WATER-DIVINING

Soultz offers weekend courses in water-divination and dowsing. The Association des Sourciers et Géobiologues d'Europe (European Association of Diviners and Geobiologists), based in the town, has 520 members from five countries. It arranges accommodation and food for interested participants. For more information call ☎ 03 89 76 15 73.

(7 m/23 ft in diameter). It contains a vivarium displaying some fascinating insects, including ants, locusts and mantis.

Lautenbach

7.5 km/5 miles NE of Guebwiller

The collegiate church St-Michel & St-Gangolphe

The village of Lautenbach grew up around a Benedictine abbey. All that now remains is a Romanesque church with a remarkable sculpted 12thC. porch. It contains a splendid pulpit and organ-loft and 15thC. stained glass windows. A statue of Christ, dating from 1491, stands at the entrance to the choir.

Murbach

2 km/1 mile W of Guebwiller

The former abbey-church of St-Léger

1, Rue de l'Église ☎ 03 89 76 91 05

Jungholtz

Around 10 km/6 miles S of Guebwiller

Horse rides

Munsch Farm
7, Rue Creuse ☎ 03 89 74 10 30
Admission charge.
Horseback excursions set off from the car park of the St Anne nursing home (lovely 14thC. chapel). Beginners are welcome, and you can even travel in a barouche if this appeals. The trail takes you through the forest, with a stop at the oldest Jewish cemetery in Alsace.

Open daily 9am-6pm (exc. during services). Built in the 12thC., this is one of the most prestigious Romanesque churches in the Rhine valley, now reduced to a chancel and transept after losing its nave in 1738. The interior features the highest vaults of their type in Alsace.

Thierenbach

7 km/4 miles S of Guebwiller

Pilgrimage to the basilica of Notre-Dame

☎ 03 89 76 95 66

Spotcheck

B6

Things to do

Moulin de Lautenbach-Zell vivarium
Musée du Florival in Guebwiller
Musée Historique du Chateau Bucheneck in Soultz

With children

Mountain bike excursions
Nef des Jouets in Soultz

Within easy reach

Route du Vin (2 km/1 mile E), pp.218-223
Route des Crêtes in the Vosges (18 km/11 miles W), pp.178-181
Ski resorts (18 km/11 miles W), pp.182-185

Tourist office

Guebwiller: ☎ 03 89 76 10 63

Open daily 10am-7pm (exc. during services). *Calendar of events available at tourist office* This magnificent Baroque basilica, with its two fine *Pietàs*, was built in 1723, but the tradition of pilgrimage to the site dates from the 8thC., and the walls are covered with over 800 ex-votos. The 1,250th anniversary of the first pilgrimage was celebrated in 1980.

The Rouffach canton,
sorcery and witches

The canton of Rouffach, located near Colmar on the RN83 towards Belfort, is crossed by two of Alsace's thematic trails, the *Route du Vin* and the *Route Romane* (Romanesque route). It's an ancient and once-fortified town which preserves vestiges of its 11th-, 12th- and 13thC. past, with lovely churches and convents numbered among its historic buildings. Where there's wine, there's a festival in Alsace, and Rouffach is no exception.

Church of Notre-Dame de l'Assomption at Rouffach

Rouffach

**21 km/13 miles
S of Colmar**

City of witches

The church of Notre-Dame-de-l'Assomption in Rouffach, built in the 12th-13thC., has arcades alternating with strong and more delicate piers, a typical feature of 12th-C. architecture in the Rhine region. You should also take a look at the 13th-14thC.

Tour des Sorcières (witches' tower) and the splendid 15th-16thC. Halle aux Blés.

Musée Historique
**6A, Pl. de la République
☎ 03 89 49 78 22**
Admission charge.
This museum recalls the tale of the Emperor Henry V, who, while staying at Château de Rouffach in 1106, abducted a young girl and took her to the castle. A throng of women advanced on the château demanding her release, and when their menfolk joined the attack, Henry fled in terror. Rouffach was also the birthplace of Marshal Lefebvre (1755-1820), the miller's son who became Duc de Dantzig and husband to the real-life 'Madame Sans-Gêne', heroine of Sardou's play.

À la Ville de Lyon restaurant
**1, Rue Poincaré
☎ 03 89 49 62 49**

Open daily (exc. Mon. & Wed. lunchtime, noon-3pm, 7pm-midnight. Philippe Boher, chef to former President Giscard d'Estaing, creates *nouvelle cuisine* in this sober but comfortable setting. The food is spectacular, with menus ranging between €19-€69.

Virgin and Child (15thC.)

Staying in the Château d'Isenbourg
☎ 03 89 78 58 50
Open daily (exc. Tues. & Sat. lunchtime). Situated in the centre of the vineyard, and overlooking the Plaine d'Alsace, this establishment offers accommodation of the highest quality, as well as a

panoramic restaurant known as Les Tonneries. Its sophisticated cuisine will set you back somewhere between €43 and €107 for a meal.

Witches' festival

☎ 03 89 78 53 15

Sat. nearest 14 July

This large and popular festival starts with a huge procession through the town. Performances are conducted on the move, and there are children's shows and a witches' market. The festivities culminate in a huge celebration in the evening.

The organic fair

☎ 03 89 78 53 15

5 days at beg. June.

Ecologically-conscious consumers will love this fair, with its magnificent mixture of colours and tastes. More than 300 exhibitors from all over Europe display organic, macrobiotic and eco-friendly produce, and the warm and friendly atmosphere contributes to a unique experience.

Stork sanctuary

Free admission.

Established in 1988, this sanctuary was created to help reintroduce storks to Alsace. Located along the attractive walk around Rouffach's ramparts, it's home to around 20 storks, looked after by volunteers and fed thanks to donations. A further 20 of the birds are at liberty to nest on local rooftops. Feeding time takes place at 5pm in summer and is a remarkable sight.

Mountain walks

Tourist office

8, Pl. de la République

☎ 03 89 78 53 15

There are 20 delightful local walks, signposted and maintained by the Club Vosgien. The club monitors 150 km/94 miles of paths and trails, departing from Rouffach, Westhalten, Osenbach, Pfaffenheim, Wintzfelden, Gueberschwihr and Soultzmatt. Details and maps can be obtained from the tourist office.

Spotcheck

B5-6

Things to do

Eco-bio fair in Rouffach
Visit wine cellars in Gueberschwihr

With children

Snail festival in Osenbach
Witches' festival in Rouffach
Donkeys in Westhalten

Within easy reach

Colmar, art town (21 km/ 13 miles N), pp.192-197
The potash basin (15 km/ 9 miles SE), pp.170-171
Vallée de Guebwiller (15 km/9 miles SW), pp.186-187

Tourist office

Rouffach:
☎ 03 89 78 53 15

Gueberschwihr

5 km/3 miles
N of Rouffach

A vineyard delight

☎ 03 89 49 31 05

This is one of the most typical vineyard villages in the region, with authentic half-timbered Renaissance

houses, lovely fortified porches and 17thC. fountains. The 12thC. Romanesque belfry is the highlight of the village, overlooking the peaceful surroundings,

carpeted with flourishing vines. Although a detour from the main *Route du Vin*, Gueberschwihr is worth the trip.

Winemakers' Open Day
Penultimate weekend in Aug. One of the most popular wine events held in Alsace, the *Fête de l'Amitié* (festival of friendship) attracts around 20,000 visitors each year. Every courtyard becomes a restaurant

or a tasting area, complete with orchestra to soothe an over-excited palate. Rue des Mouches becomes the site of a major art exhibition, and a huge procession takes place on Sunday afternoon.

Pfaffenheim

4 km/2½ miles N of Rouffach
Trail of sacred sites
Leaves from Place de la Mairie, 6-km/3¾-mile walk, gentle hills
This walk, through a vineyard and a forest, allows you to discover a range of historical religious sites, such as roadside crosses, sanctuaries, Stations of the Cross, Schauenberg (see right) and St-Léonard chapel.

CELEBRATING THE SNAIL

The snail festival held in Osenbach (10 km/ 6 miles W of Rouffach), takes place over three weekends between April and May. The less fortunate

creatures are devoured enthusiastically with other regional specialities, while others are contenders in snail races (*tiercés de l'escargot*) which take place throughout the day – the pace may be slow, but they certainly get pulses going. The festival includes a popular ball and equally popular local wine-tasting.

Prehistoric sites include the Rocher du Diable (devil's rock) and the dolmen, places full of mystery and strange energy, whuich are thought to be Druid in origin.

Schauenberg sanctuary

Access by car

The sanctuary lies high above Pfaffenheim, at the edge of a forest. Clinging to a red sandstone slope overlooking the plain, the 15thC. chapel is dedicated to the Virgin Mary and was built on the site of a former hermitage by a princess who was cured of an illness by the hermit's prayers.

Obermorschwihr

8 km/5 miles
N of Rouffach

Marbach Abbey

☎ 03 89 49 30 23
Open daily Jun.-Sept. 9am-7pm.

If you're interested in medicinal plants and infusions, or fancy sampling some homemade fruit juice, this is the place to come. The narthex houses an audiovisual exhibition on the *Guta-Sintram* codex, a 12thC. treatise on plants created in Marbach Abbey.

FIRE AND WATER

The mineral springs of Soultzmatt (6 km/4 miles S of Rouffach) were known as far back as 1271, and by the mid-17thC. the town had become a popular spa resort. Unfortunately, in 1891 it was destroyed by fire and has never been rebuilt. Today, the well known water is bottled under the name 'Lisbeth' and is available in three versions – flat, lightly sparkling or fizzy.

Huntziger live surrounded by donkeys, and can explain all about the habits and history of these gentle animals. The couple hold showings of the film *Mon Ami l'Âne* (My friend, the donkey) in their own home for their visitors, and have lots of fascinating information. Children will love the place.

Auberge du Vieux Pressoir

Domaine du Bollenberg
Open daily noon-2pm, 7-9pm (closed 20-27 Dec.).

☎ 03 89 49 62 47

This charming inn serves classic and regional food in the heart of the vineyard, and the hosts will give you a warm welcome. A meal costs around €15-69.

Wintzfelden

9 km/6 miles
W of Rouffach

Musée Lapidaire

Rue Principale
☎ 03 89 47 00 34
Admission charge.

Lovers of Romanesque and Gothic art should not miss this museum, with its important lapidary (gemstone) collection from the 12thC. Schwarzentham convent.

Gundolsheim

4 km/2½ miles
S of Rouffach

Flea market

☎ 03 89 49 61 59

This flea market, organized by the local football club, is one of hundreds of similar events that take place throughout Alsace, where bargain hunting has reached near-epidemic proportions! Gundolsheim itself was once a fortified village, with several gates, but only the Romanesque belfry now serves as a reminder of its medieval past.

Westhalten

4 km/2½ miles
W of Rouffach

Donkey sanctuary

10, Rue de la Liberté
Reservations (minimum 12 people):
☎ 03 89 78 53 15
Admission charge.

Roland and Jacqueline

The donkey festival

3rd Sunday in July

Each year a donkey festival is held in Westhalten, a pretty village surrounded by vineyards and orchards. Donkey-drivers from a wide area come to compete for prizes. Donkey rides, local arts and crafts, wine-tastings and culinary delights are all part of the fun.

Colmar,
city of beauty and art

Over the centuries Colmar has remained relatively untouched by the Reformation, the ravages of the Thirty Years War, the union with France imposed by Louis XIV, annexation by Prussia in 1871 and Germany in 1940, and the fierce winter of 1945. Home to museums, prestigious buildings and the most atmospheric Christmas markets, this is a city well worth exploring

La Petite Venise ('Little Venice')

The Isenheim altarpiece

Colmar by train
Leaves from Quai de la Sinn, opposite the Musée d'Unterlinden
☎ 03 89 24 19 82
Easter-All Saints' Day
Departures: every 30 mins. 9am-6pm.
Admission charge.
Two small, 60-seater tourist trains take visitors round the key sights of the city. In spring and late in the season passengers are protected with glass, and a simultaneous translation of the commentary brings the delightful ride alive for all.

Musée d'Unterlinden
1, Rue d'Unterlinden
☎ 03 89 20 15 58
Open daily Apr.-Oct. 9am-6pm and daily (exc. Tues.) Nov.-Mar. Closed pub. hols.
Admission charge.
Housed in a former 13thC. Dominican convent whose German name means 'under the lime trees', this is the most popular provincial museum in France. The highlight is the *Isenheim Altarpiece* (1512-1515) by Mathias Neihart (also known as Grünewald). When closed, it depicts an intensely disturbing Crucifixion used for daily contemplation – when opened on Sunday it reveals a miraculous Annunciation, Resurrection and the Virgin and Child. The museum's collection also includes medieval sculptures and paintings from the Rhine valley, archaeological finds and examples of primitive art. Not to be missed.

THE LIGHTS OF COLMAR

On Friday and Saturday, and during the Christmas and New Year celebrations, Colmar lights up as dusk falls. A central computer controls no fewer than 800 lights, revealing the full glory of the architectural heritage of the town and its old quarters. Colmar's lighting project, a glorious visual symphony that responds to different seasons, has been given an award by the Academy of Street Arts.

St-Martin's collegiate church

Place de la Cathédrale
Free admission.
Open 8am-6pm (exc. Tues. & Thurs., 8am-7.30pm). Closed Sun. am & during services.
This imposing church was completed

towards the end of the 14thC., although only one of the two planned towers was actually built. The real miracle of the building, often referred to as a cathedral, is the interior, where light, space and decoration are all harmonious and equally magnificent.

Ancien Corps de Garde

Place de la Cathédrale
Free entry daily (exc. during services) 7am-8pm.
This former guard-house (1575) is housed within the remains of a 13thC. chapel. The doorway is surmounted by a fine Renaissance loggia.

The Virgin in a Bower of Roses

Église des Dominicains
Place des Dominicains
☎ 03 89 20 68 92

Open all year Mon.-Sat. 10am-6pm, Sun. 3-6pm.
The Virgin in a Bower of Roses, the famous painting, completed in 1473 by Marin Schongauer, can be seen at the entrance to the chancel of this 14th- and 15thC. Dominican church. The church's stained glass windows are also impressive.

Maison des Têtes restaurant

19, Rue des Têtes
☎ 03 89 24 43 43
Open daily (exc. Sun. pm & Mon.) noon-3pm, 7-10.30pm.
This building owes its name to its unusual frontage, decorated with 150 rather grotesque carved heads. A bronze cooper, the work of Frédéric-Auguste Bartholdi (born in Colmar in 1834 and sculptor of New York's Statue of Liberty), crowns the gable.

Inside is an excellent hotel and restaurant, serving top-quality regional cuisine complemented by traditional décor, including magnificent wooden panelling. Menus range in price from €26-54.

Christmas markets
☎ 03 89 20 68 92

With the first weekend in Advent, the Christmas season envelopes Colmar. Traditional markets bring a festive air to the Place des Dominicains and the Place de l'Ancienne-

Douane. Particularly splendid are the Marché des Enfants (children's market) on the Place des Six-Montagnes-Noires and the Marché des Rois Mages (three wise men), held 26-31 December.

Musée Animé du Jouet et du Petit Train
40, Rue Vauban
☎ 03 89 41 93 10
Open daily (exc. Tues.)
15 Feb.-15 Dec. 10am-noon, 2-6pm, Sun. 2-6pm.
Admission charge.

Housed in a former cinema, this museum contains a remarkable collection of toys, including automata, dolls, railway engines, cars and planes, and features some rare pieces. A large puppet theatre, controlled electronically, presents performances of La Fontaine's fables that will delight children of any age.

St-Matthieu church
Grand Rue
Open 15 June-15 Oct.
10am-noon, 3-7pm
(exc. during services).

This church was built by the Franciscans between the late 13th C. and the mid-14thC. Today it serves as a Protestant church only, but its two pinnacles are a reminder of the church's twin-faith status between 1715 and 1937. A wall separates the Protestant and Catholic nave from the choir.

Au Fer Rouge restaurant
52, Grand Rue
☎ 03 89 41 37 24
Open daily (exc. Sun. & Mon.) noon-3pm, 7-10.30pm.

Patrick Fulgraff, president of an association of young European chefs, is one of France's most highly regarded chefs. Housed in a listed building, his restaurant serves

exceptional dishes, based on light and subtle flavours and sauces rather than on the traditional, heavier Alsatian recipes. A paradise for contemporary food lovers.

The *Koïfhus* or Ancienne Douane
Place de l'Ancienne-Douane
Not open to visitors.

The former Customs house features both Gothic and Renaissance architectural styles. Once the political and economic centre of Colmar, its ground floor was used to accommodate goods subject to municipal tax. The first floor houses the Salle de Décapole, in which representatives of 10 Alsatian towns united in protection of their privileges. Currently used as a conference centre, the *Koïfhus* has a magnificent Burgundian tiled roof.

Place de l'Ancienne-Douane

NO CARS PLEASE!

Cars are not welcomed in Colmar. Park your vehicle in the underground car park near the town hall (400 places, admission charge), in the free parking areas of Hasslinger and Scheurer-Kestner, or in the underground car park in Place Rapp (850 places, admission charge). This beautiful square boasts a statue of the Marshal of France (by Bartholdi), water fountains, a bandstand and a 1900s funfair. In the nearby Champ de Mars square stands another of Bartholdi's works, a fountain dedicated to Admiral Bruat.

inspired by collections in Alsace's museums or in local, private ownership. A leaflet explaining the history and original use accompanies each item.

Musée Bartholdi

Rue des Marchands
☎ 03 89 41 90 60
Open daily (exc. Tues.)
Mar.-Dec. 10am-noon,
2-5pm.
Admission charge.
Frédéric-Auguste Bartholdi was born in this 18thC. building, right in the heart of Colmar's old town, in 1834. Now a

The Lion de Belfort, *Bartholdi*

museum dedicated to the sculptor, it contains his rough sketches, designs, models, paintings and photographs. Bartholdi's worldwide fame derives mostly from the Statue of Liberty in New York (see p.49), but some examples of his work can be seen in Colmar (see box).

Boat trip on *La Lauch*

☎ 03 89 20 68 92
Leaves from landing stage, Rue Turenne
Sat. & Sun. Jun.-Sept.
from 1.30pm.
Market gardeners once delivered their produce to Colmar in flat-bottomed boats, rather like Venetian gondolas. You can follow their route along the river, admiring the half-timbered houses of fishermen and boatmen that line its banks.

The tanners' district

Old Town, Place de l'Ancienne-Douane, Rue des Tanneurs
The tanners' district owes its name to the former inhabitants, who tanned hides and washed them in the nearby river. Their 17th- and 18thC. houses can still be seen, tall, narrow and deep, built on stone foundations without cellars. The lofts were originally used to dry hides, but the industry ceased in the 19thC. A stroll through the streets provides a fascinating glimpse of the past.

Arts & Collections d'Alsace

1, Rue des Tanneurs
☎ 03 89 24 09 78
Open daily (exc. Mon. am) 9.30am-noon, 2-6.30pm.
This emporium offers a wide variety of items (porcelain, pottery, paintings, linen etc.),

The boat takes you past the delightful and famous Petite Venise (Little Venice) area, a beautiful, idyllic spot.

Maison Pfister
Rue des Marchands
Not open to visitors. Ludwig Scherer built Maison Pfister in 1537, and it is still lived in today. It's one of Colmar's most picturesque houses with its turret and flower-decked façade. The ground floor is arcaded and surmounted by a lovely wooden gallery, on one corner of which is an oriel window, and the house is decorated with frescoes and medallions.

Petite Venise
Take Rue de la Poissonnerie from the covered market and you'll find yourself in Petite Venise. This is the most romantic part of the Kruteneau quarter, where the market gardeners used to live, and from where they would embark in their flat-bottomed boats to the market. Follow Rue de la Herse along the River Lauch, where fishermen

used to place their nets, and you'll end up at the Pont St-Pierre. A perfect photo opportunity awaits.

Aux Trois Poissons restaurant
15, Quai de la Poissonnerie
☎ 03 89 41 25 21
Closed Tues. pm & Wed.

This restaurant is located in the centre of the tourist area and is housed in a lovely half-timbered house. It mostly serves fish, including pike-perch from the Rhine, trout and salmon. Gilles Seiler's memorable speciality is a delicious dish which combines three varieties of fish.

REGIONAL WINE FAIR OF ALSACE
Around 15 August, Colmar hosts the Alsatian wine fair, a celebration of wine and folklore. A great hall is devoted to wine tastings, and there are local exhibitions and displays of regional specialities. The vast hall also accommodates an open-air theatre (the biggest in Europe). Since 1946, people have enjoyed performances by the biggest international music-hall stars, and audiences usually reach around 200,000 people. Not to be missed if you're around at the time.

Musée d'Histoire Naturelle et d'Éthnographie

11, Rue Turenne
☎ 03 89 23 84 15
Open daily (exc. Tues.)
15 Feb.-15 Dec. 10am-
noon, 2-5pm, Sun. 2-6pm.
Admission charge.
This museum features both
regional and exotic flora and
fauna, together with an
important geological section
with minerals, rocks and
paleontology. There's an
impressive exhibition of
invertebrates, and displays on
ethnography and Egyptology.

The Long March

The Paris to Colmar walk
replaced the Paris to
Strasbourg route in 1981.
Since then, every year in
early June, a number of brave
and very fit hikers embark
upon the 420-km/261-mile
journey, which takes place in
all conditions and without
any breaks. Their ordeal ends
in the picturesque Place de
l'Ancienne-Douane, where
great festivities are held to
celebrate their achievement.
The revelry starts at
lunchtime on a Sunday and
continues until
late into the
night.

1ᵉʳ au 15 juillet 2000

HOMMAGE A
ARTURO BENEDETTI MICHELANGELI

Direction artistique Vladimir Spivakov

Piano: Dmitri Alexeev, Bruno Canino,
Bruno Leonardo Gelber, Jonathan Gilad,
Evgueni Kissin, Nikolaï Lugansky,
Kun Woo Paik, Ivo Pogorelich,
Sergei Tiempo, Arcadi Volodos,
Valentin Wagner.
Violon: Vladimir Spivakov, Kirill Troussov
Voix: Rachel Harnisch, Dmitri Kortchak,
Sergueï Leiferkus, Elisa Maurus
Trio Nottori
Jeunes pianistes d'Ukraine
Jeunes Talents
de la Fondation Vladimir Spivakov

12ᴱ
FESTIVAL
INTERNATIONAL
DE COLMAR

27 concerts

Ancienne Douane, Koïfhus (15e et 16e siècle) - Chapelle Saint Pierre (18e siècle)
Église Saint Matthieu (13e siècle) - Couvent des Dominicains de Guebwiller (13e siècle)
ORCHESTRE NATIONAL DE RUSSIE *Direction Vladimir Spivakov, Andrei Boreyko*
ORCHESTRE DE LA SUISSE ITALIENNE *Direction Alain Lombard, Vladimir Spivakov*
CHŒUR D'HOMMES CORO DELLA S.A.T. *Trento (Italie) Direction Mauro Pedrotti*

Renseignements: Bureau du Festival 03 89 20 68 97

LVMH   PARIS PREMIÈRE   DNA   AIR FRANCE

held in Europe. Each year
throughout July, famous
musicians and ensembles
from all over the world
gather to honour a
chosen great
master.
Concerts are

held in
some of
Colmar's
historic
buildings,
including the
Koïfhus, St-Matthieu church
or St-Pierre chapel.

King Spivakov

International Festival in Colmar

☎ 03 89 20 68 92
Admission charge.
Vladimir Spivakov is the
artistic director of this
classical music festival, one
of the top ten of its kind

Hire a boat

Marina

6, Rue du Canal
☎ 03 89 20 82 20
Information from the
Commander's office
Daily 9am-noon, 2-6pm.

After the dredging of the
Colmar canal, the town was
able to construct a small
marina. Boats can be hired
from the port to take you
down the navigable part
of the Rhône-Rhine
Canal, which is
now no longer in
use. It's a
fascinating ride,
but you do need
a permit.

Colmar-Metzeral by *Micheline* train

SNCF railway station

☎ 08 36 35 35 35
A *Micheline* railcar leaves
the Colmar station regularly
every day to take passengers
to Munster and sometimes as
far as Metzeral (p.208).
Thanks to the work of the
Vallée de Munster 'friends
of the railway' organisation,
a steam-powered train service
runs throughout the summer,
making an ideal way for
tourists to explore the
Hohneck massif.

Around Colmar,
authentic Alsace

Vineyards unfold around the capital of central Alsace like a beautiful carpet. Every outlying village has its own unique character and appeal, each contributing to the region's medieval heritage and natural beauty. This is the heart and lungs of Alsace's wine-growing country, with visual splendours that change with the seasons.

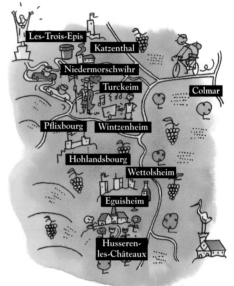

Statue of Pope Leo IX

Eguisheim
6 km/4 miles
W of Colmar
St-Odile's nephew
☎ 03 89 41 21 78
Three medieval, ruined towers rise up above the ancient village of Eguisheim. The 11th-12thC. stronghold, destroyed in 1466, was originally erected by the Eguisheim family, one of whose members became Pope Leo IX, nephew of St Odile. Walk along the ramparts and you'll travel through 12 centuries of history. Eguisheim suffered little during the World Wars, and has hardly changed since the 16thC.

Double vision
Jean-Luc
Freudenreich's
Alsatian wines
32, Grand'Rue

☎ 03 89 41 44 29
Free admission, by appt.
Although Jean-Luc followed in the footsteps of his father, he is a somewhat unusual wine grower. His wine is produced from late harvests and excellent grapes (his Cuvée Barbara, for example, is delicious), but he also combines his viticultural skills with those of a magician. Book ahead for a unique evening of tastings and tricks.

Eguisheim by Hansi

ROUTE DES CINQ CHÂTEAUX

This trail encompasses the medieval ruins of five castles, all easily accessible. Departing from Husseren or Wintzenheim, the 20-km/12¹/₂-mile circuit includes the towers of Eguisheim (three massive square keeps built in red sandstone), the Pflixbourg keep (with its wonderful view) and the imposing Château de Hohlandsbourg, built in the 13thC. and restored in the 16thC. The views along the trail are worth the walk on their own account.

Spotcheck
B5

Things to do
Route des Cinq Châteaux
Visit Eguisheim
Turckheim-Trois-Épis race
Christine Ferber's preserves

With children
Night watchman in Turckheim
Eguisheim's three castles

Within easy reach
Vallée de Munster (10 km/6 miles W), pp.204-209
The Rouffach canton (20 km/12¹/₂ miles S), pp.188-191
Vallée de Kaysersberg (15 km/9 miles W), pp.210-213

Tourist office
Eguisheim:
☎ 03 89 23 40 33

Le Caveau d'Eguisheim

3, Place du Château-St-Léon
☎ 03 89 41 08 89
Open daily noon-1.45pm, 7-9.30pm (exc. Thurs. lunchtime & Wed.).

Generous portions of *choucroute* and *baeckeofe* are among the highlights of this pretty, Alsatian-style restaurant located on the square. Booking is essential.

A tour of the town by train

Leaves from town hall car park
☎ 03 89 73 74 24
Weekends & pub. hols.

May-Jun. & July-Sept. 10am-6pm.
Admission charge.
A tourist train takes you on a 30-minute tour of the old town and the vineyards, with commentaries in French, German and English.

Eichberg and Pfersigberg

Eguisheim's 'Grands Crus' wine trail
Leaves from the signpost at the entrance to the campsite
Easy, 2-hr walk
Guided tours possible daily Jun.-July & 1-15 Sept. 3.30pm; Aug. Tues. & Sat. 3.30pm.
This wine trail introduces the visitor to the seven different grape varieties grown in the vineyards of Eguisheim, with the help of informative signs dotted around the vines. The processes involved in wine-growing and wine-producing through the various seasons are also explained. Views from the trail are magnificent.

A medieval fortress
Museum in Château du Hohlandsbourg
In Eguisheim take the Huserren-les-Châteaux path, then the Route des Cinq Châteaux
☎ 03 89 30 10 20
Guided tours daily Easter-11 Nov. 10am-7pm.
Free admission.
This is the largest and best preserved fortress in the region, built in 1279. On a clear day the view embraces Strasbourg Cathedral to the north and Basle to the south.

Husseren-les-Châteaux
3 km/2 miles W of Eguisheim
An unbeatable view
This marks the highest point in the Alsatian vineyards (380 m/1,247 ft), and the astonishingly flower-laden village has glorious views over the Plaine d'Alsace. On a clear day you can see the Rhine, Colmar, Mulhouse and Freiburg im Breisgau, at the edge of the Black Forest. Many wine producers in the area offer tastings in their cellars.

The three castles of Eguisheim
In Husseren-les-Châteaux take the Route des Cinq Châteaux
Free admission.
Three massive square keeps, spectacularly aligned along the ridge above the vines, overlook Eguisheim village. Dating from the 11th and 12thC., they are all that remains of the Châteaux of Weckmund, Wahlenbourg and Dagsbourg. Destroyed by fire, the keeps have been roughly restored. The tour takes 30 minutes.

Turckheim
5 km/3 miles W of Colmar
Musée de la Poche de Colmar
25, Rue du Conseil-Souverain
☎ 03 89 27 18 08

Open Mon.-Sat. July & Aug. 2-6pm; Sun. 10am-noon, 2-6pm; out of season Wed.-Sat. 2-6pm, Sun. 10am-noon, 2-6pm.
Admission charge.
This museum recounts the events of the fierce winter of 1944-1945, when the *Poche de Colmar*, a German 'pocket of resistance' was liberated by Général de Lattre de Tassigny, assisted by American troops (see box). The collection includes uniforms, models and dioramas.

Protected by Turenne
A medieval city
☎ 03 89 27 18 08
Turckheim is a large village which has retained its 14thC. ramparts, with three main gates still visible. In 1674, France's military genius, Turenne, won one of his most famous battles, defeating a superior imperial German army. Visit the Place Turenne, with its fountain and former

guard-house, and the lovely old church and tower. The Porte de France, a massive 14thC. tower, is crowned by a stork's nest.

Auberge de Veilleur
12, Place Turenne
☎ 03 89 27 32 22
Open daily noon-2pm, 7-9pm.

Few restaurants have so much taste and originality. The *foie gras* is hard to beat, the food is wonderfully presented and the varied menu is within most

budgets. Efficient service complements quality and freshness, and you won't be disappointed by the wine list.

The Bois Fleuri studio
46, Grand-Rue
☎ 03 89 27 32 55
Demonstrations:
July & Aug. Tues.
4.30-7pm.
Marguerite Schreck has a small, well-established studio where she creates delightful painted wooden items. Her floral art can be seen on

wardrobe doors, trees of life, lintels, shutters and cupboards, all popular in Alsatian homes.

The last night watchman
Turckheim is the only Alsatian village to retain this medieval tradition. At 10pm every evening, between 1 May and 30 October, the night watchman makes his rounds through the streets, wearing his greatcoat and carrying his halberd, lamp and horn. He stops at each street corner to shout: 'Take care of the hearth and the candle, may God and the Virgin Mary protect you. I wish you all good night.' – in French, of course!

The Brand regional wine fair
1st weekend in Aug.
This is one of the region's most popular wine fairs, at which people taste wine, eat local specialities and dance the Saturday night away among the vineyards. On Sunday afternoon, a colourful and historic procession travels through the streets with dozens of floats and folk groups, all celebrating wine and regional produce. It's a great opportunity to taste the best local wines on offer.

THE LIBERATION OF COLMAR

After France had been liberated in 1944, the *Poche de Colmar*, a pocket of German resistance, remained in Alsace. As a result the people of Colmar continued to live under German Occupation until 2 February 1945, when they were liberated by Général de Lattre de Tassigny, aided by US forces. The surrounding villages were partially destroyed in the battle, but the important historic buildings of Colmar were largely spared, as were the towns of Eguisheim, Turckheim and Niedermorschwihr.

Hiking trails around the Brand region
Wine trail through Brand vineyards
Leaves from tourist office in Turckheim

The Brand region is one of Alsace's most prestigious wine-growing areas. Its vineyards encompass more than 340 ha/ 840 acres, of which 250 ha/ 618 acres are cultivated, lying at altitudes between 200-370 m/656-1,214 ft. The sub-soil is a mixture of granite, limestone, clay and alluvium. The 2-km/1-mile circuit (1 hr) is dotted with informative panels.

A famous hillclimb
Turckheim-Trois Épis hillclimb
French & European championships
1st weekend in Sept.

This is a great spot to watch the best European drivers compete on a challenging 8-km/5-mile course. There's also a race for former competition cars.

Wettolsheim
5 km/3 miles W of Colmar
The heritage of Alsatian wine

Wettolsheim claims to be the birthplace of the wine-growing tradition, introduced in Roman times and subsequently spreading to the rest of the country. There are several wine trails through the vineyards (between 2¹/₂ and 4 hrs) and one takes you up to the ruins of the Château du Hagueneck. A wine festival is held in July.

Wintzenheim
2 km/1 mile N of Wettolsheim
Music, maestro!
Festival of Musica Mecanica
☎ 03 89 27 94 94
1st weekend in July.

In July this famous wine-growing centre, to the west of Colmar, is invaded by dozens of barrel organ players. They gather in the squares and streets of the town, filling the city with wonderful music. It's a very lively occasion.

Niedermorschwihr
2 km/1 mile N of Turckheim
Spiral belfry

Europe has a total of 60 spiral belfries, including the one in Niedermorschwihr, a village clinging to a slope among the vineyards, which dates from the 18thC. The main street is lined with old half-timbered houses, adorned with wooden balconies and oriel windows.

The Morakopf wine cellar
7, Rue des Trois-Épis
☎ 03 89 27 05 10
Open daily (exc. Mon. lunchtime & Sun.) noon-2pm, 6.30-10pm.

There are several typical cellars in this lovely spot, with its attractive buildings as pretty as doll's houses. You'll come across the Caveau des Seigneurs, Caveau des Chevaliers de Malte and Caveau du Morakopf, the latter being an especially pleasant cellar where you can taste a range of top quality wines and try a delicious *fondue vigneronne* (in which white wine is used instead of hot oil).

Christine Ferber's preserves

18, Rue des Trois-Épis
☎ 03 89 27 05 69

Christine is the queen of preserves and jams. Now internationally famous, she is the daughter of a baker and pastry chef, and has been passionate about jam-making since she was a young girl. She experiments regularly and is inventive with different flavours, such as mango and rhubarb, and has published several recipe books.

Katzenthal

3 km/2 miles
N of Niedermorschwihr

Friends of Wineck

Château de Wineck museum
☎ 03 89 27 23 17
Open in afternoon Sun. & pub. hols.
Free admission.

The 'Friends of Wineck' have rescued this castle, which was first erected around 1200. It overlooks the village and the vineyard, and its museum (open Apr.-Oct.) displays the results of research and archaeological digs that have been conducted at the site since 1971.

English Romanticism

Schoppenwihr's romantic park
6 km/4 miles N of Colmar on RN83, junction with Bennwihr station
Open daily Apr.-Nov. 10am-noon, 2-7pm.
Admission charge.

Enjoy a stroll through this lovely park with its water features, rare scents, castle ruins, swans and ducks. An exhibition of rare plants is held during the last weekend of April.

Les Trois-Épis

15 km/9 miles
W of Colmar

Le Galz monument

Walk from Trois-Epis
The view over the Plaine d'Alsace and the Black Forest is quite magnificent – on a clear day you can see Sundgau and Jura. At the summit is a huge monument sculpted by Valentin Jaeg commemorating the return of Alsace to France in 1918. It's an hour's walk (there and back), mostly on the flat, and the route is easy and pleasant.

THE MIRACLE OF TROIS-ÉPIS

On 3 May 1491, a blacksmith from Orbey stopped to pray before the image of the Virgin Mary in Niedermorschwihr. The Virgin appeared to him, holding in her left hand a lump of ice symbolising the devastation of the area if its inhabitants continued in their ungodliness. In her right hand she held three ears of corn, symbols of the fruitful harvest that would result from their repentance. When the blacksmith recounted his vision, a sanctuary was established on the site. It is now an important pilgrim destination.

The New Year market

The *Marché de l'An Neuf* actually takes place between Christmas and New Year. Its stalls are packed with local produce and arts and crafts – mulled wine, gingerbread, pastries, pottery, lace and regional fabric. A sprinkling of snow adds the final magical touch to this fairytale landscape.

The Munster and Metzeral valleys,
a seductive landscape

The locals of the Vallée de Munster have a reputation for modesty, but even they describe their valley as one of the most welcoming in the Vosges region. Endowed with a rich and colourful heritage, it also benefits from the nearby mountain with its wonderful walks, attractive ski resorts, memorable gastronomic delights and popular festivals. The 16 *communes* that make up the area are full of tradition and atmosphere.

Munster

19 km/12 miles SW of Colmar

Follow your nose
Route du Fromage (cheese trail)
From Munster to Hohrod, Wettstein, Schlucht, Schnepfenried and Petit Ballon. Map available from tourist office

The *Route du Fromage* takes you round the farm-inns of the Munster valley, past sites of great beauty and into the high pastures where the *marcaires* (dairy farmers) keep their flocks. It's here that the celebrated Munster cheese is

produced. Tasty and strong-flavoured with its distinctive yellow-orange crust, it's a prime speciality of the area.

A cheese town with no cheese-maker
Information:
☎ 03 89 77 31 80

Munster gave its name to the local cheese, but ironically contains no cheese producers within its town limits. It does have plenty of storks, however, nesting on the roofs at the junction of the roads leading to Col de la Schlucht and the Metzeral valley. Spend some time on Place du Marché with

Storks in Munster

its town hall, dating from 1550, the former abbots' palace, and the 19thC. Protestant church of St-Léger.

Église Saint-Léger

Getting back in shape
Hôtel-restaurant
À la Verte Vallée
10, Rue Alfred-Hartmann
☎ 03 89 77 15 15
Open daily all year

You can't avoid relaxing in this modern 107-room hotel, set in a lovely tree-covered park with nearby lake. Two indoor swimming pools are complemented by a sauna,

Turkish bath, jacuzzi, fitness centre, therapy and beauty room plus solarium – leaving you no excuse not to feel a lot better when you leave! Excellent food can be enjoyed on the terrace on warmer days.

Headquarters of the Ballons des Vosges regional nature reserve

1, Cours de l'Abbaye
☎ 03 89 77 90 34
Open May-Sept.
Wed.-Sun. 9.30am-12.30pm, 2-6.30pm.
Free admission.
The Maison du Parc (park office) is full of ideas of how to enjoy the wonderful environment of the nature reserve. It provides a wealth of information (some interactive) on the area's history, geology, natural and cultural heritage. It's the essential first port of call for your mountain holiday.

Sentier des Roches (GR 531)

6 km/4 miles
W of Munster
Starting from Munster, head towards Gérardmer. At Stosswihr, aim for Ampferbach, leaving your car at the Auberge des Cascades following the *Sentier des Roches* (rock path – part of the GR 531), which takes a good 3 hours. On the walk you'll see the lovely Stoltzabloss waterfalls and cross the glacial cirque of Frankenthal. The path that leads to the Col de la Schlucht is challenging, but the views are beyond compare. This trail is only for the fittest, most experienced hikers, and requires proper footwear.

MUNSTER TOURTE DE LA VALLÉE

This famous deep-dish pie is made with lean, chopped pork, marinated in white

wine and mixed with onion, garlic, a little *pain au lait* (sweet bun), egg and nutmeg. This mixture is wrapped in filo pastry, then cooked in a terracotta dish in a hot oven for 30-35 minutes. It's delicious served with a fresh green salad. Each farm-inn has an individual interpretation of the recipe, and the *tourte* is a key part of the *repas de marcaire* which they serve.

Gunsbach

5 km/3 miles
NE of Munster
Albert Schweitzer Museum

8, Rue de Munster
☎ 03 89 77 31 42
Guided tour (donations welcome)
Open daily (exc. Sun.)
9-11.30am,
2-4.30pm.

Spotcheck
A5

Things to do

Route du Fromage
Farm-inns
Albert Schweitzer's house
Mountain lakes
Sentier des Roches

With children

The water trail in Gunsbach
Transhumance in Metzeral

Within easy reach

Colmar (15 km/9 miles E), pp.192-197
Route des Crêtes (ridge route) (15 km/11 miles W), pp.178-181
Route des Vin (10 km/6 miles E), pp.218-223
Ski resorts (12 km/7 miles W), pp.182-185

Tourist office

Munster: ☎ 03 89 77 31 80

During his stays in Europe, Albert Schweitzer, winner of the Nobel Peace Prize in 1952, lived here in Gunsbach. Now a museum and archive, the house displays furniture, books, photos, and other memorabilia illustrating the great man's talents – as theologian, clergyman, organist, writer and missionary doctor.

Souvenirs of Africa
Musée d'Art Africain
Rue du Munster
☎ 03 89 77 31 42
Guided tour by appt.;
donations welcome.
Near Albert Schweitzer's
home, this museum houses
evocative mementoes brought
back from Africa by Emma
Hausknecht, a native of
Colmar, who was a nurse in
Schweitzer's hospital in
Lambaréné (Gabon) from
1927 to 1957. The collection
includes weapons, stones,
ivory and ebony sculptures,
African clothing and
antelope horns.

THE *MARCAIRE'S* MEAL
In the farm-inns, the traditional dairy-farmers
dinner is solid and plentiful: *tourte de la vallée*
(see p.205), *kassler* (smoked pork roll) or
roïgabrageldi (sliced potatoes cooked for two
or three hours in butter with streaky bacon and
onions). With a fresh green
salad, Munster cheese,
a slice of *tarte aux
myrtilles* or other
fruit in season, plus
a pitcher of the
local Edelzwicker
wine, it's a feast for
the gods!

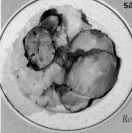

Roïgabrageldi

A church open to all
**In the centre of the
village**
Open during the day.
This church has been a place
of worship for both Catholics
and Protestants since 1751.
It is one of a number of
Alsatian churches open to
both faiths, and has been
expanded and transformed on
several occasions. The organ,
installed in 1961, was entirely
remodelled by Alfred Kern
from Strasbourg, following the
plans of Albert Schweitzer,
himself a talented organist.

Walking on water
☎ 03 89 77 38 83
*Leaves from Rue du Stade
in Gunsbach. 4-km/2¹/₂-
mile walk (around 2¹/₂ hrs).*
An interesting and educational
trail which focuses on a watery
theme. It consists of 13 stages,

each marked with a notice
board explaining the role of
water in that particular spot,
together with its history and
function. The trail takes you
through lovely countryside
along the banks of the River
Flecht and it's an ideal day
out for families. Leaflets are
available from the town hall.

soultzbach-les-Bains
6 km/4 miles
E of Munster
An historic circuit
Car park opposite church
☎ 03 89 71 11 16
*Guidebook available
from town hall*
This pretty medieval village
has 16 notice boards, helping
those on the history trail to
discover more about its

traditions and colourful past. The trail (around 45 mins) includes the former Château de Hattstatt-Schauenbourg and St-Jean-Baptiste church, both dating from the 15thC., the Ste-Catherine chapel, the Lion fountain and timber-framed houses.

Wasserbourg
12 km/7 miles
SE of Munster
The Petit Ballon
Walk to the Petit Ballon
Leaves from centre of Wasserbourg

A signposted route through the forest leads from this tiny village (population 400) to the Petit Ballon mountain (1,272 m/4,173 ft), taking around 2 hours on foot and much less by car. This is the land of *marcaires* (dairy farmers) with their farm-inns and dairies. The high pastures of the Ried

and of Kahlenwasen command amazing views, and the whole circuit is very scenic.

An evening on the mountain
Kahlenwasen farm-inn
Along the forest route from Wasserbourg or Sondernach
☎ 03 89 77 32 49
Open from Wed. before Easter to 11 Nov. (closed Wed.).
This authentic mountain farm lies in a wonderful setting. Its terrace affords dramatic views and the ambiance of the high-altitude inside the restaurant (1,100 m/3,609 ft) is unforgettable. Kahlenwasen is more farm than bistrot, and is quite delightful as a result. Try the cheese, it's wonderful.

Muhlbach-sur-Munster
5 km/3 miles
SW of Munster
A hard profession
Musée de la Schlitte
11, Rue de la Gare
☎ 03 89 77 61 08
Open daily July & Aug. 10am-noon, 3-6pm; out of season by appt.
Admission charge.
Located on the village square, this museum focuses on the work of *schlitteurs* (sledgers) and other woodworking trades. *Schlitteurs* transported wood on sledges along a track of beech sleepers. The carter would then take over and take the wood to the saw mill. The museum has a reconstruction of a sledge track as well as a collection of sledges and other objects relating to the forest and the wood industry.

Handmade cheese and other delights
From Munster head for Metzeral, turning left in Breitenbach on to a signposted forest path (6 km/4 miles)
Lameysberg farm-inn
☎ 03 89 77 35 30
Open daily (exc. Mon. pm & Tue.) Feb.-15 Nov.
This farm-inn is the place to come to try the *tourte de la vallée*, served with a green salad or as a starter as part of your *repas du marcaire*. Try the delicious Munster cheese, the *barykas* (mountain cheese) and the butter too, and visit the dairy to find out how they are made.

The Lac Vert

*15 km/9 miles
NW of Munster*
**The green lake
and its goblins**

The best way to get to the Lac Vert is by car, from the road leading to the Col de la Schlucht. The lake itself is full of aquatic plants whose movement produces the celebrated deep green colour, particularly in July. Swimming is prohibited and fishing regulated (information from the park office in Munster, p.204). The *Route du Tanet* passes through the area known as Kerbholz, in which, according to legend, goblins make their cheeses

on 29 September, the same day as dairy farmers traditionally leave their mountain pastures and return to their villages.

FRANKENTHAL WEDDING FESTIVAL

**Les Mariés de
Frankenthal**
Stosswihr
2 km/1 mile W of Munster
2nd weekend in Aug.

Each year a couple launch the local folk festival by taking the guise of a bride and groom. After the service they leave the church in a carriage and the festivities really begin. The locals don traditional costume and there are displays of vintage cars and antique farm equipment, folk music and delicacies such as freshly caught trout. The day culminates with a firework display.

Metzeral

*6.5 km/4 miles
SW of Munster*
The *transhumance*
☎ 03 29 63 22 92

At the end of May the shepherds take their herds and head up to the high pastures (1,254 m/4,114 ft), where they will spend the summer. The cattle all sport cowbells and the *maircaires* (dairy farmers and cheese-makers) dress in traditional costume. This festival of *transhumance* (changing pastures) is attended by a crowd of villagers and tourists. After a 3-4 hour walk, the participants enjoy a relaxing *repas de marcaire*.

The Christlesgut farm-inn

*From Munster or
Metzeral head to
Breitenbach, climbing the
Route du Stemlisberg*
☎ 03 89 77 51 11
Open daily 15 May-1 Nov.
This old farm lies in a large clearing at 850 m/2,789 ft. Originally built in 1820, it has been renovated and now serves local dishes (*choucroute, baeckeofe* and cheeses) and sells preserves and honey. It's the departure point for a number of waymarked walking trails (between 30 mins and 3¹/₂ hrs).

Mountain lakes

*3 km/2 miles
from Metzeral*
**Fischboedle and
Schiessrothried
lakes**
*Around 4 hrs there and
back on foot.*
On leaving Metzeral, make for Mittlach. Park your car on the right at the entrance to the village and take a signposted path on your right, the *Route François*, along the Wormsa river. The manmade

Fischboedle lake (790 m/ 2,592 ft) was created in 1850 and is the smallest but most picturesque lake in the Vosges region. A winding path leads to Schissrothried lake (920 m/ 3,019 ft), below the Hohneck summit. The walk takes about an hour there and back.

Stosswihr

2 km/1 mile
W of Munster
Auberge du Marcaire
Hotel-restaurant
82, Rue Saegmatt
☎ 03 89 77 44 89
Open daily noon-10pm; closed 1 Nov.- 1 Mar.
As its name suggests, this is a great place to enjoy a *repas du marcaire* (dairy farmer's meal). The farm-inn is friendly and welcoming – a common characteristic in the area – with a great atmosphere.

The menu is varied and interesting, and you can wash down a delicious and hearty meal with a high-quality wine.

Hohrod

5 km/3 miles
NW of Munster
What a view!
Hotel-restaurant d'Altitude Panorama
4, Route du Linge
☎ 03 89 77 36 53
Open daily all year noon-2pm, 7-9pm (for meals). This hotel commands impressive views of the Munster valley, Petit Ballon and Hohneck. The delights of its superb setting are exceeded only by the quality of its food. Fresh fish, mushrooms and Alsatian specialities all feature on the menu (€15-34). The rooms are well furnished with regional furniture, and there's even a swimming pool.

Breitenbach

4 km/2½ miles
SW of Munster
Making mountain cheeses
Saesserlé Farm
☎ 03 89 77 49 46
Open daily all year. Visit by appt.
Free admission.
You will be warmly welcomed at this spotless cheese factory, where demonstrations of making *tomme* cheese are held as well as tastings.

The Kaysersberg valley,
beauty and charm

Kaysersberg

This attractive valley lies close to Colmar, and includes the flower-decked villages of Kientzheim, Sigolsheim and Ammerschwihr. Kaysersberg itself is a small, charming city, overlooked by a medieval château. Take time to explore this magnificent region.

Ammerschwihr

3 km/2 miles
SE of Kaysersberg
Golf for all budgets
Route de Labaroche
☎ 03 89 47 17 30
Admission charge.
This golf course is not only affordable, but also attractive and challenging (the most difficult course in Alsace, in fact). Test your skills over 9 or 18 holes in a lovely natural setting on the hillside. You'll have to be fit to finish the long course, sometimes uphill and close to streams and woods. Start training as soon as possible.

A magnificent house
Restaurant Aux Armes de France
1, Grand'Rue
☎ 03 89 47 10 12
Open daily (exc. Wed. & Thurs.) noon-1.30pm and from 7.30pm.
This is one of Alsace's largest mansions, a wonderfully furnished building jealously guarded by the Gaertner family. The top-quality cuisine is traditional, rich, sophisticated and varied, and excellent service enhances a memorable evening. Meals cost approximately €60-80.

Sigolsheim
5 km/3 miles
E of Kaysersberg
National monument to the *Première Armée*
From the car park, climb the 124 steps to the top of the hill. The cemetery contains the graves of 1,684 French soldiers from the 1st Army, who lost their lives in the region in 1944. The red sandstone wall around the vines is impressive, as is the panoramic view over the plain, the mountains and the town of Colmar, and its surrounding villages.

A feast of bilberries
La Pommeraie Farm
D10 towards Ingersheim
☎ 03 89 78 25 66
Admission charge.
Remember to bring a basket to this bilberry farm, where

the fruit is exceptionally large and tasty. The farm also grows a variety of apples, pears and other seasonal fruit, making shopping here a very pleasurable experience.

Kientzheim

2 km/1 mile
E of Kaysersberg

Staying at the Abbaye d'Alspach

2, rue du Maréchal-Foch
☎ 03 89 47 16 00
Open daily
(closed Jan. & Feb.).
This establishment stands impressively at the edge of the ramparts in a peaceful, calm location. The 24 comfortable rooms are available at affordable rates (€46-69), and it's an address

to remember when planning where to eat in the confusingly large number of restaurants in Kaysersberg.

Paul Blanck and Son's wine cellar

32, Grand'Rue
☎ 03 89 78 23 56
Open daily (exc. Sun.)
9am-noon, 1.30-6.30pm.
This is one of the many excellent traditional wine cellars in Alsace. Tastefully decorated, it's the ideal spot to try a delicious glass of Gewurztraminer, Tokay Pinot Gris or Pinot Noir.

The art of the wine-maker

Musée du Vignoble et du Vin d'Alsace
Château de la Confrérie de St-Étienne (St Stephen's Brotherhood)
1A, Grand'Rue
☎ 03 89 78 21 36
Open daily 1 Jun.-31 Oct. 10am-noon, 2-6pm.
Admission charge.

The former mansion of Baron Lazare von Schwendi (1522-1584), reputed to have brought Tokay vines from Hungary to Alsace, now houses the museum of Alsatian wine and wine-growing. Dedicated to the history of the area's important wine industry, the collection includes a monumental wine press and rare, now obsolete, antique wine-making tools.

LALLI'S GRIMACE

Kientzheim is historically the town of the Decapolis (the ten towns which formed the league of defence against the powers of the nobility). It has retained medieval fortifications, among them the *Porte Basse* – a fortified gate topped by a grinning head. This depicts the famous *Lalli*, who stuck out his tongue at the enemy, who were deterred by the portcullis and drawbridge. Kientzheim's church, dating from the 13th-14thC., has a remarkable Gothic tower as well as the tombstone of Lazare von Schwendi.

Spotcheck
B5

Things to do
Golf course in Ammerschwihr
Visit Kaysersberg
Wine-tasting in Kientzheim cellars

With children
Picking bilberries in Sigolsheim
Christmas in Kaysersberg

Within easy reach
Colmar (12 km/7½ miles E), pp.192-197
Pays Welche region (5 km/3 miles W), pp.214-217
Ski resorts (10 km/6 miles W), pp.182-185

Tourist office
Kaysersberg:
☎ 03 89 78 22 78

KAYSERSBERG CASTLE

In Roman times Kaysersberg was known as *Caesaris Mons* (the emperor's mountain), due to its strategic position on the route between ancient Gaul and the Rhine valley. The castle, whose restored ruins still dominate the town, was later purchased by Frederick II, the German emperor from the Hohenstaufen dynasty.

Frédéric II

Tympanum of Ste-Croix church

Kaysersberg

12 km/7¹/₂ miles W of Colmar

A pearl of a city

Albert Schweitzer was born in Kaysersberg, which has retained much of its medieval character. The ruins of a fortified castle overlook the historic wine-growing town, with its 12th-15thC. church and fortified bridge. The town is full of interesting architecture, including old houses, a German Renaissance town hall (1604), a Renaissance well and fountains. A lovely spot to linger, and in summer it's a car-free zone.

The mementoes of Albert Schweitzer

Musée Albert Schweitzer
126, Rue du Général-de-Gaulle
☎ 03 89 47 36 55
Open daily 2 May-31 Oct. & pub. hols. 9am-noon, 2-6pm.

Admission charge.
One of the museum's rooms is devoted to the creation of the hospital in Lamaréné (Gabon) by Dr Schweitzer in 1913. It contains an array of documents, photographs, personal mementoes and various African objects, brought from Gabon by the great humanist.

Museum of religious heritage and traditions

Musée d'Histoire Locale
64, Rue du Général-de-Gaulle
☎ 03 89 78 22 78
Open daily 1 July-31 Aug., 10am-noon, 2-6pm; May-Jun. & Sept.-Oct., Sat. 2-6pm, Sun. 10am-noon, 2-6pm.
Admission charge.
Located on the first floor of a patrician dwelling dating from 1521, this museum houses a collection of religious art from the 14th to 18thC. Other objects on display include tools associated with local crafts, such as coopering.

Hôtel-Restaurant Chambard

9, Rue du Général-de-Gaulle
☎ 03 89 47 10 17
Open daily (exc. Tues. lunchtime & Mon.).

Only in Alsace can you find places such as this. The panoramic dining room overlooks the main street, and each table has its own lamp and secluded atmosphere. The food is excellent, the setting wonderful, and the hotel's calm atmosphere is complemented by a restrained décor. With menus ranging frm €38-68, it's certainly a spot to remember.

Christmas in Kaysersberg
☎ 03 89 78 22 78

As December arrives, Kaysersberg sets out its festive and colourful Christmas market stalls around the church, in what is a truly idyllic setting. Local wooden houses, garlanded with Christmas decorations, are illuminated at night, making the markets even more attractive as dusk falls. Music, song, mulled wine, the smell

EXPERIENCE THE REAL KAYSERSBERG

Information at tourist office in Kaysersberg
☎ 03 89 71 30 11
The tourist office has developed a programme of 'authentic' experiences, comprising 6 days and 7 nights in a hotel or B&B on a half-board basis, with dinners organised in local restaurants.

Visitors can also stay in *gîtes* and have locally-prepared food delivered. Cultural and sporting activities are arranged at preferential rates for holders of a 'valley passport', available from the local tourist office.

of spices and smoked pork all contribute to the atmosphere. Thousands of people visit the market, making it a lively and festive place.

Schlossberg cellar
20, Rue du Général-de-Gaulle
☎ 03 89 47 17 87
Open daily 10am-midnight (exc. Mon. lunchtime & Tues.).
This charming old wine cellar with its subtle, rustic décor is a great place to taste the most delicious *pierrades* (fondues). With musical accompaniment provided by the family's mynah bird (who can whistle a mean *Marseillaise*). You won't forget this spot in a hurry.

Hassenforder Restaurant
129, Rue du Général-de-Gaulle
☎ 03 89 47 13 54
Open daily all year 10am-midnight.

Kientzheim

Roger Hassenforder was a very eccentric character in French cycling in the 1950s. Today, when not out hunting, he can be found in his restaurant, assisting his staff and mingling with the guests, regaling the lucky diners with amusing anecdotes from his Tour de France days. A colourful character, he and his delicious regional cuisine are certainly worth a detour.

The Pays Welche
and the lakes of the Hautes Vosges

Nestling above the Kaysersberg valley, the mountainous Pays Welche region is an enclave of French language speakers in an area full of varied dialects. It's green and densely forested, and dotted with beautiful lakes. Its rural traditions are deep rooted, even today. Wood in all forms is plentiful, and the orchards that thrive at a medium altitude produce delicious and varied *eaux-de-vie*.

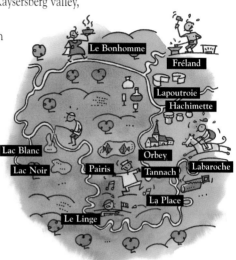

Le Bonhomme
Fréland
Lapoutroie
Hachimette
Lac Blanc
Orbey
Lac Noir
Pairis
Tannach
Labaroche
La Place
Le Linge

Lac Blanc

2 km/1 mile from the Col du Calvaire, towards Orbey
A glacial lake
The 'white lake' sits in the wonderful setting of a glacial cirque. Its name derives from the high granite cliffs which surround it. Located at an altitude of 1,054 m/3,458 ft and with a depth of 72 m/ 236 ft, it's an excellent fishing spot (for information contact the Orbey tourist office).

Not far away is the 'Château Hans', an unusual rock shaped like a fortress, with a spectacular view over the lake.

Lac Noir

100 m/328 ft below Lac Blanc
Savage beauty
The black lake, at an altitude of 954 m/3,130 ft, also lies in the glacial cirque, but is smaller and shallower than its neighbour. A hydroelectric power station pumps water up to Lac Blanc, recouping energy as it pours back down. Walking around the lake (follow the yellow crosses) takes around an hour and there's a wonderful view of the Val d'Orbey and the plain from a rocky promontory.

Orbey-Pairis

3 km/2 miles W of Orbey
Lakeland fish farm
J P Guidat
310, Noirrupt district
☎ **03 89 71 28 37**
Admission charge.
Guided tour.

ST-NICHOLAS MARKET

In the small village of Lapoutroie, the locals organise a market to honour St Nicholas, held on or around his feast day, 6 December. St Nicholas is said to have been a rich traveller who gave gifts or money to the needy. On his feast day, which commemorates the anniversary of his death, he hands out presents to the well-behaved children of Alsace, while *Père Fouettard* punishes the naughty ones. Fill your basket with fresh mountain produce at the stalls, but don't forget sweets for the children.

This fish farm is situated in a lovely, natural setting. Its waters flow down from Lac Noir, and you'll see the young trout pouncing on their food at feeding time.

Orbey-Tannach

1 km/¹/₂ mile
S of Orbey
The water festival
1st weekend in July.
The *Fête de l'eau* opens with a giant welcoming scarecrow. The locals gather to join in the folk festival, accompanied by tunes from the spinet. Food is an important feature and the main dish is *compiche* (like *choucroute*, but made with whole cabbage leaves). There's much drinking (and not just water), eating, dancing and singing – all in French, of course.

Orbey

8 km/5 miles
SW of Kaysersberg
Musée du Val d'Orbey
97A, Rue Charles-de-Gaulle
☎ 03 89 71 27 65
(Mme Laurent)
Admission charge.
The museum focuses on the popular arts, crafts and traditions of the region and reconstructs daily life in days gone by with its collection of furniture and other domestic items. Historic trades, such as cheese-making and weaving, are also featured.

Le Bonhomme

12 km/7¹/₂ miles
W of Kaysersberg
Auberge du Vallon
☎ 03 89 71 35 45
Open daily 8am-10pm.
Located in Le Bonhomme, which marks the beginning of the Pays Welche, this inn is a place to remember. It has an authentic atmosphere, whether you sit out on the terrace in summer, or inside on cooler or romantic snow-covered days. Warm the cockles of your heart with a delicious fondue.

Spotcheck

A-B5

Things to do

Water festival in Orbey
Musée des *Eaux-de-Vie* in Lapoutroie
Woodcrafts in Labaroche

With children

Horse-riding in Labaroche
Fish farm in Orbey

Within easy reach

Vallée de Kaysersberg (10 km/6 miles E), pp.210-213
Colmar (20 km/12 miles E), pp.192-197
Route des Crêtes (8 km/5 miles W), pp.178-181

Tourist office

Orbey: ☎ 03 89 71 30 11

Brézouard farm-inn

Alt. 840 m/2,756 ft, access from Le Bonhomme
☎ 03 89 47 23 80
Open daily (exc. Wed.)
15 Feb.-15 Nov.
This large, attractive farm lies at the entrance to the Hautes Vosges and its lower pastures. It serves *repas marcaires* to order, specialising in terrines and preserves. You can also enjoy a spot of fishing in the Béhine or the Weiss rivers (ask at the inn for more information).

Lapoutroie

2 km/1 mile N of Orbey

Musée des Eaux-de-Vie

85, Rue du Général-Duffieux

☎ 03 89 47 50 26

Admission charge.

ESSENTIAL
EAUX-DE-VIE

The variety of *eaux-de-vie* available in Alsace is remarkable, and most local families enjoy a drop or two on special occasions. The delicious, sweet liqueur can be made with cherries (*Kirsch*), wild strawberries, prunes, plums, quetsch, pears, raspberries, elderberries or blackberries. Home distillers, whose numbers are in decline, are allowed to produce their own *eau-de-vie* once a year, but the right to do so is non-transferable, and so the privilege will cease within a few years. It will be a sad loss.

The museum is housed in a former staging post dating from the 18thC. It displays one of the world's most spectacular collections of French liqueurs from the 1950s, explaining all the stages (and some of the secrets) involved in making these highly prestigious liqueurs, notably those made by René Miscault. A tasting follows your visit.

Hôtel-Restaurant du Faudé

28, Rue du Général-Duffieux

☎ 03 89 47 50 35

Open all year (exc. Nov.) noon-2pm, 7-9pm.

The Baldinger family runs a comfortable, cosy hotel with a warm, attractive décor – very welcome on chilly winter nights. Rich, traditional food and impeccable service, with menus ranging from €13-61.

Graine au Lait cheese-maker

333A, La Croix-d'Orbey

☎ 03 89 47 55 50

Open daily 9am-noon, 2-5pm.

Free admission.

Enjoy demonstrations and free tastings at this cheese-maker, where you'll learn about the art and craft of making farm cheeses.

Guided tour of the Miclo distillery

311, Gayire district

☎ 03 89 47 50 16

Open Mon.-Fri. 8am-noon, 2-6pm.

Free admission by appt.

This is a perfect example of a small, traditional distillery. If you time your visit well, you can watch the high-quality liqueurs being made and then finish off your tour by tasting the various flavours of *eau-de-vie* – in moderation, of course!

Labaroche

7 km/4 miles E of Orbey

Horse-riding at the Hacienda ranch

267, Chapelle district

☎ 03 89 49 86 39

Admission charge.

If you fancy exploring the beautiful countryside on horseback, hire a mount from

the Hacienda ranch and follow the bridle paths that wind through the woods and meadows. Gentle instruction is available for those unfamiliar with the saddle.

In memoriam
Le Linge memorial and museum (World War I)
Col du Linge (access via Trois-Épis or Orbey)
☎ 03 89 77 29 97
Open daily 15 Apr.-1 Nov. 9am-12.30pm, 2-6pm.
Free admission to museum.

An impressive World War I memorial stands where fierce fighting raged between 20 July and 15 October 1915. German forces entrenched on top of the hill (Le Linge or *Lingekopf*) were attacked by French troops, who fought their way up the steep slope. In the resulting carnage over 17,000 men were killed. Today, you can see the remains of the German defences and remnants of the French trenches.

Conservation centre of timber trades
Woodworking and rural heritage complex
In Labaroche
☎ 03 89 78 94 18

Open daily (exc. Mon.) 9am-noon, 2-6pm.
Admission charge.
This attractive, educational complex keeps alive the traditional woodworking crafts of the region. A fascinating site, it took over 50,000 hours to complete and is full of workshops and machinery.

Hachimette
5 km/3 miles W of Kaysersberg
Le Cellier de Montagne
4, Route de l'Europe
☎ 03 89 47 23 60
Open daily (exc. Tues.) 9am-12.30pm, 2.30-7pm.
Stock up on delicious local farm produce, including honey, preserves, salt meat, cheese, fruit, vegetables and yoghurt.

Fréland
4 km/2½ miles N of Lapoutroie
Customs and traditions of the Pays Welche
Musée des Arts et Traditions Populaires
2, Rue de la Rochette
☎ 03 89 71 90 52
Guided tour with commentary 1 June-30 Sept., 10am, 3pm & 4.30pm (3pm out of

season, exc. Wed.).
Admission charge.
This museum illustrates regional traditions and the historical way of life in the Pays Welche, with a collection of items contributed by the local people themselves.

Musée de la Forge
90, Grand'Rue
☎ 03 89 47 58 30
Open daily 8am-7pm.
Visit by appt.
Admission charge.
The museum is housed in a former late 19thC. water-powered forge, still in perfect working order. It recreates the blacksmith's trade, for which all the machines are powered by a large paddle wheel which provided electricity for the house over 100 years ago. It's a fascinating sight.

Route du Vin,
a delightful tour

The celebrated *Route du Vin* (wine route) weaves its way from north to south, focusing heavily on the areas around Ribeauvillé and Riquewihr. Villages emerge from the dense vines like a chain of islands, with the summit of every ridge providing another photo opportunity. The trail is characterised by its glorious scenery and there are some wonderful wines to discover.

Bennwihr
*6 km/4 miles
NW of Colmar*
A martyred village
This village was entirely destroyed during battles of the *Poche de Colmar* (a zone of German resistance), in the winter of 1944-45. Only a war memorial stands amid the ruins, featuring two women, one from Alsace, the other from Lorraine, holding hands. In the neighbouring village of Mittlewihr (2 km/1 mile N), you'll find the Mur des Fleurs Martyres (wall of martyred flowers), which was decorated with red, white and blue flowers throughout the German occupation as a token of loyalty to France.

Illustration by Hansi

or Hansi (see p.41), are displayed in this museum. A second Maison Hansi recently opened in Colmar (5, Rue Mercière, ☎ 03 89 41 96 79).

Musée du Dolder
Rue du Général-de-Gaulle
☎ **03 898 47 92 15**
(M. André Hugel)
Open daily 15 June-5 Sept. 9.15am-noon, 1.30-6.15pm.
Admission charge.
Housed in the Tour du Dolder, a gate built in 1291, this museum is dedicated to the way of life and traditions of the town. It features prints,

Riquewihr
*3 km/2 miles
NW of Bennwihr*
Musée Hansi
16, Rue du Général-de-Gaulle
☎ **03 89 47 97 00**
Open 10am-6.30pm (exc. Mon.).
Admission charge.
Over 150 works by the famous Alsatian artist and cartoonist Jean-Jacques Waltz,

THE OLDEST WORKING BARREL IN THE WORLD!

☎ 03 89 47 92 15
Open daily (exc. Jan.)
9am-noon, 1-6pm.
Free admission.
As you stroll through the streets of Riquewihr, pause at 3, Rue de la 1re Armée-Française, where Hugel and Sons have a wine cellar. The *foudre Cathérine* (Catherine tun) is said to be the oldest barrel still in use in the world. Made from oak in 1715, it's adorned with carvings weathered by time. An authentic working monument – spare a moment to drink the noble barrel's health.

furniture, tools, mementoes and a magnificent collection of weapons from the 15th and 16thC.

Musée de la Tour des Voleurs

Rue des Juifs
☎ 03 89 47 92 15
(M. André Hugel)
Open daily 15 Apr.-12 Nov. 9.15am-noon, 1.30-6pm.
Admission charge.

A former prison, the 'thieves' tower' museum includes a chilling torture chamber, the guard's room and lodgings. It's a remarkable building with a fascinating collection of early 20thC. photographs.

Musée d'Histoire des PTT d'Alsace (post and telecommunications)

Château des Princes
☎ 03 89 47 93 80
Open daily (exc. Tues.)
10am-noon, 2-6pm.
Admission charge.
This museum, housed in a 16thC. château, charts the story of 2,000 years of communication in Alsace. Starting in Gallo-Roman times, it moves through the age of the medieval foot messenger to the technological advances of more recent times – mail, airmail, telegraph and telephone. An impressive stamp collection and postal uniforms bring the past vividly to life.

A local micro-brewery

8, Av. J-Preiss
☎ 03 89 49 06 72
Open Easter-31 December, 2-6pm; July & Aug. 10am-noon, 2-6pm.
Free admission.

Spotcheck
B4-5

Things to do

Pfifferdaj (fiddlers' festival)
Riquewihr, the 'pearl of the vineyards'
Musée d'Histoire des PTT

With children

Stork and otter sanctuary
Around Riquewihr by tourist train

Within easy reach

Colmar (15 km/9 miles S), pp.192-197
Sélestat (15 km/9 miles E), pp.154-155
Château de Haut-Koenigsbourg (10 km/6 miles W), p.158

Tourist office

Ribeauvillé:
☎ 03 89 73 62 22

Gilbert Holl has bravely become a micro-brewer in the land of vineyards and wine. His Hollbeer can be tasted at the

brewery as well as in many of the region's fashionable bars, such as Century in Muntzenheim, east of Colmar. It's a delicious and refreshing change from the grape – so give it a try.

Musée de la Diligence
Rue des Écuries-Seigneuriales
☎ 03 89 47 93 80
Open daily (exc. Tues.)
1 Apr.-15 Nov.
10am-noon, 2-6pm.
Admission charge.
This intriguing museum features a variety of coaches from the 18th and 19thC.

The collection, which includes models, log-books, signs, postillion uniforms, boots and stamps, is housed in the former baronial stables.

Touring Riquewihr by tourist train
Leaves from town hall
☎ 03 89 73 74 24
Open Easter-end Oct. (check times at tourist office) *Commentary in four languages.*
Admission charge.
Discover the medieval town of Riquewihr, the 'pearl of the vineyards', from this tourist train. It travels past some splendid medieval and Renaissance architecture, from the narrow Rue des Juifs to the Château des Princes de Wurtenberg-Montbéliard, then past a Protestant church, the Maison au Nid de Cicognes, the Maison de l'Ours Noir, the Dolder tower and the ancient communal baths.

Zellenberg
3 km/2 miles
NE of Riquewihr
High on the hill...
The village of Zellenberg overlooks Riquewihr, perched on a vine-clad hill. An historic trail leads you around the lovely old buildings of this unusual wine-growing village, with some magnificent views over the Plaine d'Alsace on one side and the vineyards on the other. Once you visit Zellenberg, it's easy to appreciate why it was known as 'Alsace's little Toledo' during the Middle Ages.

Hunawihr
2 km/1 mile
NW of Zellenberg
Through the 'pearls of the vineyard'
The 'Grand Cru' trail (15 km/ 9 miles) links six *communes* – Zellenberg, Beblenheim, Bennwihr, Mittelwihr and Riquewihr. You can absorb the beautiful, natural world of the vines on foot, wandering

deep into the heart of medieval Alsace on this enjoyable and educational route. The village of Hunawihr itself has an interesting fortified church and a cemetery dating from the 14th-15thC.

Stork and otter sanctuary
☎ 03 89 73 72 62
Open daily 1 Apr.-
11 Nov., 10am-noon,
2-6pm; Sat. & Sun.,
pub. hols. & June-Aug.
10am-6pm (or 7pm).
Admission charge.
The sanctuary is home to
200 animals, including storks,
but also has an aquarium
displaying the amazing talents
of the anglers of the natural
world, such as cormorants,
otters, penguins and
seals.

Ribeauvillé

N of Hunawihr
Touring Ribeauvillé by tourist train
☎ 03 89 73 74 24
Daily Easter-Oct. 10am-
6pm; evenings in July
& Aug. 8.30-10pm.
*Leaves from car park at
entrance to town*
Tour the old town by tourist
train, with a commentary in

six languages. Groups (at least
15 passengers) can book a
tour of the Grand'Rue and
Hunawihr via the vineyard,
or visit the old town and a
wine cellar, where tastings are
arranged.

Musée Municipal
Place de la Mairie
☎ 03 89 73 20 00
Open daily (exc. Mon. &
Sat.) 1 May-1 Nov.
10am-noon, 2-3pm.
Free admission.
The museum houses a local
history collection, including
furniture and magnificent
17thC. gold plate, the
treasury of the rulers of
Ribeaupierre. On the first
floor you'll find a
printing plate of a
Japanese scene, a
copy of the original
made for the 1900
Universal Exhibition – where
it won the gold medal.

Medieval street in Ribeauvillé

Hôtel-Restaurant Clos St-Vincent
Route de Bergheim
☎ 03 89 73 67 65
Open 12.15-1.30pm,
7.15-8.30pm (closed
Mon., Wed, & Thurs.
lunchtimes, & Tues.).
This top-quality establishment
has amazing views over the
Plaine d'Alsace. The food is
excellent, with a subtle mix of
classic and modern influences
bringing an original touch to
local specialities. Menus range
from €28-39.

The ruined châteaux of Ribeaupierre
*Leave from the 'Au
Zahnacker' car park,
Place de la République*
Following the marked trail
(red symbols), climb to an
altitude of 508 m/1,667 ft,

The fortresses of St-Ulrich and Girsberg

where you'll find the castle of St-Ulrich. After pausing to admire the magnificent views, head to the ruins of the 12thC. castle of Girsberg. Only the keep still stands at the third ruin – the 12thC. castle of Haut-Ribeaupierre (642 m/2,106 ft). This 9-km/6-mile trail should take around 3 hours to complete.

Museum of wine and viticulture
Musée de la Vigne et de la Viticulture
2, Route de Colmar
☎ 03 89 73 61 80
Tour & reservations daily 9am-noon, 2-6pm.
Free admission.
This private museum is housed in the basement of a wine cellar – in fact, the oldest co-operative cellar in France. It chronicles the life and skills of the wine-grower, from the first grafting of the vine to the bottling of the wine.

Pfifferdaj, the day of the pipers
1st weekend in Sept.
The *Pfifferdaj* ('day of the fifes') is one of the most popular and attractive festivals in Alsace. It features a torch-lit procession and dancing on the Saturday, with a demonstration of medieval grape-pressing. On Sunday morning there are concerts in all the squares, a medieval feast and a large procession. Festivities come to an end with free wine-tasting from the Fontaine du Vin (wine fountain).

Dusenbach
2 km/1 mile NW of Ribeauvillé
Pilgrimage to Notre Dame
Above Ribeauvillé Access via Strenbach valley.
In medieval times, this was the most popular pilgrimage in Alsace.

It started when Eguenolphe de Ribeaupierre brought back a statue of the Virgin from the Orient and placed it in a specially-constructed chapel. Two other chapels were built nearby, and all were destroyed and rebuilt no less than three times. In 1903, a neo-Gothic church was added.

Bergheim
4 km/2¹/₂ miles
NE of Ribeauvillé
Living heritage
Once a medieval refuge for criminals on the run (only witches were denied sanctuary), Bergheim is now one of Alsace's best-preserved historic market towns.
At 9pm on Sundays in summer, the night watchman arrives with his storyteller, the primary school teacher, accompanied by pupils in costumes of blouses and black tulle skirts embroidered with daisies. They recount the history of the town, and singers and musicians entertain the audience with the illuminated ramparts of its surrounding wall providing a wonderful backdrop.

The witch trials of Alsace
Musée de la Sorcellerie
5, Place de l'Église
☎ 03 89 73 85 20
Open daily by appt.
Admission charge.
Here you'll find the first part of a permanent exhibition dedicated to the witch trials held in Bergheim from 1582 to 1683. Artefacts include a relief showing the town between 1550 and 1650, and details of the trial of Cathérine Bassler, accused of witchcraft.

Winstub du Sommelier
51, Grand-Rue
☎ 03 89 73 69 99
Open daily (exc. Wed.)
noon-1.30pm & from 7pm.
Antje and Patrick Schneider have created a warm and welcoming atmosphere in their *winstub*, located in this old building. They serve top-quality food, including a memorable *presskopf* and a delicious dish of duck confit on *choucroute*, complemented by excellent wines. An à la carte meal will cost around €23.

Rodern
4 km/2¹/₂ miles
N of Bergheim
Pinot Noir festival
3rd weekend in July
During this festival, the main street of Rodern is lined with refreshment stalls and bars celebrating the famous Pinot Noir grape. A town dance is held on Saturday night, followed on Sunday morning by the blessing of the grape by the parish priest. Open-air feasting follows, and the rival merits of *choucroute* and Strasbourg sausages served with potato salad are a dilemma for the hungry visitors. A further challenge appears in the form of *fleschnaka* (snail meat). Unsurprisingly, the Pinot Noir flows freely.

St-Hippolyte
1.5 km/1 mile
N of Rodern
At the foot of Haut-Koenigsbourg
St-Hippolyte sits against the backdrop of the Haut-Koenigsbourg and the surrounding vineyards. The first village of the Upper Rhine on the *Route du Vin* (when approached from the Lower Rhine), this large and attractive village boasts 17thC. half-timbered houses, a Renaissance fountain and a Gothic church. Its name derives from the Roman martyr, Hippolyte, whose relics were brought back by Fulrad when the abbot of St-Denis founded the monastery.

Val d'Argent,
silver valley

Silver, copper and other metals, including gold, have been mined in the valley of St-Marie-aux-Mines since the Middle Ages. Mining reached its height during the 16th and 17thC.

Textile museum

Ste-Marie-aux-Mines
36 km/22 miles NW of Colmar

La Maison de Pays
Place du Prensureux
☎ 03 89 58 56 67
Open daily Jun.-Sept. 10am-noon, 2-6pm.
Admission charge.
The museum focuses on the three key activities of this small industrial town – mining, mineralogy and weaving. There's a local and international collection of rocks, a workshop showing the different processes involved in making fabric and an exhibition on the history of mining, with models, archives and a collection of tools.

Back to school
Musée de l'École
8, Echery
☎ 03 89 58 56 67
Visit by appt.
Admission charge.
This small museum, a faithful reconstruction of a French classroom of the 1930s, houses school documents dating back to the 18thC.

All that glistens is not gold…
St-Louis-Eisenthur silver mine
4, Rue Weisberger
☎ 03 89 58 62 11
Open all year by appt.
Admission charge.
Tour: 2¹/₂-3 hrs.
The Neueberg historic mining trail, which takes about 45 minutes, leads visitors to the remains of various silver mines. You can also descend into the

A MINING HERITAGE
The St-Barthélemy silver mine
Chemin de la Sermonette
☎ 03 89 58 72 28
Open daily July-Sept., Easter Sun. & Mon. & last two Sundays in June,

ANCIENNE MINE D'ARGENT
St BARTHELEMY

9.30am-noon, 2-6pm.
Admission charge.
Tour lasts 1-2 hrs.
This disused mine, which operated at its height in the 16thC., has now been converted into a museum. In its galleries the daily life of miners who worked nearly 400 years ago is reconstructed, assisted by an excellent running commentary. There are also collections of tools used to extract the precious metal with explanations of the various processes involved.

'subterranean pearl' of the Val d'Argent, opened in 1549, a 1-km (0.6-mile) circuit taking around an hour to complete. Bring comfortable shoes, old clothes and a warm sweater.

in 1990, is recounted in this museum, which also explores major technological developments during the period.

Historic and botanical trail

Leaves from car park on the RD459 in Ste-Croix-aux-Mines
☎ 03 89 58 80 50
Leaflet from tourist office
The trail, just under 4km/2¹/₂ miles long and taking around 2¹/₂ hours, traces the daily routine of Martin, a forester in the St-Pierremont forest. There are 15 markers, along with informative panels about the trees.

Ste-Croix-aux-Mines

2 km/1 mile E of Ste-Marie-aux-Mines
Musée de la Scierie Vincent
2A, Rue M.-Burrus
☎ 03 89 58 78 18
Open daily Jun.-Sept. 10am-7pm (Oct.-May by appt.).
Admission charge.
The history of this sawmill, which opened in the 19thC. and closed

Thannenkirch

15 km/9 miles SE of Ste-Croix-aux-Mines
Life is just a bowl of cherries…
The cherry festival
☎ 03 89 73 10 19
2nd weekend in July.

Things to do

Musée de la Scierie Vincent (sawmill museum)
Visit a silver mine
Cherry festival in Thannenkirch

With children

Musée de l'École in Ste-Marie-aux-Mines
Historic and botanical trail in Ste-Croix-aux-Mines

Within easy reach

Haut-Koenigsbourg (20 km/ 12¹/₂ miles S), p.158
Route des Crêtes (15 km/ 9 miles SW), pp.178-181

Tourist office

Ste-Marie-aux-Mines:
☎ 03 89 58 80 50

A charming summer resort, nestling among cherry orchards, Thannenkirch hosts an annual festival in celebration of a cherry tart known as *griottin*. A country market (*merdoll*) takes place, with stalls selling arts and crafts, antiques and local food and wines, and there are dramatic re-enactments of traditional mountain life, as well as the erection of the *keelwatann*, a celebratory fir tree burnt at the end of summer.

A tranquil haven
Taennchel botanical trail
Above Thannenkirch
Information:
☎ 03 89 73 10 19
This trail, devised by the Friends of Taennchel, takes visitors through the wonderful Taennchel massif. The natural beauty of the area, as well as its peacefulness and glorious scents, make this a calming and inspiring walk.

Mulhouse,
a great industrial heritage

Mulhouse was an independent republic which was returned to France in 1798. It underwent huge economic development in the 19thC., when it became known as the 'Manchester of France'.

Place de la Réunion

The city is now home to several of Europe's most important and fascinating technical museums, as well as historic and cultural sites. There are also good spots for relaxation.

Musée National de l'Automobile

192, Av. de Colmar
☎ 03 89 33 23 23
Open daily (exc. 25 Dec. & 1 Jan.) 10am-6pm.
Admission charge.
Europe's premier automobile museum houses 500 fabulous vintage cars, collected by the Schlumpf brothers. They include Rolls-Royces, Alfa Romeos, Mercedes, Ferraris and no less than 200 Bugattis, among them two *Royales*. One of these, the *Napoléon*, was Ettore Bugatti's personal car, considered to be the most prestigious car of all time.

A parade of vintage cars

☎ 03 89 35 48 48
Early Aug.

THE TOWN OF 1000 CHIMNEYS

In 1746, entrepreneurs Samuel Koechlin, J.-Jacques Schmaltzer, J.-Jacques Feer and J.-Henri Dollfus established a business manufacturing '*indiennes*' (printed calico), the height of contemporary fashion. The industry expanded further in 1798 when Mulhouse became re-united with France, and the town was said to possess over 1,200 factory chimneys. Spinning, weaving, chemistry and machine technology all developed dramatically as industrialisation grew across Europe.

Every year, in early August, vintage car fans fill the streets of Mulhouse to enjoy a 3-day festival. Among the many and varied events are shows, exhibitions, rally driving and workshops. The climax comes

with a huge parade of cars from international museums, some of which have taken on a cult or almost mythical status.

Musée Électropolis

55, Rue du Pâturage
☎ 03 89 32 48 60
Open daily (exc. Mon. & pub. hols.) 10am-6pm.
Admission charge.

This collection by the French Railways (SNCF) features some fascinating examples of locomotives from 1844 to the present, such as the *St-Pierre* teak steam engine and the drawing-room carriage of Napoleon III's aides-de-camp. It also has the engine holding the record for the fastest speed ever achieved on rails.

This is the first museum in Europe to be dedicated to electricity. It takes visitors through the various stages of its production, using models, interactive displays and machinery. The highlight is the *Grande Machine*, the huge Brown-Boveri Sulzer generator of 1901, made from 170 tonnes of steel, cast-iron and copper, which supplied the DMC factory with electricity.

Musée Français du Chemin de Fer

2, Rue A.-Glehn
☎ 03 89 42 25 67
Open daily Oct.-Mar. (exc. 1 Jan., 25-26 Dec.) 9am-5pm; Apr.-Sept. 9am-6pm.
Admission charge.

Musée du Sapeur-Pompier

2, Rue A.-Glehn
☎ 03 89 42 25 67
Open 1 Apr.-30 Sept., 9am-6pm; 1 Oct.-31 Mar., 9am-5pm.
Admission charge.

The fire brigade museum is located in the same building as the French Railways museum. It explores the history of firefighting, and illustrates the technological development of the equipment, including fire engines, hand pumps, helmets and uniforms. The watchtower and the telephone exchange of Mulhouse's former fire station have been reconstructed.

Spotcheck
B6

Things to do

Musée Électropolis
Roman baths
Musée de l'Impression sur Étoffe
Christmas in Mulhouse

With children

Zoological and botanical park
Musée National de l'Automobile
Musée Français du Chemin de Fer

Within easy reach

The Sundgau region (20 km/12½ miles SE), pp.168-169
Ecomuseum of Haute Alsace in Ungersheim (14 km/9 miles NW), p.170
Route de la Carpe frite (20 km/12½ miles S), p.168

Tourist office
☎ 03 89 35 48 48

Musée de l'Impression sur Étoffe

14, Rue J.-J.-Henner
☎ 03 89 46 83 00
Open daily Oct.-Apr. (exc. 1 Jan, 1 May & 25 Dec.), 10am-6pm; May-Sept., 9am-6pm.

The museum of printed fabric reveals the process and history of printing on cotton, for which Mulhouse is famous. It displays various engraving

and printing techniques which evolved over the years, and conducts demonstrations of the impressive machinery.

Musée des Beaux-Arts

4, Place Guillaume-Tell
Open daily (exc. Tues.)
June-Sept. 10am-noon,
2-5pm, Thurs. 10am-6pm.
Admission charge.
The Steinbach villa contains the work of artists from several different eras and schools. It includes religious art from the Middle Ages and paintings by Boucher and Courbet.

Musée Historique

Hôtel de Ville, Place de la Réunion
Open daily (exc. Tues.)
1 July-30 Sept., 10am-
noon, 2-6pm; 1 Oct.-
30 June, 10am-noon,
2-5pm.
Admission charge.
The history of Mulhouse is recounted through archaeological collections and displays of pottery, jewellery, coins, weapons, coats of arms, paintings, manuscripts and models.

NIGHTLIFE IN MULHOUSE

Mulhouse has a choice of four entertainment venues, not counting the exhibition park (Parc des Expositions). The Filature is a concert venue and home to the symphony orchestra and the Ballet du Rhin, as well as to national companies. The Sinne Theatre has performances by the *Tréteaux de Haute Alsace* and the Alsatian Theatre. Entrepôt 50's facilities include a concert hall-cum-café and a café-theatre, and the Noumatrouff's shows and events are popular with young people. Information on all venues is available at the tourist office.

Théâtre

The museum includes reconstructions of interiors to help evoke the historic town of Mulhouse.

St-Étienne temple

Heritage trail

*Leaves from
Place de la Réunion
Leaflet from tourist office.*
This fascinating trail (*sentier du Vieux Mulhouse*) leads you through the heart of the old town, encompassing the St-Étienne temple, the town hall, Paul Curie's house, the library, the Cour des Chaînes

Town hall

(manufactory of printed calico) and the Cour de Lorraine, as well as the Ste-Marie-Barfüsserkirchem church (13thC.) and the Feer family mansion.

Maison de la Céramique

25, Rue J. Hofere
☎ **03 89 43 32 55**
Open daily (exc. Mon. & pub. hols.) 10am-noon, 2-6pm; Sun. 2-6pm.
Admission charge.
This international art centre, the only one of its kind in France, is devoted to contemporary ceramics. It runs a unique range of courses, and each year hosts five major exhibitions bringing together work by artists from all over the world.

Zoological and botanical park

51, Rue du Jardin-Botanique
☎ **03 89 31 85 10**
Open May-Aug. 9am-7pm; Apr. & Sept. 9am-6pm.
Admission charge.
This large park (25 ha/ 62 acres) enjoys a magnificent setting and is one of the most beautiful in Europe. Over 190 species and 1,200 animals shelter here, some of them very rare (for example, the Siberian tiger, Persian panther, bald ibis and Madagascar lemur). More than 2,000 plant varieties flourish in the landscaped gardens.

The 19thC. trail

Leaves from
Rue de la Bourse
Leaflet from tourist office.
After taking a look in the Hôtel de la Société Industrielle (social and urban planning came early to Mulhouse), admire the magnificent villas of 19thC. industrialists Mantz, Risler, Thierry-Mieg, Vaucher-Lacroix and Schoff. The former weaving-mill of Grosheintz and Hartmann comes next, followed by the St-Étienne church, Steinbach square, the Gangloff building and the municipal theatre.

Christmas in Mulhouse

Place de la Réunion
☎ **03 89 35 48 41**
From last week in Nov. to 31 Dec. The historic centre of Mulhouse has some wonderful, and unique, illuminations during the festive season. There's also a delightful Christmas market, and events include a festive Christmas procession and a number of concerts and shows.

Forest discovery trails

Park your car in the Waldeck sportsfield
☎ **03 89 32 58 58**
There are 25 km/ 16 miles of paths to enjoy, of which 13 km/ 8 miles have been way-marked by the Club Vosgien and 8 km/5 miles are reserved for mountain bikes. The trails include two jogging loops, a botanical path to Thannenwald, five shelters and a number of picnic and relaxation areas, equipped with benches and tables.

Roman baths

7, Rue Pierre-et-Marie-Curie
☎ **03 89 32 69 00**
Open mid-Sept. to mid. May (closed Sun. & pub. hols.)
This splendid leisure complex includes a sauna, hot bath,

Turkish bath, hot and cold pools and massage showers, with certain days reserved for men-only, women-only and mixed attendance. The (mixed) baths stay open until 10.30pm on Tuesday.

Jardin des Scenteurs

Access via Rue de l'Arsenal or Rue des Franciscans
☎ 03 89 32 58 58
Open all day.
Admission charge.
Opened in 1981, these scented gardens were among the first in France designed specifically for the visually handicapped. They are now home to a wonderful collection of over 170 scented plants. Signs are in Braille, and the paving is specially adapted.

A swimming bonanza

Watersports complex
53, Boulevard Stoessel
☎ 03 89 43 47 88
Open daily in summer, 10am-8pm.
Admission charge.
This huge watersports complex is on the banks of the River Ill, near the football stadium and the ice-rink. It houses a large pool (50 m x 20 m/164 ft x 66 ft), a family pool, a diving pool and an area for handicapped swimmers.

A revolving panoramic restaurant

Tour de l'Europe
☎ 03 89 45 12 14
Closed Sun. pm & Mon.
Relax and enjoy some delicious *nouvelle cuisine*, together with a fantastic view over Mulhouse and the surrounding area. It's an ever-changing experience: the view turns

through a complete circle in 20 minutes. The Tour de l'Europe is open for lunch and dinner, in summer or winter, and well worth a visit.

Rixheim

3 km/2 miles E of Mulhouse
Musée du Papier Peint

28, Rue Zuber
☎ 03 89 64 24 56
Open daily (exc. Tues., 1 Jan., 1 May, Good Friday & 25 Dec.), 10am-noon, 2-6pm; Jun.-Sept. 9am-noon, 2-6pm.

Admission charge.
This museum houses one of the largest international collections of wallpapers from the 18thC. to the present day. It has magnificent examples of the exotic wallpaper that was exported throughout the 19thC., to adorn the walls of the most fashionable salons.

Riedisheim

3 km/2 miles E of Mulhouse
La Poste Kieny restaurant

7, Rue du Général-de-Gaulle
☎ 03 89 44 07 71
Closed Sun. pm, Mon. & Tue. lunchtime.

This restaurant offers a warm welcome, a lovely décor and an excellent menu that focuses on meat dishes and imaginative desserts. It also has a fine cellar.

Wallach park
Rue des Sapins
☎ 03 89 32 58 58
Open daily 9am-dusk.
Free admission.
Alfred Wallach, an important local industrialist, donated the park to the town. It combines excellent sporting facilities with a pleasant garden in which to stroll and relax, including a substantial lawn. The rose garden contains no fewer than 136 species, while the woodland has an

attractive rest area with statues and benches. Take a moment to unwind before exploring the labyrinth at the edge of the wood.

Lutterbach

2 km/1 mile
W of Mulhouse

Micro-brewery

6, Rue du Houblon

☎ 03 89 57 48 48

Visit by appt. Restaurant open daily (exc. Mon.), 11am-10pm.

Free admission.

The historic Lutterbach brewery, built in 1648, finally closed down in 1968 and was demolished in 1971. The *commune* of Mulhouse has helped to revive the brewing industry by supporting the micro-brewery that makes Lutterbier – an unpasteurised, 100 per cent malt beer, which definitely merits sampling.

Kingersheim

2 km/1 mile
N of Mulhouse

Tropical aquarium of the Musée Océanographique

9, Rue du Hagelbach

☎ 03 89 53 72 72

Open daily (exc. Thurs., 25 Dec. & 1 Jan.) 2-6pm.

Admission charge.

The aquarium houses both saltwater and freshwater fish, including natives of the Pacific and Indian Oceans, the Caribbean and the Red Sea, along with piranha, discus fish and elephant fish from Africa.

Reiningue

5 km/3 miles
W of Mulhouse

Reiningue and the Doller watersports complex

Rue de Wittenheim

☎ 03 89 55 40 15/
03 89 59 02 40

Open daily 15 Mar.-31 Oct. 9am-5pm.

Admission charge.

A pleasure zone for those who love sailing and the great outdoors. It's a peaceful spot, and just relaxing by the water is a delight, although swimming is forbidden. Sailing classes can be arranged, and are conducted by qualified instructors using a technique approved and developed by the French sailing association.

PASSPORT TO THE MUSEUMS OF THE UPPER RHINE

A pioneering tourist initiative has been developed in this very European region. The 'passport' is a

cross-border document that allows free and unlimited entry to over 130 museums in the adjoining countries of France, Germany and Switzerland. It's reasonably priced and well worth considering. For more information ☎ 03 89 45 86 11.

The Ill, the Rhine and the Ried,
a watery terrain

The Ried, stretching between the Ill and the Rhine, is a huge and fertile alluvial plain, with large villages characterised by their proximity to forest and water. The Ried of the Upper Rhine is rich in corn and wheat, with large industrial zones situated along the river.

Ottmarsheim

10 km/6 miles
E of Mulhouse
Carolingian architecture in Alsace
The abbey-church
At the edge of the forest of Hardt, the 11thC. octagonal church features characteristic Carolingian architecture. It's the only Alsatian replica of the Palatine chapel of Aachen, built by Charlemagne. The rotunda is surrounded by circular galleries on two levels, and the church has beautiful, harmonious proportions.

Volgelsheim

33 km/21 miles
N of Ottmarsheim
The tourist railway of the Rhine
CFTR, Vogelsheim station
☎ 03 89 71 51 42
Open Sat., Sun. and festivals, from Easter weekend to end Sept. The old carriages of this tourist train have delightful

open platforms for the first stage of this combined 'rail and water' trip. You have an unimpeded view of a typical Rhine landscape as the railway hugs the Grand Canal d'Alsace and crosses some wonderful forests. The trip then continues on board a 1930s-style boat.

Neuf-Brisach

1 km/¹/₂ mile
W of Vogelsheim
An historic fortress
Musée Vauban
7, Place de la Porte-de-Belfort
☎ 03 89 72 51 68
Open 1 Apr.-31 Oct. daily (exc. Tues.), 10am-noon, 2-5pm.
Admission charge.
The Musée Vauban is a mine of information on the 17thC. octagonal stronghold built by Sébastien le Prestre de Vauban, Louis XIV's military

engineer and architect. Having ceded Vieux-Brisach to the Germans, Louis XIV commissioned Vauban to build a fortress, in order to guard the river-crossing. The museum houses documents, portraits and photographs from the past 300 years. A relief map of Neuf-Brisach is complemented by a *son et lumière* show.

Vauban, military engineer

Things to do

Musée de l'Instrumentation
Optique in Biesheim
Musée Vauban in Neuf-
Brisach
Auberge de l'Ill in Illhaeusern

With children

Tourist railway of the Rhine
Parc l'Eldorado in Artzenheim

Within easy reach

Colmar (20 km/12 miles
W), pp.192-197
Mulhouse (25 km/
16 miles SW), pp.226-
231

Tourist office

Neuf-Brishach:
☎ 03 89 72 56 66

Biesheim

3 km/2 miles
N of Volgelsheim

Musée Gallo-Roman

Place de la Mairie
☎ 03 89 72 01 58
Open Wed. & Fri.-Sun.,
2-6pm, Thurs. 9am-1pm.
Admission charge.
This museum focuses
upon the ancient
military site
where many
vestiges
of Roman
legionary camps
have been found.
Its displays give
fascinating insights
into military
activities, funeral rites
and daily life for people
living under Gallo-Roman
rule. A wonderful gold
ingot, the only one ever to
be found in Gaul, is one of
the highlights of the
collection.

Musée de l'Instrumentation Optique

Place de la Mairie
☎ 03 89 72 01 59
Open Wed. & Fri.-Sun.,
2-6pm, Thurs. 9am-1pm.
Admission charge.
The developments made in
the world of optics over the
last three centuries are
charted in a very unusual
collection. Over 300 objects,
such as microscopes, sextants,
telescopes and lasers are
featured in this enthralling,
museum, which should really
not be missed.

Artzenheim

8 km/5 miles
N of Biesheim

4,500 species of plants

Parc l'Eldorado
Rue du 42e RIF
☎ 03 89 71 67 14
Open Apr.-Oct. Wed.-
Sun., 2-7pm.
Admission charge.
Enjoy a stroll in this
park with its
4,500 rare plant
species from all
over the world,
including European
and Canadian
maples and Japanese
cedars. Wildlife is
also represented with
over 150 birds and
animals, such as goats, ducks,
geese and racing pigeons.

Illhaeusern

12 km/7¹/₂ miles
NW of Artzenheim

Auberge de l'Ill

2, Rue Collonges
☎ 03 89 71 89 00

Closed Mon.,Tues. & Feb.
Booking essential.
This is one of France's top
restaurants, in an idyllic
riverside location. The
Haeberlin brothers'
reputation is founded on their
sophisticated cusine and
wonderful setting, and menus
include fillet of pike-perch
cooked in red wine and frogs'
legs with cep mushrooms.
Pricey, but a wonderful
experience.

THE BOATMEN'S FESTIVAL

Traditionally, Illhaeusern, an old fishing village,
celebrates its boatmen in a festival during the
second weekend in July. On Saturday evening the
locals eat *flammekueche* and dance under canvas
near the Grenouillère lake, pausing for a dramatic
firework display. On Sunday afternoon the
procession of boatmen
on board their distinctive,
flat-bottomed boats
takes place. Times
have changed, however,
and today only one
professional fisherman
remains in Illhaeusern.

This guide was written by HERVÉ BRIDE, ROLAND KALTENBACH AND ANNE-MARIE MINIVIELLE, with the help of CHRYSTEL ARNOULD, PIERRE CHAVOT, JULIE COT AND AURÉLIE JOIRIS.

Illustrated maps: PHILIPPE DORO

Cartography: © IDÉ INFOGRAPHIE (THOMAS GROLLIER)

Translation and adaptation: JANE MOSELEY (Email: janecafmoseley@hotmail.com)

Additional design and editorial assistance: CHRISTINE BELL, CATHERINE BRADLEY, BEN CRACKNELL, JANE MOSELEY, SHEILA MURPHY AND MICHAEL SUMMERS.

We have done our best to ensure the accuracy of the information contained in this guide. However, addresses, telephone numbers, opening times etc. inevitably do change from time to time, so if you find a discrepancy please do let us know. You can contact us at the address below.

Hachette UK guides provide independent advice. The authors and compilers do not accept any renumeration for the inclusion of any addresses in these guides.

Please note that we cannot accept any responsibility for any loss, injury or inconvenience sustained by anyone as a result of any information or advice contained in this guide.

First published in the United Kingdom in 2002 by Hachette UK

Distributed in the United States of America by Sterling Publishing Co., Inc. 387 Park Avenue South, New York, NY 10016-8810

A CIP catalogue for this book is available from the British Library

ISBN 1 84202 167 2

Hachette UK, Cassell & Co., The Orion Publishing Group, Wellington House, 125 Strand, London WC2R 0BB

Printed in Slovenia by DELO tiskarna by arrangement with Prešernova družba, d. d.

ADDRESS BOOK

CONTENTS

Practical information

Comité régional du tourisme d'Alsace
(Alsace Regional Tourism Committee)
BP 172
67004 Strasbourg Cedex
☎ 03 88 25 01 66
✆ 03 88 52 17 06
crt@tourism-alsace.com
www.tourisme-alsace.com

Agence de développement touristique du Bas-Rhin (ADT 67)
(Lower Rhine Tourist Development Agency)
9, rue du Dôme
BP 53
67061 Strasbourg Cedex
☎ 03 88 15 45 88 or
03 88 15 45 85 (reservations)
✆ 03 88 75 67 64
alsace-tourism@sdv.fr

Association départementale du tourisme du Haut-Rhin (ADT 68)
(Departmental Association of Tourism in Upper Rhine)
Maison du tourisme
1, rue Schlumberger
BP 337
68006 Colmar Cedex
☎ 03 89 20 10 68 or
03 89 20 10 62 (reservations)
✆ 03 89 23 33 91
www.tourisme68.asso.fr.fr
adt@rmcnet.fr

Maison de l'Alsace
39, av. des Champs-Élysées
75008 Paris
☎ 01 53 83 10 00
✆ 01 45 63 84 08

BOOKING ACCOMMODATION

Service de réservation loisirs et tourisme vert en Alsace
(Reservation service for rural tourism and activities in Alsace)
7, pl. des Peupliers
67000 Strasbourg
☎ 03 88 75 56 50
✆ 03 88 23 00 97

Service loisirs-accueil
(Activities and accommodation service)
BP 371
68006 Colmar
☎ 03 89 20 10 62
✆ 03 89 23 33 91

Relais départemental du tourisme rural
(Departmental association of rural tourism)
7, pl. des Meuniers
67000 Strasbourg
☎ 03 88 75 56 50
✆ 03 88 23 00 97

Association des Fermes-auberges
(Association of Farm-inns)
BP 371
68006 Colmar Cedex
☎ 03 89 20 10 68
✆ 03 88 23 33 91

Procampal
Camping Clair Vacances
68127 Sainte-Croix-en-Plaine
☎ 03 89 49 27 28
✆ 03 89 49 21 55

Accueil jeunes Alsace
Maison des associations
1, pl. des Orphelins
67000 Strasbourg
☎ 03 88 24 03 09
✆ 03 88 24 04 98

VVF Vacances
13, rue du 22-Novembre
67000 Strasbourg
☎ 03 88 22 24 44
✆ 03 88 22 70 40

Parc naturel régional des Vosges du Nord
(Northern Vosges Nature Reserve)
Maison du parc
BP 24
67290 La Petite-Pierre
☎ 03 88 01 49 59
✆ 03 88 01 49 60

Parc naturel régional des Ballons des Vosges
(Nature Reserve of the Ballons of Vosges)
Maison du parc
1, cour de l'Abbaye
68140 Munster
☎ 03 89 77 90 20
✆ 03 89 77 90 30

A.R.I.E.N.A.
(Regional association for environmental education)
36, Enwihr
67600 Muttersholtz
☎ 03 88 85 11 30
✆ 03 88 85 17 87

Office national des Forêts
(National Forest Office)
14, rue du Maréchal-Juin
67084 Strasbourg Cedex
☎ 03 88 76 76 40
✆ 03 88 76 76 50
www.ski-nordic-france.com

Club Vosgien
(ramblers association)
16, rue Sainte-Hélène
67000 Strasbourg
☎ 03 88 32 57 96
✆ 03 88 22 04 72

Comité départemental de cyclotourisme du Bas-Rhin
(Lower Rhine Bicycle Touring Committee)
Maison des Sports
15, rue de Genève
67000 Strasbourg
☎ 03 88 21 10 58
✆ 03 88 24 14 03

Ligue d'Alsace de cyclotourisme Maison des jeunes de Colmar
(Alsace Bicycle Touring League)
17, rue de Schlumberger
68000 Colmar
☎ 03 89 41 26 87
✆ 03 89 23 20 16

Délégation départementale tourisme équestre Bas-Rhin
(Lower Rhine Departmental Horse Riding Society)
Roland Adam
4, rue des Violettes
67201 Eckbolsheim
☎ 03 88 77 39 64
✆ 03 88 76 05 46

Délégation régionale et départementale tourisme équestre Haut-Rhin
(Upper Rhine Regional and Departmental Horse Riding Society)
Maison des associations
6, rte d'Ingersheim
68000 Colmar
☎ 03 89 24 43 18
✆ 03 89 23 15 08

VNF
(Waterway Tourism in France)
5, port du Rhin
BP 20
67016 Strasbourg Cedex
☎ 03 90 41 06 06
✆ 03 88 60 31 77

**Ligue d'Alsace de
canoë-kayak**
*(Canoe-Kayaking
League of Alsace)*
Maison des sports
15, rue de Genève
67100 Strasbourg
☎ 03 88 21 10 66
✆ 03 88 24 14 03

**Ligue d'Alsace
de vol libre**
*(Hang-gliding League of
Alsace)*
Gilbert Nicolini
42B, rue de Brisgau
68121 Urbès
☎ 03 89 82 71 01

**Comité départemental
de ski du Bas-Rhin**
*(Lower Rhine Departmental
Skiing Association)*
Maison des Sports
4, rue Jean-Mentelin
67000 Strasbourg
☎ 03 88 26 94 00
✆ 03 88 26 94 01

**Comité régional du
massif des Vosges**
*(Regional Association
of the Vosges Massif)*
24, av. Aristide-Briand
68200 Mulhouse
☎ 03 89 43 25 50
✆ 03 89 32 14 32

**Pêcher dans le
Bas-Rhin**
(Fishing in the Lower Rhine)
33A, rue de la Tour
67200 Strasbourg
☎ 03 88 10 52 20
✆ 03 88 10 52 29

**Pêcher dans le
Haut-Rhin**
(Fishing in the Upper Rhine)
29, av. de Colmar
68200 Mulhouse
☎ 03 89 60 64 74
✆ 03 89 60 64 75

Getting there

BY PLANE

AIRLINES

British Airways
☎ 0845 77 333 77
www.britishairways.com

Air France
☎ 0 820 820 820
www.airfrance.fr

AIRPORTS

Strasbourg International
Rte de Strasbourg
67960 Entzheim
☎ 03 88 64 67 67
✆ 03 88 68 82 12

**EuroAirport Basel -
Mulhouse-Freiburg**
68300 Saint-Louis
☎ 03 89 90 31 11
✆ 03 89 90 25 77

BY TRAIN

Rail Europe
☎ 08705 848 848
www.raileurope.co.uk

SNCF (French railways)
www.voyages-sncf.com

MAIN STATIONS

**Strasbourg, Colmar,
Mulhouse.**

BY CAR

MAPS

Michelin Maps
nos. 87 and 242,
scale 1/200 000

IGN Map
'Top 100' nos. 12 and 31,
scale 1/100 000

CAR HIRE

Ada
☎ 08 36 68 40 02
www.ada-sa.fr

Avis
☎ 08 02 05 05 05
www.avis-location.fr

Budget
☎ 08 00 10 00 01
www.budget.com

Europcar
☎ 08 03 35 23 52
www.europcar.com

Rent a car
☎ 08 36 694 695
www.rentacar.fr

Hertz
☎ 01 39 38 38 38
www.hertz.fr

USEFUL ADDRESS

These pages contain over 180 accommodation options in Alsace, divided into the following categories: campsites, youth hostels, farm-inns, walking shelters, bed & breakfasts and hotels. Addresses within each category are listed alphabetically. The number of triangles indicates the price range of each entry and refers to the cost per night per person in the case of youth hostels and gîtes. The price indication in the hotel category is based on a double room.

▲ under €30
▲▲ €30-45
▲▲▲ €45-61

▲▲▲▲ €61-92
▲▲▲▲▲ over €92

CAMP SITES

CERNAY

Camping municipal
Les Acacias
Rte de Belfort
☎ 03 89 75 56 97
🖷 03 89 39 72 29
Open Apr.-Sept.
204 sites

COURTAVON

Plan d'eau de Courtavon
Rte de Liebsdorf
☎ 03 89 08 12 50
Open May-Sept.
70 sites

DAMBACH-LA-VILLE

Camping municipal
Rte d'Ebersheim
☎ 03 88 92 48 60
Open 15 May-Sept.
120 sites

NIEDERBRONN-LES-BAINS

Heidenkopf
Rte de Bitche
☎ 03 88 09 08 46
🖷 03 88 09 04 97
clubvosgien@aol.com
Open all year.
58 sites

OBERNAI

Camping municipal
Le Vallon de l'Ehn
Rte d'Ottrott
☎ 03 88 95 38 48
🖷 03 88 48 31 47
Open all year.
150 sites

RIBEAUVILLÉ

Camping municipal
Pierre-de-Coubertin
Rue de Landau
☎ 03 89 73 66 71
Open 15 Mar-15 Nov.
260 sites

RIQUEWIHR

Camping intercommunal
Chemin du stade
☎ 03 89 47 90 08
🖷 03 89 49 05 63
Open Easter to end of Oct.
150 sites

ROUFFACH

Camping municipal
☎ 03 89 49 78 13
🖷 03 89 78 03 09
Open 21 May-Sept.
30 sites

SAVERNE

Camping municipal
Rue Knoepffler
☎ and 🖷 03 88 91 35 65
Open Apr.-Sept.
144 sites

WASSELONNE

Camping municipal
Rte de Wangenbourg
☎ and 🖷 03 88 87 00 08
Open 15 Apr.-15 Oct.
100 sites

YOUTH HOSTELS

COLMAR

Mittelharth
2, rue Pasteur
☎ 03 89 80 57 39
🖷 03 89 80 76 16
100 beds

MULHOUSE

37, rue de l'Illberg
☎ 03 89 42 63 28
🖷 03 89 59 74 95

STRASBOURG

Parc du Rhin
Rue Cavaliers
☎ 03 88 45 54 20
🖷 03 88 45 54 21
220 beds

René Cassin
9, rue Auberge-de-Jeunesse
☎ 03 88 30 26 46
🖷 03 88 30 35 16
260 beds

FARM-INNS

BELLEFOSSE

▲▲
Ban de la Roche
Véronique Wilbacher
66, rue Principale
☎ 03 88 97 35 25
5 rooms

LE HOHWALD

▲▲
Du Wittertalhof
Bernard Hazemann
15, rue du Wittertalhof
☎ 03 88 08 31 24
4 rooms

LUTTENBACH

▲
Kahlenwasen
(see p.207)
Guy Lochert
Petit Ballon
☎ 03 89 77 32 49
11 rooms

LUTTENBACH-PRÈS-MUNSTER

▲
Geisbach
Paul Erte
4, chemin du Geisbach
BP 5
☎ 03 89 77 32 63
5 rooms

NATZWILLER

▲▲▲
Auberge du Segersthal
Dominique Radmacher
☎ and 🖷 03 88 97 95 82
3 rooms

ROMBACH-LE-FRANC

▲▲
Creux-Chêne
Ginette Wenger
6, La Hingrie
☎ 03 89 58 95 43
🖷 03 89 58 42 46
5 rooms

SONDERNACH

▲▲
Rothenbrunnen
Jean-Claude Lochert
☎ 03 89 77 33 08
🖷 03 89 77 09 42
7 rooms

STOSSWIHR

▲▲
Trois Fours
Rte des Crêtes
☎ 03 89 77 31 14
🖷 03 89 77 97 33
8 rooms

▲▲
Auberge du Marcaire
82, rue Saegmatt
☎ 03 89 77 44 89
Open daily noon-10pm.
Closed 1 Nov.-1 Mar.
15 rooms

WISSEMBOURG

▲▲
Moulin des Sept Fontaines
Claude Finck
Drachenbronn
☎ 03 88 94 50 90
📠 03 88 94 54 57
11 rooms

WALKING SHELTERS

ALTENACH

▲
Philipp Edgarg
4, rue Sainte-Barbe
☎ 03 89 25 12 92
1 x 12-bed dormitory,
1 x 16 bed dormitory

BREITENBACH

▲
Frédéric Dischinger
(see p.208)
Christlesgut
☎ 03 89 77 51 11
14 beds

DAMBACH

▲
Rummel
16/a Neudoerfel
☎ 03 88 09 23 13
16 beds

DIEBOLSHEIM

▲
Albert Decock
85, rue Jean-de-Beaumont
☎ 03 88 74 80 59
📠 03 88 74 66 72
27 beds

LA PETITE-PIERRE

▲
S. Rummler
BP 13
22, rue Principale
☎ 03 88 70 45 30
📠 03 88 70 42 02
Open all year.
20 beds

LE BONHOMME

▲
Schelcher-Petitcolas
140, La Hollée
Les Bagenelles
☎ 03 89 47 51 38
📠 03 89 73 77 96
12 beds

LICHTENBERG

▲
Mairie
Place de l'Église
☎ 03 88 89 96 06
📠 03 88 89 96 91
44 beds

LUTTENBACH

▲
Philippe Schneider
Chemin du Baechle 119
☎ 03 89 77 13 04
18 beds

OBERBRONN

▲
Christelle Leingang
Camping municipal
Eichelgarten
☎ 03 88 09 71 96
Open all year.
60 beds

OBERSTEINBACH

▲
Evelyne Berring-Flaig
29, rue Principale
☎ and 📠 03 88 09 55 26
25 beds

STOSSWIHR

▲
Thierry Hiniger
Auberge du Schantzwasen
☎ 03 89 77 30 11
📠 03 89 77 99 10
www.auberge-
schantzwasen.com
60 beds

WANGENBOURG-ENGENTHAL

▲
Clodong Liliane
Refuge du Grand Tétras
2, impasse des Papillons
☎ 03 88 87 34 34
📠 03 88 87 32 06
Open all year.
15 beds

B&Bs

BARR

▲▲
Gérard Ball
39, rue de l'Altenberg
☎ and 📠 03 88 08 10 20
9 beds

EGUISHEIM

▲▲
Monique Freudenreich
4, cour Unterlinden
☎ and 📠 03 89 23 16 44

ACCOMMODATION

GUEBERSCHWIHR

▲▲
Christiane Scherb
1, rte de Rouffach
☎ and 🖷 03 89 49 33 70
12 beds

ITTERSWILLER

▲▲
Betty Hungerbuhler
101, rte du Vin
☎ 03 88 85 50 57
7 beds

LAUTENBACH

▲▲
Ringler/Peyrelon
44, rue Principale
☎ 03 89 76 39 21
or 06 60 89 15 83
3 beds

MARCKOLSHEIM

▲▲
Roger Jaeger
3, rue du Violon
☎ and 🖷 03 88 92 50 08
4 beds

ORBEY

▲▲
Fabienne Batot
33, le Busset
Ferme du Busset
☎ and 🖷 03 89 71 22 17
13 beds

RORSCHWIHR

▲▲
André Ackermann
25, rte du Vin
☎ 03 89 73 63 87
🖷 03 89 73 38 16
6 beds

THANNENKIRCH

▲▲
René Dumoulin
15, rue Sainte-Anne
☎ 03 89 73 12 07
8 beds

HOTELS

ALTKIRCH

▲▲
Auberge Sundgovienne
Rte de Belfort
☎ 03 89 40 97 18
🖷 03 89 40 67 73
Closed 23 Dec.-1 Feb.
29 rooms.

BALDENHEIM

▲▲▲
À l'Étoile
11, rue de Baldenheim
Rathsamhausen
☎ 03 88 92 35 79

🖷 03 88 82 91 66
Open all year.
8 rooms

BARR

▲▲▲
Domaine Saint-Ulrich
106, rue de la Vallée
☎ 03 88 08 54 40
🖷 03 88 08 57 55
Open all year.
30 rooms

BISCHOFFSHEIM

▲▲▲
Le Bischenberg
17, rue Raiffeisen
☎ 03 88 49 28 28
🖷 03 80 49 28 00
Closed in Aug. & Christmas
to New Year's Day.
86 rooms

BOUXWILLER

▲▲▲
La Cave du Tonnelier
84 A, Grand-Rue
☎ 03 88 70 72 57
🖷 03 88 70 95 74
cour-du-tonnelier@libertysurf.fr
Closed 23 Dec.-23 Jan.
16 rooms

COLMAR

▲▲▲▲▲
Europe
15, rte de Neuf-Brisach
Horbourg-Wihr
☎ 03 89 20 54 00
🖷 03 89 41 27 50
Open all year.
138 rooms

▲▲
Arcantis-Hexagone
38, rte de Sélestat
☎ 03 89 41 23 33
🖷 03 89 41 53 81
www.acom.fr/arcantis
Open all year.
44 rooms

▲▲
Le Jardin du Bonheur
23, rte de Neuf-Brisach
☎ 03 89 23 63 36
🖷 03 89 24 94 42
Closed 15 Jan.-28 Feb.
14 rooms

DAMBACH-LA-VILLE

▲▲
Au Raisin d'Or
28bis, rue Clemenceau
☎ 03 88 92 48 66
🖷 03 88 92 61 42
Closed Mon., Tues. lunchtime.
15 Dec. & 1 Feb.
8 rooms

DORLISHEIM

▲
Le Forum Relais Routier
4, av. de la Gare
☎ 03 88 38 14 28
🖷 03 88 38 88 94
Open all year.
11 rooms

EGUISHEIM

▲▲▲▲
Hostellerie du Pape
10, Grand-Rue
☎ 03 89 41 41 21
🖷 03 89 41 41 31
www.hostellerie-pape.com
info@hostellerie-pape.com
Closed 5 Jan.-9 Feb.
33 rooms

▲▲▲
Auberge Alsacienne
12, Grand-Rue
☎ 03 89 41 50 20
🖷 03 89 23 89 32
Closed 20 Dec.-15 Feb.
19 rooms

ESCHAU

▲▲
Au Cygne
☎ 03 88 64 04 79
🖷 03 89 64 33 83
Open all year.
15 rooms

FERRETTE

▲▲
Hôtel-restaurant Collin
4, rue du Château
☎ 03 89 40 40 72
🖷 03 89 40 38 26
Open all year.
7 rooms

GERTWILLER

▲▲
Aux Délices
176, rte de sélestat
☎ 03 88 08 95 17
🖷 03 88 08 17 41
14 rooms

GUEBWILLER

▲▲▲
Du Lac
244, rue de la République
☎ 03 89 76 63 10
🖷 03 89 74 24 84
77 rooms

HAGUENAU

▲▲▲
Europe Hôtel
15, av. Professeur-René-Leriche
☎ 03 88 93 58 11
🖷 03 88 06 05 43
europe.hotel@visit-alsace.com
Open all year.
82 rooms

HAGENTHAL-LE-BAS

▲▲▲▲
Jenny
84, rue d'Higenheim
☎ 03 89 68 50 09
📠 03 89 68 58 64
Closed 22 July-6 Aug.
26 rooms

HOHROD

▲▲▲
Panorama
4, route du linge, Hohrodberg
☎ 03 89 77 36 53
📠 03 89 77 03 93
Closed Mar., Nov. &
Christmas
30 rooms

INGWILLER

▲▲▲
Aux Comtes de Hanau
139, rue du Général-de-Gaulle
☎ 03 88 89 42 27
📠 03 88 89 51 18
11 rooms

ISSENHEIM

▲▲
Demi-Lune
9, rue de Rouffach
☎ 03 89 76 83 63
📠 03 89 74 90 29
Closed 22 Dec.-5 Jan.
12 rooms

KAYSERSBERG

▲▲▲
Belle Promenade
5, pl. Gouraud
☎ 03 89 47 11 51
📠 03 89 78 13 40
Closed 5-31 Jan.
14 rooms

▲▲
Château
38, rue du Général-de-Gaulle
☎ 03 89 78 24 33
📠 03 89 47 37 82
Closed 15 Feb.-5 Mar.
& 1-8 July.
8 rooms

KIENTZHEIM

▲▲▲
Hostellerie Schwendi
2, pl. Schwendi
☎ 03 89 47 30 50
📠 03 89 49 04 49
Open all year.
17 rooms

▲▲▲
**Hostellerie de l'Abbaye
d'Alspach** *(see p.211)*
2, rue du Maréchal-Foch
☎ 03 89 47 16 00
Open daily (closed Jan.-Feb.)
24 rooms

LA PETITE-PIERRE

▲▲▲▲
Aux Trois Roses
19, rue Principale
☎ 03 88 89 89 00
📠 03 88 70 41 28
Open all year.
42 rooms

LAPOUTROIE

▲▲▲
Faudé
28, rue du Général-Dufieux
☎ 03 89 47 50 35
📠 03 89 47 24 82
www.faude.com
info@faude.com
Closed 2 weeks in Mar.
& beg. Nov.-beg. Dec.
31 rooms

LAUTERBOURG

▲▲
Au Cygne
39, rue du Général-
Mittelhauser
☎ 03 88 94 80 59
📠 03 88 94 61 90
Closed Feb.
18 rooms

MARLENHEIM

▲▲
Hostellerie Reeb
2, rue du Docteur-Schweitzer
☎ 03 88 87 52 70
📠 03 88 87 69 73
35 rooms

MARMOUTIER

▲▲
Aux Deux Clefs
30, rue du Général-Leclerc
☎ 03 88 70 61 08
📠 03 88 70 69 75
Open all year.
15 rooms

MASEVAUX

▲▲
L'Hostellerie Alsacienne
16, rue du Maréchal-Foch
☎ 03 89 82 45 25
📠 03 89 82 45 25
Open all year.
12 rooms

MITTELHAUSBERGEN

▲▲▲
Au Tilleul
5, rte de Strasbourg
☎ 03 88 56 18 31
📠 03 88 56 07 23
www.autilleul.com
autilleul@wanadoo.fr
Closed 18 Feb.-7 Mar.
& 16 July-1 Aug.
12 rooms

ACCOMMODATION

MOLSHEIM

▲▲
Auberge du Cheval Blanc
5, pl. de l'Hôtel-de-Ville
☎ 03 88 38 16 87
🅕 03 88 38 20 96
Open all year.
13 rooms

MULHOUSE

▲▲▲▲
Best Western Bourse
14, rue de la Bourse
☎ 03 89 56 18 44
🅕 03 89 56 60 51
bourse.hotel@wanadoo.fr
Closed 21 Dec.-8 Jan.
50 rooms

▲▲▲▲
Bristol
18, av. de Colmar
☎ 03 89 42 12 31
🅕 03 89 42 50 57
www.hotelbristol.com
hbristol@club-internet.fr
70 rooms

▲▲▲
Au Cheval Blanc
27, rue Principale
Baldersheim
☎ 03 89 45 45 44
🅕 03 89 56 28 93
www.hotel-cheval-blanc.com
cheval-blanc@wanadoo.fr
Closed 22 Dec.-3 Jan.
83 rooms

▲▲
Saint-Bernard
3, rue des Fleurs
☎ 03 89 45 82 32
🅕 03 89 45 26 32
21 rooms

▲
Schœnberg
14, rue Schœnberg
☎ 03 89 44 19 41
🅕 03 89 44 49 80
15 rooms

MUNSTER

▲▲▲▲
À la Verte Vallée
(see p.204)
10, rue Alfred-Hartmann
☎ 03 89 77 15 15
Open all year.
107 rooms

▲▲
Aux Deux Sapins
49, rue du 9ᵉ-Zouaves
☎ 03 89 77 33 96
🅕 03 89 77 03 90
www.alsanet.com/2sapins
Closed 20 Nov.-20 Dec.
19 rooms

MUTZIG

▲▲
Le Felsbourg
21, av. du Général-de-Gaulle
☎ 03 88 38 13 28
🅕 03 88 48 84 34
Open all year.
16 rooms

NATZWILLER

▲▲▲
Auberge Metzger
(see p.143)
55, rue Principale
☎ 03 88 97 02 42
Closed Sun. evening, Mon.,
3 weeks in Jan., last week in
June, & Christmas week.
16 rooms

NEUF-BRISACH

▲▲
Aux Deux Roses
11, rte de Strasbourg
☎ 03 89 72 56 03
🅕 03 89 72 90 29
Open all year.
47 rooms

NIEDERBRONN-LES-BAINS

▲▲▲
Lully
33-37, rue de la République
☎ 03 88 09 01 42
🅕 03 88 09 05 90
Closed Feb. school hols.
& Christmas.
40 rooms

OBERNAI

▲▲▲▲▲
À la Cour d'Alsace
3, rue de Gail
BP 64
☎ 03 88 95 07 00
🅕 03 88 95 19 21
www.com-alsace.com
info@com-alsace.com
Closed 25 Dec.-22 Jan.
43 rooms

▲▲▲▲
Le Parc
169, rte d'Ottrott
☎ 03 88 95 50 08
🅕 03 88 95 37 29
www.hotel-du-parc.com/
leparc@imaginet.fr
Closed Dec.
56 rooms

ORBEY

▲▲
Le Saut de la Truite
391, ld Remomont
☎ 03 89 71 20 04
🅕 03 89 71 31 52
Closed Jan. & Feb.
21 rooms

▲▲
Au Vieux Tonneau
3, route du Vin
☎ 03 88 82 03 51
🅕 03 88 82 73 50
Closed 12 Feb.-5 Mar.
15 rooms

OTTROTT

▲▲▲
**Hostellerie du
Mont-Saint-Odile**
Mont Saint-Odile
☎ 03 88 95 80 53
🅕 03 88 95 82 96
Open all year.
140 rooms

PFAFFENHOFFEN

▲▲▲
À l'Agneau
3, rue de Saverne
☎ 03 88 07 72 38
🅕 03 88 72 20 24
Closed 16 Aug.-8 Sept.
18 rooms

RHINAU

▲▲
Aux Bords du Rhin
10, rte du Rhin
☎ 03 88 74 60 36
🅕 03 88 74 65 77
Closed 19 Feb.-9 Mar.
& 2-11 July.
21 rooms

RIBEAUVILLÉ

▲▲▲
Les Vosges
2, Grand-Rue
☎ 03 89 73 61 39
🅕 03 89 73 34 21
www.vosges-hotel.com
Closed 5 Jan.-15 Mar.
18 rooms

RIQUEWIHR

▲▲▲
La Couronne
5, rue de la Couronne
☎ 03 89 49 03 03
🅕 03 89 49 01 01
Open all year.
40 rooms

RIXHEIM

▲▲
Le Relais de Rixheim
1, petit chemin de
Sausheim
☎ 03 89 64 59 01
🅕 03 89 64 59 02
Open all year
42 rooms

ROSHEIM

▲▲
Hôtel Alpina
39, rue du Lion
☎ 03 88 50 49 30
🖷 03 88 49 25 75
Open all year
10 rooms

SCHERWILLER

▲▲▲▲
Auberge Ramstein
1, rue du Riesling
☎ 03 88 82 17 00
🖷 03 88 82 17 02
Closed Feb. school hols.
15 rooms

SÉLESTAT

▲▲▲▲▲▲
**Hôtel-restaurant Abbaye
La Pommeraie**
8, av. Foch
☎ 03 88 92 07 84
🖷 03 88 92 08 71
Open all year.
13 rooms

SEWEN

▲▲
Au Relais des Lacs
30, Grande-Rue
☎ 03 89 82 01 42
🖷 03 89 82 09 29
Closed Jan.
13 rooms

SOULTZMATT

▲▲▲▲
Vallée Noble
☎ 03 89 47 65 65
🖷 03 89 47 65 04
www.valleenoble.com
vallee.noble@wanadoo.fr
32 rooms

STRASBOURG

▲▲▲▲
Hôtel du Dragon
12, rue de l'Écarlate
☎ 03 88 35 79 80
🖷 03 88 25 78 95
Open all year.
32 rooms

▲▲▲▲
Hôtel Aux Trois Roses
7, rue de Zurich
☎ 03 88 36 56 95
🖷 03 88 35 06 14
Open all year.
33 rooms

▲▲▲
Hôtel Gutenberg
31, rue des Serruriers
☎ 03 88 32 17 15
🖷 03 88 75 76 67
Closed 1-15 Jan.
42 rooms

▲▲▲
Couvent du Franciscain
18, rue du Faubourg-de-Pierre
☎ 03 88 32 93 93
🖷 03 88 75 68 46
www.hotel-franciscain.com
info@hotel-franciscain.com
43 rooms

▲▲▲
Au Cerf d'Or
6, pl. de l'Hôpital
☎ 03 88 36 20 05
🖷 03 88 36 68 67
Closed 24 Dec.-2 Jan.
37 rooms

THANN

▲▲▲
Cigogne
35-37, rue du Général-
de-Gaulle
☎ 03 89 37 47 33
🖷 03 89 37 40 18
Closed 8-28 Feb.
27 rooms

▲▲
Kléber
39, rue Kléber
☎ 03 89 37 13 66
🖷 03 89 37 39 67
Closed Feb.
25 rooms

WISSEMBOURG

▲▲
De la Gare
23, av. de la Gare
☎ 03 88 94 13 67
🖷 03 88 94 06 88
Closed Aug.
18 rooms

▲▲
À l'Escargot
40, rte Nationale
☎ 03 88 94 90 29
🖷 03 88 54 29 92
Open all year.
15 rooms

WOERTH

▲▲
**Hôtel-auberge
Aux 7 Chênes**
34, rte de Lembach
☎ 03 88 09 38 09
🖷 03 88 09 38 09
Closed 2 weeks in Feb.,
2 weeks in Oct. & Christmas
10 rooms

ZELLENBERG

▲▲▲▲
Schloessberg
50 a, rue de la Fontaine
☎ 03 89 47 93 85
🖷 03 89 47 82 40
Open all year.
9 rooms

ACCOMMODATION

The following pages contain over 48 restaurants, farm-inns and winstubs, in which to try local cuisine and regional specialities. The entries are listed alphabetically by location. The number of lozenges indicates the average price of a meal at each entry.

◆ under €15
◆◆ €15-30
◆◆◆ €30-45

◆◆◆◆ €45-76
◆◆◆◆◆ over €76

ALTKIRCH

◆◆
Caveau du Tonneau d'Or
33, rue Gilardoni
☎ 03 89 40 69 79
Closed 15-30 Aug., 24 Dec.,
2 Jan. & Mon.

AMMERSCHWIHR

◆◆◆◆
Aux armes de France
(see p.210)
1, Grand-Rue
☎ 03 89 47 10 12
Open daily (exc. Wed.
& Thurs.), noon-1.30pm
& from 7.30pm.

◆◆◆
Aux Trois Merles
5, rue de la 5e-D.-B.
☎ 03 89 78 24 35
🖷 03 89 78 13 06
Closed Nov., Jan. & Feb.,
Sun. evening, Mon. & Wed.
evening.

ARTZENHEIM

◆◆◆
Auberge d'Artzenheim
30, rue du Sponeck
☎ 03 89 71 60 51
🖷 03 89 71 68 21
Closed 15 Feb.-15 Mar.,
Sun. evening, Mon., & Tues.
evening.

AVOLSHEIM

◆
À la Vignette
☎ 03 88 47 48 28
Closed Mon. evening & Tues.

BARR

◆
Caveau Folie Marco
30, rue du Docteur-Sultzer
☎ 03 88 08 89 65
Closed Wed. & Sat. evening.

BERGHEIM

◆◆
Au Sommelier
51, Grand-Rue
☎ 03 89 73 69 99
Closed Sun.

BOERSCH

◆◆◆
Le Châtelain
41, rue Monseigneur-Barth
☎ 03 88 95 83 33
🖷 03 88 95 80 63
Closed Mon. & Tues. lunchtime.

BOURBACH-LE-BAS

◆◆
À la Couronne d'Or
9, rue Principale
☎ 03 89 82 51 77
🖷 03 89 82 58 03
Closed Mon.

CARSPACH

◆◆
Auberge Sundgovienne
Rte de Belfort
☎ 03 89 40 97 18
Closed Mon. & Tues. lunchtime.

COLMAR

◆◆◆
La Maison des Têtes
(see p.193)
19, rue des Têtes
☎ 03 89 24 43 43
Open daily (exc. Sun. evening
& Mon.), noon-3pm,
7-10.30pm.

◆◆◆
Au Fer Rouge *(see p.194)*
52, Grand-Rue
☎ 03 89 41 37 24
Open daily (exc. Sun. &
Mon.), noon-3pm, 7-10.30pm.

◆◆◆
Aux Trois Poissons
(see p.196)
15, quai de la Poissonnerie
☎ 03 89 41 25 21
Closed Tues. evening & Wed.

◆◆◆
Le Rapp'
1-3-5, rue Weinemer
☎ 03 89 41 62 10
🖷 03 89 24 13 58
www.rapp-hotel.com
rapp-hot@calixo.net
Open daily.

◆◆
Brasserie-restaurant Heydel
45, rue des Clefs
☎ 03 89 41 41 20
Closed Mon.

EGUISHEIM

◆◆◆
Le Caveau d'Eguisheim
(see p.199)
3, pl. du Château-Saint-Léon
☎ 03 89 41 08 89
Open daily, noon-1.45pm,
7-9pm (exc. Wed., & Thurs.
lunchtime).

ENTZHEIM

◆◆
Steinkeller
34, rte de Strasbourg
☎ 03 88 68 98 00
🖷 03 88 68 64 56
www.strabourg.com/pere-
benoit
hotel.perebenoit@wanadoo.fr
Closed Sat. lunchtime, Sun.
& Mon. lunchtime.

FELDBACH

◆◆
Au Cheval Blanc
1, rue de Bisel
☎ 03 89 25 81 86
🖷 03 89 07 72 88
Closed Mon. & Wed.

GŒRSDORF

◆
Au Panorama
232, rue Principale
☎ 03 88 09 30 91
Closed Mon.

GUEBWILLER

◆◆
La Taverne du Vigneron
7, pl. Saint-Léger
☎ 03 89 76 81 89
Closed Mon. & Tues
lunchtime.

GUNSBACH

◆
**Auberge Schwartzenburg,
chez Dédé**
17, rue du Muklélé
☎ 03 89 77 42 40
Closed Mon.

HAGENTHAL-LE-BAS

◆◆◆
Chez Jenny
84, rue d'Hegenheim
☎ 03 89 68 50 09
Closed Sun. evening & Mon.

HANDSCHUHEIM

◆
Auberge À l'Espérance
(see p.137)
5, rue Principale
☎ 03 88 69 00 52
Open Wed.-Sun. evenings.

HOERDT

◆
À la Charrue *(see p.124)*
30, rue de la République
☎ 03 88 51 31 11
Open daily at lunchtime
(exc. Mon.), & Fri.-Sun.
evenings.

HUNAWIHR

◆
Auberge du Tonnelier
1, rte de Ribeauvillé
☎ 03 89 73 74 25
Closed Tues. evening & Wed.

HUNINGUE

◆◆
Tivoli
15, rue de Bâle
☎ 03 89 69 73 05
✆ 03 89 67 82 44
www.tivoli.fr
Closed Sat. lunchtime & Sun.

ILLHAEUSERN

◆◆◆◆◆
L'Auberge de l'Ill *(see p.233)*
2, rue Collonges
☎ 03 89 71 89 00
Closed Mon., Tues. & Feb.
Booking essential.

◆◆◆◆
Auberge Napoléon
7, rue Montorge
☎ 04 76 87 53 64
✆ 04 76 87 80 76
auberge-napoleon.fr
Closed Sun., Mon., Tues.
& Wed. lunchtime; closed
29 July-19 Aug.

INGERSHEIM

◆◆
La Pierre Rouge
73, rue de la République
☎ 03 89 27 05 85
✆ 03 89 80 93 24
Closed Wed.

INGWILLER

◆◆
Aux Comtes de Hanau
(for details see p. VII)
Closed Mon. & Wed. evening.

◆◆
Au Château de Brumath
81, rue du Maréchal-Foch
☎ 03 88 89 46 65
Closed Fri.

ISSENHEIM

◆
Auberge Jean-Luc Wahl
58, rte de Rouffach
☎ 03 89 76 86 68
Closed Sun. evening & Mon.

ITTERSWILLER

◆◆
La Couronne
19, rte du Vin
☎ 03 88 85 50 65
Closed Thurs.

KATZENTHAL

◆◆
**Caveau-restaurant
'Chez Bacchus'**
20, Grand-Rue
☎ 03 89 27 32 25
Open all year, Thurs.-Sat.
from 6.30pm, Sun. lunchtime
& evening; 14 July-30 Sept.,
every evening (exc. Tues.) &
Sun. lunchtime; closed 1st
week in July, 3 weeks in Nov.
& 3 weeks in Jan.

KAYSERSBERG

◆◆◆◆
**Restaurant gastronomique
Chambard** *(see p.213)*
9, rue du Général-de-Gaulle
☎ 03 89 47 10 17
Open daily (exc. Tues.
lunchtime & Mon.).

◆◆
Au Lion d'Or
66, rue du Général-de-Gaulle
☎ 03 89 47 11 16
✆ 03 89 47 19 02
www.auliondor.fr
Closed Tues. evening & Wed.

◆◆
**Taverne Alsacienne
'S'Riwerla'**
4, rue du Général-de-Gaulle
☎ 03 89 47 16 16
✆ 03 89 47 18 23
Closed Tues.

◆
Caveau du Schlossberg
(see p.213)
20, rue du Général-de-Gaulle
☎ 03 89 47 17 87
Open daily 10am-midnight
(exc. Mon. lunchtime &
Tues.).

◆
Restaurant Hassenforder
(see p.213)
129, rue du Général-de-
Gaulle
☎ 03 89 47 13 54
Open daily 10am-midnight.

RESTAURANTS

KRUTH

◆◆

Auberge de France
20, Grand-Rue
☎ 03 89 82 28 02
📠 03 89 82 24 05
Closed Thurs.

KRAUTERGERSHEIM

◆

Le Chou' Heim
2, rue Clemenceau
☎ 03 88 48 18 10
Closed Mon. evening &
Wed. evening.

LA PETITE-PIERRE

◆

Au Lion d'Or
15, rue Principale
☎ 03 88 01 47 57
📠 03 88 01 47 50
Open daily (exc. Jan. &
end Jun.).

LA WANTZENAU

◆◆

Au Moulin
2, impasse du Moulin
☎ 03 88 96 20 01
Closed Sun. evening.

LANGENSOUTZBACH

La Taverne Alsacienne
☎ 03 88 54 08 55
Closed Mon.

LAPOUTROIE

◆◆◆◆

Restaurant du Faudé
(see p.216)
28, rue du Général-Dufieux
☎ 03 89 47 50 35
Open daily (exc. Sun. evening
& Mon.), noon-2pm, 7-9pm;
closed Nov.

LAUTERBOURG

◆◆◆

À la Poêle d'Or
35, rue du Général-
Mittelhauser
☎ 03 88 94 84 16
📠 03 88 54 62 30
Closed Wed. & Thurs.

LE BONHOMME

◆

L'Auberge du Vallon
(see p.215)
☎ 03 89 71 35 45
Open daily, 8am-10pm.

LEMBACH

◆

À l'Orée du Bois
25, rte de Woerth
☎ 03 88 94 41 33
Closed Wed. lunchtime.

LIPSHEIM

◆◆◆

À l'Ange
30, rue Jeanne-d'Arc
☎ 03 88 64 07 78
📠 03 88 64 98 71
Closed at Christmas.

LIEPVRE

◆◆◆

Auberge Vieille Forge
Bois L'Abbesse
☎ 03 89 58 90 54
Closed Sun. evening & Mon.

LUTTER

◆◆

L'Auberge Paysanne
24, rue de Wolschwiller
☎ 03 89 40 71 67
Open all year (exc. Mon.).

MARLENHEIM

◆◆◆◆

Le Cerf
30, rue du Général-de-Gaulle
☎ 03 88 87 73 73
📠 03 88 87 68 08
info@lecerf.com
Closed Tues. & Wed.

MARKSTEIN

◆◆

Wolf
☎ 03 89 82 64 36
📠 03 89 38 72 06
www.multimania.com/
wolfmarkst/
wolf/markst@aol.com
Open daily.

MASEVAUX

◆◆

Hostellerie Alsacienne
16, rue du Maréchal-Foch
☎ and 📠 03 89 82 45 25
Closed Sun. evening & Mon.

MERKWILLER-PECHELBRONN

◆◆

Auberge Le Puits VI
(see p.109)
20, rue de Lobsann
☎ 03 88 80 76 58
Open Wed. evening to Sun.
evening.

◆◆◆

**Auberge du Beachel-
Brunn**
3, rte de Soultz
☎ 03 88 80 78 61
📠 03 88 80 75 20
Closed Sun. evening, Mon.
evening & Tues.

MOLSHEIM

◆

Burewinstubel
15, rue de la Monnaie
☎ 03 88 38 14 84
Open Sat. & Sun.

MULHOUSE

◆◆◆

Le Belvédère
80, av. de la 1ᵉ-D.-B.
☎ 03 89 44 18 79
Closed Sun. evening,
Mon. evening & Tues.

◆◆

**Restaurant Panoramique
Tournant de la Tour de
l'Europe** *(see p.230)*
☎ 03 89 45 12 14
Closed Sun. evening & Mon.

◆

**Aux Caves du
Vieux Couvent**
22, rue du Couvent
☎ 03 89 66 47 87
📠 03 89 66 47 87
Closed Sun. evening & Mon.

MUSSIG

◆◆

Auberge à l'Illwald
Rte de Marckolsheim
Le Schnellenbuehl
☎ 03 88 85 35 40
Closed Tues. & Wed.

◆

Le Caveau
64A, rue du Maréchal-Foch
☎ 03 88 38 57 66
Closed Mon. evening & Sat.
lunchtime.

MUTZIG

◆

Au Nid de Cigogne
25, rue du 18-Novembre
☎ 03 88 38 11 97
Closed Tues. evening & Wed.

NEUWILLER-LÈS-SAVERNE

◆◆

Au Chasseur
☎ 03 88 70 33 19
Closed Mon. afternoon & Tues.

NIEDERMORSCHWIHR

◆◆

La Croix d'Or
Les Trois-Épis
☎ 03 89 49 81 61
📠 03 89 78 90 48
Closed Tues.

◆

Caveau des Seigneurs
124, rue des Trois-Épis
☎ 03 89 27 12 75
Closed Tues.

◆
Le Caveau du Morakopf
(see p.202)
7, rue des Trois-Épis
☎ 03 89 27 05 10
Open noon-2pm, 6.30-10pm
(exc. Sun. & Mon. lunchtime).

OBERBRONN

◆◆
Au Cerf
23, rue Principale
☎ 03 88 09 12 21
Closed Sept.

OBERMORSCHWIHR

◆
À la Couronne
☎ 03 89 49 30 69
Closed Sun. evening & Mon.

OBERSTEINBACH

◆
Alsace Villages
☎ 03 88 09 50 59
Closed Wed. evening & Thurs.

ODEREN

◆◆
Auberge du Vieux Moulin
11, rue Gorth
☎ 03 89 82 10 40
Closed 15 Aug.-1 Sept.

ORBEY

◆◆
Les Terrasses du Lac Blanc
348, Lac Blanc
☎ 03 89 86 50 00
🆏 03 89 86 50 05
Open daily in high season.

◆◆
La Croix d'Or
13, rue de l'Église
☎ 03 89 71 20 51
www.hotel-croixdor.fr
thhotelcroixdor@minitel.net
Closed Tues.

◆
Restaurant Wetterer
206A, Basses-Huttes
☎ 03 89 71 20 28
🆏 03 89 71 36 50
Closed Wed.

ORSCHWILLER

◆◆
Au Fief du Château
20, Grand-Rue
☎ 03 88 82 56 25
www.fief-chateau.com
info@fief.chateau.com
Closed Wed.

OSTHEIM

◆◆
Au Nid de Cigognes
2, rte de Colmar

☎ 03 89 47 91 11
🆏 03 89 47 99 88
Closed Sun. evening & Mon.

OTTROTT-LE-HAUT

◆◆◆◆
Hostellerie des Châteaux
11, rue des Châteaux
☎ 03 88 48 14 14
🆏 03 88 95 95 20
Closed Mon.

PFULGRIESHEIM

◆◆◆
Bürestubel
8, rte de Lampertheim
☎ 03 88 20 01 92
🆏 03 88 20 48 97
Closed Mon. & Tues.

RIBEAUVILLÉ

◆◆◆
**Restaurant Clos
Saint-Vincent** *(see p.221)*
Rte de Bergheim
☎ 03 89 73 67 65
Open 12.15-1.30pm, 7.15-
8.30pm (closed Mon. Wed. &
Thurs. lunchtimes & Tues.).

◆◆
Les Catalpas
48, rte de Bergheim
☎ 03 89 73 62 19
🆏 03 89 73 62 19
Closed Sun. evening & Mon.

◆◆
Caveau de l'Ami Fritz
1, pl. de l'Ancien-Hôpital
☎ 03 89 73 68 11
🆏 03 89 73 30 63
Open daily

RIEDISHEIM

◆◆◆
La Poste Kieny *(see p.230)*
7, rue du Général-de-Gaulle
☎ 03 89 44 07 71
Closed Sun. evening, Mon.
& Tues. lunchtime.

RIQUEWIHR

◆◆◆
Le Schœnenbourg
Rue du Schœnenbourg
☎ 03 89 49 01 11
🆏 03 89 47 95 88
www.calixo.net/schoenenbourg
schoenenbourg@calixo.net
Open daily

◆◆
Relais de Riquewihr
6, rue du Général-de-gaulle
☎ 03 89 47 89 88
🆏 03 89 47 97 91
Closed Mon.

RESTAURANTS

ROSHEIM

◆◆◆

Hostellerie le Rosenmeer
45, av. de la Gare
☎ 03 88 50 43 29
Closed Sun. evening, Mon.,
3 weeks in winter & 2 weeks
in summer.

ROUFFACH

◆◆◆◆

Les Tonneries
(see p.189)
Panoramic Restaurant in the
Château d'Isenbourg Hotel
☎ 03 89 78 58 50
Closed Wed. & Sat. evenings.

◆◆◆

À la Ville de Lyon
(see p.188)
1, rue Poincaré
☎ 03 89 49 62 49
Open daily (exc. Mon. & Wed.
lunchtime), noon-3pm, 7pm
to midnight.

SAVERNE

◆◆

Taverne Katz *(see p.114)*
80, Grand-Rue
☎ 03 88 71 16 56
Open daily, 10am-10pm.

SCHWEIGHOUSE-
SUR-MODER

◆◆◆

Restaurant La Cassolette
(see p.123)
27, rue du Général-de-Gaulle
☎ 03 88 72 61 12
Closed Mon. evening, Tues.
evening & Wed.

SÉLESTAT

◆◆◆

Abbaye La Pommeraie
8, bd du Maréchal-Foch
☎ 03 88 92 07 84
🅕 03 88 92 08 71
Closed Sun. evening.

◆◆

**Restaurant Jean-Frédéric
Edel** *(see p.154)*
7, rue des Serruriers
☎ 03 88 92 86 55
Open daily (exc. Tues. Wed.
& Sun. evening).

◆

Au Bon Pichet
10, pl. du Marché-aux-Choux
☎ 03 88 82 96 65
Closed Sun. & Mon. evening.

STRASBOURG

◆◆◆◆

Le Jardin de l'Europe
Parc de l'Orangerie
☎ 03 88 61 36 24
🅕 03 88 60 30 25
www.strasbourg.com/jardin-
europe
Closed Sun. evening & Mon.

◆◆◆

Au Pont Saint-Martin
15, rue des Moulins
☎ 03 88 32 45 13
🅕 03 88 75 77 60
Closed Wed.

◆◆

La Choucrouterie
(see p.132)
20, rue Saint-Louis
☎ 03 88 36 07 28
Open every evening from
6.30pm (exc. Sun. & 3 weeks
in summer).

◆◆

**Micro-brasserie
de la Lanterne**
5, rue de la Lanterne
☎ 03 88 32 10 10
Closed Mon.

◆◆

Buffet de Lagare
32, pl. de la Gare
☎ 03 88 32 68 28
Open daily.

◆◆

Interhotel de la Tour
18, rue de la Tour
☎ 03 88 29 41 41
🅕 03 88 29 57 70
www.hotel-tour.com
inter-hotel-de-la-
tour@wanadoo.fr
Closed Sat. lunchtime & Sun.

◆◆

Aux Contades
5, rue René-Hirschler
☎ and 🅕 03 88 35 26 73
Closed Sat.

◆

À la Tête de Lard
3, rue Hannong
☎ 03 88 32 13 56
🅕 03 88 32 64 91
Closed Sat. lunchtime & Sun.

THANN

◆◆◆

Moschenross
42, rue du Général-de-gaulle
☎ 03 89 37 00 86
🅕 03 89 37 52 81
Closed Mon.

TURCKHEIM

◆

Auberge du Veilleur
(see p.201)
12, pl. Turenne
☎ 03 89 27 32 32
Open daily, noon-2pm,
7-9pm.

URMATT

◆

**Le Clos du Hahnenberg
'Chez Jacques'**
65, rue du Général-de-gaulle
☎ 03 88 97 41 35
🅕 03 88 47 36 51
www.closhahnenberg.com
clos.hahnenberg@wanadoo.fr
Closed Mon.

VIEUX-FERRETTE

◆◆

Sundgauer Käs Keller
(see p.166)
☎ 03 89 40 42 22
Open daily 11am-10pm;
closed Sun.

WESTHALTEN

◆◆◆

Auberge du Vieux Pressoir
(see p.191)
Domaine du Bollenberg
☎ 03 89 49 62 47
Open daily noon-2pm, 7-9pm
(closed 20-27 Dec.).

WILDENSTEIN

◆

Auberge du Bramont
6, rte du Bramont
☎ 03 89 82 28 55
Open daily.

WINDSTEIN

◆◆

Windstein
8, rte d'Obersteinbach
☎ 03 88 09 24 18
🅕 03 88 09 24 60
Closed Mon.

WISSEMBOURG

◆

**La Taverne
de la Petite venise**
3, rue de la République
☎ 03 88 54 30 70
Closed Tues.

ZELLENBERG

◆◆◆

Maximilien
19 A, rte d'Ostheim
☎ 03 89 47 99 69
🅕 03 89 47 99 85
Closed Sun. evening & Mon.

FARM-INNS

BREITENBACH

▲
Lameysberg Farm-inn
(see p.207)
☎ 03 89 77 35 30
Open daily (exc. Mon. evening & Tues.) Feb.-15 Nov.

COL DU PLATZERWASEL-SCHNEPFENRIED

◆
Uff-Rain *(see p.179)*
Signposted from D27, before you reach Platzerwasel
☎ 03 89 77 67 68

HOHENBOURG

◆
Le Gimbelhof *(see p.107)*
At the foot of the Château
☎ 03 88 94 43 58
Open Wed. & Sun. noon-2pm, 6.30-9pm.
Refreshment room open all day.

LE BONHOMME

◆
Brézouard Farm-inn
(see p.215)
☎ 03 89 47 23 80
Open daily (exc. Wed.), 15 Feb.-15 Nov.

LE MARKSTEIN

◆
Salzbach Farm-inn
(see p.179)
On the D27 towards La Schlucht
☎ 03 89 77 63 66

MARLENHEIM

▲
Auberge du Cabri
Nordheim
☎ 03 88 87 56 87
📠 03 88 87 61 65

WINSTUBS

COLMAR

◆◆
Au Cygne
15, rue Édouard-Richard
☎ 03 89 23 76 26
Closed Mon.

◆◆
Winstub Brenner
1, rue de Turenne
☎ 03 89 41 22 33
Closed Tues. evening & Wed.

HUNAWIHR

Winstub Suzel
2, rue de l'Église
☎ 03 89 73 30 85
Closed Tues.

MULHOUSE

Winstub Henriette
9, rue Henriette
☎ 03 89 46 27 83
Closed Sun.

STRASBOURG

Le Tire-Bouchon
(see p.128)
5, rue des Tailleurs-de-Pierre
☎ 03 88 23 10 73
Open daily.

Chez Yvonne *(see p.135)*
10, rue du Sanglier
☎ 03 88 32 84 15
Closed Sun., Mon. lunchtime, 14 July & 15 Aug.

Hailich Graab *(see p.135)*
15, rue des Orfèvres
☎ 03 88 32 39 97
Closed Sun. & Mon.

Muensterstuewel
(see p.135)
8, pl. du Marché-aux-Cochons-de-Lait
☎ 03 88 32 17 63
Closed Sun. (open Sun. lunchtime in Dec.), Mon. (open last 2 Mon. in Dec.), 18-28 Feb. & 19 Aug.-12 Sept.

Le Clou *(see p.135)*
3, rue du Chaudron
☎ 03 88 32 11 67
Closed Wed. lunchtime & Sun.

Zum Strissel
5, pl. de la Grande-Boucherie
☎ 03 88 32 14 73
📠 03 88 32 70 24
Closed Sun. & Mon.

TURCKHEIM

Auberge du Veilleur
(see p.201)
12, pl. Turenne
☎ 03 89 27 32 32
Open daily noon-2pm, 7-9pm.

RESTAURANTS

HACHETTE TRAVEL GUIDES

VACANCES

Alsace-Vosges	1 84202 167 2
The Ardèche	1 84202 161 3
The Basque Country	1 84202 159 1
Brittany	1 84202 007 2
Catalonia	1 84202 099 4
Corsica	1 84202 100 1
The Dordogne & Périgord	1 84202 098 6
The French Alps	1 84202 166 4
Languedoc-Roussillon	1 84202 008 0
Normandy	1 84202 097 8
Poitou-Charentes	1 84202 009 9
Provence & the Côte d'Azur	1 84202 006 4
Pyrenees & Gascony	1 84202 015 3
South West France	1 84202 014 5

A GREAT WEEKEND IN …

Focusing on the limited amount of time available on a weekend break, these guides suggest the most entertaining and interesting ways of getting to know the city in just a few days.

Amsterdam	1 84202 145 1
Barcelona	1 84202 170 2
Berlin	1 84202 061 7
Brussels	1 84202 017 X
Dublin	1 84202 096 X
Florence	1 84202 010 2
Lisbon	1 84202 011 0
London	1 84202 013 7
Madrid	1 84202 095 1
Naples	1 84202 016 1
New York	1 84202 004 8
Paris	1 84202 001 3
Prague	1 84202 000 5
Rome	1 84202 169 9
Venice	1 84202 018 8
Vienna	1 84202 026 9

Forthcoming titles:
Budapest
Seville

ROUTARD

The ultimate food, drink and accommodation guides for the independent traveller.

Andalucia & Southern Spain	1 84202 028 5
Athens & the Greek Islands	1 84202 023 4
Belgium	1 84202 022 6
California, Nevada & Arizona	1 84202 025 0
Canada	1 84202 031 5
Cuba	1 84202 062 5
Ireland	1 84202 024 2
North Brittany	1 84202 020 X
Paris	1 84202 027 7
Provence & the Côte d'Azur	1 84202 019 6
Rome & Southern Italy	1 84202 021 8
Thailand	1 84202 029 3